HEALING RHINOS AND OTHER SOULS

ISBN-13: 978 – 1492324928
ISBN-10: 1492324922

©2013 Stephanie Rohrbach

STEPHANIE ROHRBACH

HEALING RHINOS AND OTHER SOULS

The Extraordinary Fortunes of a Bushveld Vet

To Walter

With Special Thanks to Topsy and Family

And to all the women and men who made this book possible through their generous contributions. Without your memories, anecdotes, observations, ideas, inspiration, laughter, tears, humour, criticism, corrections, encouragement, help, photographs, drawings, generosity, hospitality, patience, warmth, love and care, Walter's life-story would not have been written.

Thank you – Baie dankie – Ke a leboga – Vielen Dank

A WORD BEFOREHAND

This is not a work of fiction, nor is it, strictly speaking, a biography. It is a life-story, a memoir, and a collection of anecdotes. It is a story told by many voices, a picture painted with words.

It is the story of Walter Eschenburg, who was a much respected if unorthodox vet, a loving husband, father and grandfather, a great storyteller and talented painter, a person who loved and understood nature and all her creatures, a reluctant businessman, a somewhat exuberant driver, a humble man and a wonderful friend to many. Ultimately, this is a story about a man who was simply himself, all his life. It is the story of a life well lived.

Like any great weaver of stories, Walter embellished and embroidered; he condensed stories and characters, and perhaps caricatured them a little. He drew life in the most vivid colours and attempted to capture the essence of each person and event, the essence of life.

If two artists paint a portrait of the same person their pictures will never look the same, as each infuses the painting with own memories, thoughts, emotions and spirit. Similarly, anecdotes and memories are always personal, because we all take in the world through our own eyes, have lived distinct lives and thus see different pictures.

To paint somebody else's life's picture, to be its chronicler and to capture its essence, by default, a great degree of artistic license is required.

Some names have been changed, and some stories have been told so many times that they have developed lives of their own. Some might remember events differently, others perhaps recognise themselves and say, 'But I never said that!'

If there are any mistakes or misunderstandings, people not mentioned or important stories not told, the fault is entirely mine and I am solely to blame. It is possible: although I wrote this book with the best intentions, it is a personal story. It is my picture of Walter.

Thank you.

THE BEGINNING

THE BEGINNING

Walter Eschenburg settled into his favourite blue armchair and began to talk. He was briefly interrupted by the call of an eagle owl somewhere outside in the garden. Listening to it with a smile, he continued telling me the story of his life. He talked of his journeys and adventures as a wildlife vet in South Africa, and unearthed childhood memories pertaining to a time when he and his family were marooned at a castle in rural Germany during the Second World War.

He spoke with a certain kind of urgency, as if he knew that time was limited, and the desire to tell his story was palpable.

I now think it was the same urgency that I had felt a few days before. 'If I want to do this book with Walter, then I must do it now', I remember thinking. I'd phoned him that same morning to ask if he was still interested. The idea, and I can't remember whose it actually was, had been bandied about for years, but always deferred. Finally, it seemed, all procrastination was put aside. 'Yes, of course,' Walter had replied, 'the sooner, the better. When are you coming?'

While Walter and I were sitting in the Eschenburgs' lounge, Topsy was rummaging around in the kitchen behind us, an assortment of dogs at her feet. She was clearing up the little that was left of a delicious supper, occasionally adding snippets to our conversation she casually overheard.

All possible desires relating to food had been satisfied and occasionally Walter rubbed his stomach with one of his broad, strong hands. The buttons of his shirt were perilously close to bursting off; Topsy's exquisite cooking had left its traces over the years.

My thoughts wandered back to the first time I had met Walter. It had nothing to do with food, but with castrating two young horses. I was spending some time at a large cattle farm and horse-riding enterprise in the Waterberg, a remote area in the northern regions of the South African bushveld. Triple-B Ranch and Horizon Horse Trails were only a short drive away from the Eschenburgs' home in Vaalwater, and Walter had been their vet and advisor in all matters related to horses, cattle and dogs for many years.

'Oh, you'll love Walter,' Shane had said.

Shane did not only understand horses, but people too. One of a rare breed, a real horseman, he was in charge at Horizon together with his wife Laura. Leaning against the rails of the paddock, his Australian Akubra hat drawn deep to protect his eyes from the sun, he continued, 'Walter has been our vet ever since we moved here, and he is the best; there is no doubt. I don't know what we would do without him. But you'll see for yourself.'

The two colts were ready, but luckily unaware of what was about to happen to them. They were just content being allowed to graze on the lawn outside the kitchen, where the castrations would take place.

'We always do these little ops on the grass here,' Shane said. 'It was Walter's idea. There is less dust and therefore less risk of infection.'

We watched two young English lads, guests spending their holidays at Horizon, milling about. Coming from London, they had only just lost their air of investment bankers. They were a tad inexperienced in bush matters, but keen to give everything a go. Up for a new and exciting challenge, they had volunteered to assist. At their riding stables back home they were not allowed anywhere near a horse when the vet was around. But Horizon was different; here they could become part of a working cattle farm, ride horses to their hearts' content and learn from Shane, a quiet man who in his modesty shrugged off all comparisons with the famous horse whisperer.

'We'll see how they cope,' Shane said now. He had seen it all before.

'Oh, there comes Walter.'

A cloud of dust rose from the access road, which was flanked by rows of tall eucalyptus trees.

'Walter can be rather unorthodox,' he explained, 'but you'll see, he just knows. And as I said, he is brilliant. I have never seen anybody else administer anaesthetics the way he does. If at all possible I only let Walter do anything to my animals.'

A battered blue *bakkie* came to an abrupt halt in the middle of the yard. The driver's door opened with a squeak and a tall and somewhat portly gentleman alighted. His dirt-speckled glasses sat slightly askew on the bridge of his nose and his shirt and khaki shorts were spattered with what could only have been dried blood. He ran one of his hands through his shock of white hair as he looked around.

As expected, the operations went well. Within an hour the two young horses were standing again, still slightly dazed but already interested in the grass.

The two young Englishmen presented a different picture. Geoff, the taller and louder one, sat on the steps leading up to the kitchen holding his head in his hands, while Chris was lying on his back in the grass, eyes closed and breathing heavily. Both of them looked decidedly off-colour, with a tinge of green around the gills on their sunburnt faces.

Walter just grinned. It wasn't the first time that some young guys had volunteered to assist, and he had learned that it was always better to have somebody a little more seasoned around. Women in general dealt better with castrations than men. These two had actually done all right, held the ropes when he dropped the colts and watched with interest when he got the *emasculator* ready. But things had turned pear-shaped for Chris and Geoff when he'd thrown the severed testicles to the dogs that had been waiting patiently. It was one of their special treats and even now Fred and Dingo were licking their lips.

'Walter always does that, and the dogs know,' Shane said. 'Suppose he's got a wicked sense of humour. But did you notice how sure he is with every movement he makes? That's what I call experience.'

It had indeed been apparent that each and every move was deliberate, that Walter had done the operation uncountable times.

How many years of practice does a vet need before he gets this kind of experience, this confidence, I wondered.

'Walter, how about a cup of coffee?' Shane asked now.

'Hey? Sorry, did you say something?'

'Ah, yes, a coffee would be great. Why do you even ask? And yes, two sugars please, a good South African coffee.'

Within minutes of being introduced I was invited to spend the next weekend with the Eschenburgs. Only later did I learn that Walter and Topsy had made it their habit to pick up 'strays' and indulge them with the hospitality they had become famous for. It was, as they say, the beginning of a long and wonderful friendship.

Ten years later, Walter was sitting in his blue armchair, with Tessa, his old, black Labrador snoring by his side. While telling me his story, covering seventy-five years of a life lived to the full, he made sure more than once that the dictaphone was switched on, that not a word was lost.

Every now and then he ran his fingers through his still full head of white hair. As usual, his glasses were anything but clean, yet his eyesight seemed as sharp as ever, not missing the slightest of movements when out in the bush. It was his ears that were giving him and the rest of the world trouble. '*Ja*, *Oom* Walter has become a little hard of hearing lately,' people would say and Topsy, knowing him better than most after nearly fifty years of marriage, would answer, 'Yes, none so deaf as those that will not hear…'.

As always I thoroughly enjoyed my time with the Eschenburgs. Days started early; at five o'clock we were up, feeding the cattle, the horses and the birds. We did the rounds, using the excuse of visiting patients to go for long drives around the Waterberg, bumping at high speed along corrugated dirt roads. We clambered through the bushes to see ancient rock paintings, and we stopped for an unusual bird call, a spoor on the road, a pair of kudu or yet another interesting tree. We assisted one of Walter's cows giving birth to twins, treated a foal with septicaemia and tried to find the cause for the slight lameness of an endurance horse which, Walter was convinced, lay with its unbalanced rider.

There was time to talk to each and every person we met along the way, and all seemed delighted to catch up with the Doc. Every evening we had a long chat to George, who had been working for the Eschenburgs for a lifetime. We checked on the horses and the cows, made sure there were no snakes lying hidden in the chicken coop and watched Topsy feed her bush babies before she proceeded to fill our stomachs with yet another delicious meal.

After a week, I was sad to leave. I promised to put all the recordings on paper and start writing the book, while Walter would try to remember more. Then, sometime in the not too distant future, we'd get back together again, discuss the final structure and fill the gaps.

Little did I know then that life had different plans, that this was the last time I would ever see him.

JOURNEYS

MEMORIES

We spent the war in Juchow, all six years of it. It has left very profound memories. There were sad times, when you realised the war was still on. There were so many killed. But that was in between good times for us children. To us, it seemed that things happened at Juchow that never happened anywhere else in the world. I suppose we didn't really understand the extent of the horrors that had overcome Europe; it had all become part of our life. And life carried on. It had to carry on.

Now, after more than sixty-five years, these memories are in part as fresh as if it all had happened only yesterday, although some of what I am going to relate may be a little blurred by the passage of time.

But maybe I should start at the beginning.

It was in January 1939, when I first got an inkling of impending change. We were by then a family of five. Hermann, the eldest, was born in 1931. I followed in '34 and Elsa, the baby, was only a few months old when Germany was first talked about as a place to be visited. We were living at *Uhlenhorst*, my father's farm on the outskirts of Johannesburg. The fields where flowers were grown for the market, the stable for the little herd of dairy cows and the peach orchards, these were our world then.

For a German speaking South African family, talk of Germany was nothing unusual, but one day I overheard my parents discussing a letter that had arrived unexpectedly. My father was asked to visit his parents in Lübeck, together with his wife and children - us.

There seemed to be some argument about when, and who should go. My mother was apparently not too eager to leave her home, which she was very proud of, in the care of the new farm manager and his family, the Van Veterens. They had only recently emigrated from Holland and begun to work for my father. He was very happy to have them around, because they were extremely hardworking and thrifty, but my mother had not really warmed to them. 'I don't know what it is,' she'd say, 'but I just don't trust them.' Eventually though, my father convinced her that it would be fine. After all we'd be away for a couple of months at the most.

The Van Veterens had two little boys of ages between my brother Hermann and me, whom we didn't play with very much. Like our mother, we regarded them with a certain degree of suspicion, mainly because we didn't understand them. We spoke German at home and had learned Afrikaans, but the Van Veterens only spoke High Dutch, and that sounded very *snaaks,* strange to our ears.

Our mistrust went so far that one day Hermann suggested we hide our favourite toys before going to Germany, so that the Van Veteren boys wouldn't be able to play with them whilst we were away. This led to a lot of burying and exhuming over the next few days, subjecting our recently received Christmas presents to some rough treatment. When my mother caught on to the scheme, she explained that it was still some months before our planned departure in May and promised to warn us in time.

May was still so far away that for some time the trip was hardly spoken about. Life went on at Uhlenhorst as usual. Cows had to be milked, and flowers watered and picked before they were treated and bundled, packed in special boxes and taken to the market, or directly to the florists in Johannesburg.

Normally it was my father who took the flowers to town, but on occasion Mr Ouwens, the previous farm manager, who had been working for my father for years and was trusted implicitly, was charged with this task.

On one of those occasions, a Chinese flower buyer at the market had asked Willem Ouwens to lend him three Pound Sterling, the currency in the country at the time. Willem was hesitant at first, but he was also young and ambitious and the offer of a good interest on the loan, fifty per cent for the week, clinched the deal. On his way home, he must have felt a little apprehensive, for his salary was gone; what should he tell his wife? He needn't have worried.

On the following Monday, Willem got his money back plus interest. In fact, he got a lot more than he had bargained for. The Chinese man had been so pleased with his loan that he gave Willem a piece of paper with numbers on it and strict instructions on what to do with them. He was to go to the dog races that coming Friday and play the numbers exactly as indicated on the paper. He had to reinvest his winnings on each subsequent race, but not on the third. Willem did as he was told, played as instructed and arrived home with sufficient money in his pocket to buy a new Ford truck. He gave in his notice the next day. Although he'd always got on well with my father, the prospect of being his own boss was just too tempting.

Most of the land at Uhlenhorst was under irrigation, but some of the flower beds were watered by bucket or watering can, the water drawn from a deep hole in the ground. This was forbidden territory for us, but temptation was great and on hot days I'd watch my brother and his friends skinny-dip.

Needless to say, the day came when I had to try it myself. Approaching the waterhole with its steep sides, I slipped on the muddy ground and fell in head first.

Luck would have it that Hermann, who would turn out to be my guardian angel more than once, was not too far away. He saw the splashing and pulled me out by the feet. I survived this adventure unscathed, but it left me with a healthy respect for water for the rest of my life.

Hermann had been named after our father, who hailed from an illustrious family in Lübeck, a city on the German coast of the Baltic Sea. He'd studied agriculture and then, in 1927, left Germany and immigrated to South Africa. He soon found a piece of land he liked close to Johannesburg and bought the farm, Rietfontein 33, in 1929. He christened it Uhlenhorst, a German name that referred to the many owls living in the large eucalyptus trees surrounding the old farm house.

The same year he met my mother, Ursula Wilhelmi, a South African born of German parents, at her mother's farm Driefontein. It was love at first sight and after they got married, she moved with him to Uhlenhorst, which they soon developed into a flourishing dairy and flower farm.

Eventually, May approached. I had all but forgotten about the holiday, but one day Hermann and I came into the house and saw a large glass bowl on the dining room table. It was half filled with water and a funny contraption was floating in it.

'What's this, Mammie?' we asked.

'This, my boys, is a kind of prophecy,' she smiled.

'Prophecy? What's a prophecy, Mammie?'

'Can't you see? It's a sailing ship! And I should think it means that there is a ship waiting for all of us in Cape Town, to sail on to Germany.'

She had us speechless, but only for a second or two. Neither Hermann nor I knew exactly where Germany was, or how long it would take to get there.

It was questions here and explanations there; suitcases and cabin trunks were brought into the house, clothes sorted and household goods packed away. In short, a lot of unusual activity ensued.

A couple of days later we found another surprise.

'Mammie, why is there a train on the table?' The model locomotive had a bunch of flowers sprouting from the chimney.

'Well, you see, before we can sail on the ship we have to travel to Cape Town, and this train will take us there.'

'When?'

'The day after tomorrow.'

'Oh, then we must hide our toys now!' I immediately wanted to rush out to bury Hermann's red lorry and my little Plymouth panel van, the spitting image of father's new delivery truck, but we had to wait until after lunch. I for one was so excited that I could hardly eat, and finally the long awaited task was tackled.

We didn't know then that seven long years would pass before we'd be welcomed home by these two toys in the sandpit next to our dilapidated home, to which we'd return after the end of the world's most gruesome war.

I remember saying good byes to Amma, our grandmother, and all our relations on mother's side, some of whom we would never see again. When Aunty Freya, mother's sister, took us to Park Station in Johannesburg, I couldn't believe my eyes. Holding tight onto my mother's hand, I walked along the train, which I thought was gigantic. It had a black engine and more brown coaches than I could count. Little farm boy that I was, I was suitably impressed. Eventually, we found our compartment and the train jerked into motion.

To me it all felt like the beginning of a great adventure. We saw so many new things, which our parents patiently explained to us; the changing landscapes, grasslands with horses and cattle, maize fields, streams, rivers, dams, pans with water birds, even some springbuck and later, in the Karoo, lots of sheep.

It was during this journey that our father became more real to us. On the farm, we only saw him at mealtimes or when he drove off to town in his green panel van. At night he either took his produce to the market or fell asleep. Here on the train and later on the ship he turned into the all-knowing hero that only a small boy could appreciate.

He told us about Germany, and our aunts, uncles, cousins and grandparents we'd be visiting. He explained each and everything we saw, and then, to our great amusement, he'd suddenly fall asleep. He had the ability to take a nap anywhere, at any time, only to wake up a few minutes later, wide-awake. Under some circumstances this was a great asset to him, but we were always highly entertained, when he woke up, say during a church service, and disturbed the congregation with a distinct, '*Ja*', as he sat up straighter.

We arrived at Cape Town harbour. I still remember the great ships, cranes and tugs, and the porters who spoke a different kind of Afrikaans to what we were used to. And of course the sea, and Table Mountain which loomed over the city, covered by its cloudy tablecloth. The smell of ships has become an everlasting memory for me, somewhat musty and claustrophobic, and seagulls with their loud cries will always remind me of my first encounter with the sea.

Soon it was time to board the *Pretoria*, which belonged to the German Africa Line and had black, white and red lines across the funnel. We walked up the long, slightly moving gang plank; it was a gala occasion, with brass bands playing and streamers being thrown from deck to shore. Thousands of people seemed to be at the quay seeing the ship off, all waving and shouting, '*Bon voyage, bon voyage!*' and, it being a German ship, '*Leinen los* – Cast off!*'
Hermann and I set out to explore the ship over the next few days. We admired the large swimming pool and watched in delight how our father excelled at the many deck games. He won the clay pigeon shooting contest hands down, and all the diving competitions. We beamed with pride. Our father was a real hero!

After some days at sea, the *Pretoria* passed her sister ship, the *Windhuk*, which was on her way from Germany to South Africa. Soon after dark and close to the equator, everybody was called on deck and I was treated to the first great firework display of my life. Both ships were bathed in colourful lights, and great Catherine wheels and coloured crackers were set off. As soon as the ships were close, rockets were shot across each other's bows, while all the time the ship's band was playing popular music. What a memory!

Flying fish! The wave of new impressions and discoveries just didn't end. I had never even heard of flying fish before and couldn't imagine what they should look like. My parents had tried to point them out for a

23

long time before I actually saw one. I had expected something large and couldn't believe that these little animals didn't get lost forever in the huge sea. We observed them singly and in groups coming out of the water and gliding over long distances next to the ship.

'Are they also going to Germany?' I remember asking my father.

We had left Uhlenhorst in early winter. It hadn't been really cold yet, but the veld had been dry, changing colour to yellow, brown and grey. Much to our amazement, we arrived in Europe to a vibrant green spring. This brilliant, almost luminous green was a colour we had never seen before.

Herring gulls started circling the ship, swooping and diving for scraps of food thrown overboard. Passengers were excited now about their imminent arrival but many hours were still to pass steaming up the river Elbe before we'd reach our destination.

In Hamburg, grandfather Eschenburg was waiting for us and together we'd continue on our journey to Lübeck.

FAMILY MATTERS

Nearly two months after their arrival in Germany, Walter's mother Ursula stood at the window in her room on the second floor of the Villa Eschenburg. In the distance she could see the lazy waters of the river Trave snaking its way through Lübeck. It was the artery that brought life to the oldest German city on the Baltic Sea, a prominent member of the Hanseatic League.

Ursula watched the barges, heavily laden with timber, steam up the river. Commerce with other states bordering the Baltic, particularly Scandinavia, was the foundation of the city. It was also, she had learned only recently, the corner stone of the Eschenburgs' business and the fabulous wealth and subsequent influence and power the family had acquired over the last few centuries.

Her thoughts wandered back to the memorable Sunday afternoon in the summer of 1929, when she'd first met Hermann Eschenburg. Immediately she had liked the tall and handsome, quiet man who had been brought to Driefontein by a common friend. Her mother loved nothing more than a good party, and on weekends, the hoi polloi of early Johannesburg would gather at her farm.

Amongst the guests was usually a number of young German bachelors, recent immigrants mostly, and Ursula's mother no doubt had entertained high hopes that her daughter would one day find a suitable match amongst them. She had been particularly taken by young Hermann Eschenburg, whom she thought was a really good catch, and she was only too delighted when he proposed to Ursula soon after they'd met.

Hermann had never spoken much about his previous life in Germany, but over the years Ursula had managed to piece together her husband's history. And now, that she had met his family, she understood; her mother's instincts had not betrayed her.

One day, while wandering through the grand villa, marvelling at its large banqueting hall, the tall windows, the stuccoed ceilings and the conservatory with its glass roof, Ursula's sister-in-law had informed her surreptitiously, 'You know, our father is the third richest man in Germany.'

When Ursula later, somewhat intrigued, had asked Hermann about it, he'd only grumbled, 'Last time she bragged about it, she said he was the fifth richest. Who cares anyway? It's got nothing to do with us.'

Hermann had not been back to Germany since immigrating to South Africa more than ten years previously. From what Ursula could gather, it had not been a happy departure. Being the oldest son, he should have inherited the family business, but his younger brother Wolfgang apparently had shown more interest and aptitude for business affairs and quickly become their father's *Liebling*, his favourite.

Hermann had chosen to study agriculture in Munich and been promised an estate the family owned in Pomerania; vast lands of gently undulating hills and forests, fields and pastures. He had been looking forward to living there, had dreamed of building a large manor house. He'd produce the best potatoes, breed excellent cattle and horses. Horses had always been his great love, and women of course. So much so, that he constantly got into trouble for what his father called his 'womanising affairs'.

Ursula didn't know exactly what had happened. She had a feeling it was a matter of broken hearts, but she knew better than to press her husband for answers. She, for her part, was very glad that things had worked out the way they had. Whatever the reasons, the estate in Pomerania was handed over to a cousin and Hermann had set sail for greener pastures. He'd travelled to South America, had explored Chile, Brazil and the Argentine for opportunities before venturing to South Africa. With the compensation that was given to him instead of his inheritance, he had bought Uhlenhorst.

'And that's where I'd like to be now,' Ursula thought, while gazing out the window. She was longing for their red patch of earth and the wide African sky, the vast empty spaces and the strong sense of community. More than anything else though, she felt free in South Africa, or at least a lot more free than in Lübeck, this German city with all its so-called sophistication and snobbism. Also, she was used to being active and working hard, not sitting around idly as she was expected to do here.

From her vantage point, Ursula could now see a small group approaching the Villa Eschenburg from the street corner. Her heart skipped a beat; there were her children, together with Marie, their nanny. She smiled while she observed Walter and Hermann walking ahead, dressed in their finest outfits, followed by Marie who carried little Elsa in her arms. Elsa was nearly a year old now; time really flew by.

Ursula remembered how, when she was pregnant with Elsa, Hermann had wished for a little sister and Walter, tired of always being the 'little brother', desperately had hoped for a boy. Somewhere they had heard that the outcome of the pregnancy could be influenced by a trick, and so Hermann had sprinkled sugar onto the windowsill to make sure that his wish would come true. Walter, not to be outdone, had quickly wiped the sugar off and then replaced it with salt; he'd get a little brother, he was convinced.

Walter stormed into the room only minutes later, ran up to Ursula and gave her a big hug.

'Mammie, I really don't like going out with Marie.'

'Why, my boy? It's good for you to go outside and get some fresh air.'

'*Ja*, Mammie, I know, but why do we always have to wear shoes? They hurt my feet. And Marie says we have to be clean and tidy before we go out. I hate being clean and tidy. And then she scrubs my ears and my neck until it hurts. I really don't like it.'

Ursula laughed. Walter and Hermann were real little farm boys, used to running wild at home, where shoes were only worn on Sundays, for church.

'And when we walk with her through the park,' Walter continued, 'we are not allowed to run around. It's so boring, Mammie, when can we go home?'

'Soon, my darling, soon.'

'You always say that!'

'Shush! Why don't you and Hermann go and see Grandfather?'

While Walter and Hermann visited their grandfather in the so-called *Herrenzimmer*, the gentlemen's room, Ursula paced up and down with Elsa in her arms. She was waiting for her husband, who had gone out with his brother to have a look at the company's vast timber yards on the river. She wanted to talk to him, tell him that she felt the time had come to go back home.

Ursula knew Hermann enjoyed himself here in Lübeck, now that he had made peace with his family. He had been devastated when he had left Germany, but now he was happy with his lot. He had told Ursula only the previous evening how often he thought of their Uhlenhorst and how he blessed fate for his move there. He was independent, had built up his own farm from scratch and loved his life there. Life as a businessman in the closed Lübeck society would not have been for him. If he was honest, he'd said, as much as he enjoyed this meeting up with old friends and family, savouring the sophisticated city life for a while, there was a bit of *Heimweh* for South Africa. A yearning to go home.

But there was more, Ursula felt, more than just the desire to go home and see her family again. It was the political situation that worried her. She was not a political person, never got involved in any form of political discussions, but she was not comfortable with the Nazi ideology, a fact that she didn't dare speak out aloud. She listened patiently when people told her how Germany had come out of the economic depression; that things seemed to be looking up; that people were employed and that there was more law and order. But the anti-Semitic utterances she seemed to hear everywhere went against her grain. They always made her think of her beloved Auntie Juliet, who lived in Johannesburg and was half Jewish; and it wasn't only Juliet, they had lots of Jewish friends and business partners back home.

Even more disturbing was that in recent weeks there had been a lot of talk about war. She wasn't quite sure what it was all about, but she did know, could feel it in her bones, that it was time to go home. It felt as if there was a dark cloud looming on the horizon.

Ursula halted in her movement. She had made up her mind. Tomorrow she would go to the offices of the German Africa Line and enquire about their return passage. Maybe, just maybe, there would be space on another ship, an opportunity for an earlier departure.

GRANDFATHER ESCHENBURG

I remember Grandfather Eschenburg as a rather imposing man – he always intimidated me a little. We had to bow and click our heels when we entered his room, the Herrenzimmer, where he spent a lot of time in the company of his dachshund Männe.

He seemed to enjoy our company though, and liked to educate us about our family's history. The Eschenburgs had been residing in Lübeck since the 15th century, he told us, when Laurentz Eskeburg, probably of Scandinavian origin, had arrived there. Ever since, the family had grown and prospered. Originally tanners and tradesmen, they became timber merchants, citizens, senators and academics.

Our great grandfather apparently had been mayor of Lübeck twice, while grandfather himself, never really interested in politics, had been the president of the chamber of industry and commerce for many years.

Grandfather particularly liked to impress us with stories about his father rubbing shoulders with the German *Kaiser* Wilhelm II, a privilege reserved for noblemen and only the most important dignitaries. The emperor apparently visited the Villa Eschenburg regularly and the children, including our father, had to stand to attention.

'You know, when your grandmother Hedwig was young,' he'd tell us, 'she was a very beautiful lady. She was so beautiful, that when the Kaiser was in town, he demanded her as his *Tischdame*, his dinner partner. Let me tell you, I was not amused.'

But my absolute favourite of grandfather's stories was the one about the sailing race. In 1912, he'd built a state-of-the-art racing yacht, which he called "Heti". He had decided that he needed to compete in the *Kaiserliche Yachtregatta*, the emperor's annual sailing race. And then, one year, he won against the Kaiser's boat and subsequently was offered a noble title.

'No, thank you,' was his proud reply. 'I prefer being the first citizen of Lübeck and not the last noble man.'

He was quite a man, our Grandfather Eschenburg!

UNINTENDED CONSEQUENCES

As the European summer came to an end, the storm clouds over Europe continued to gather. There was talk of trouble in Poland.

Ursula had gone to the shipping line's offices and found out that the *Windhuk*, the *Pretoria's* sister ship, was departing as scheduled. There would be space for her family, but it would mean leaving two weeks earlier than planned. Only too eager and now hopeful, she consulted with her husband and his family.

'No, you are mad to cut your visit short,' they told her in unison. 'Stay here. Even if there is a war with Poland, which is unlikely, it will take our army two to three days to sort out and then Poland will be mopped up.'

'But I'm worried that…' Ursula ventured.

'No ifs and buts,' grandfather Eschenburg said. 'You have only just arrived; I haven't seen my son in over ten years and now you want to take him away sooner than planned? I object.'

With this, the discussion was ended. Ursula relented reluctantly.

They stayed on in Lübeck and it soon became apparent that their visit would last much longer than planned. Indeed, Germany invaded Poland on the first of September 1939. As a consequence Great Britain and France declared war on Germany two days later.

Suddenly it was clear that the so-called trouble in Poland was not going to be 'mopped up' quickly and it didn't seem likely that there would be a ship traveling to South Africa any time soon. A naval war had begun and all civilian voyages had been cancelled, including the *Pretoria's* passage to Cape Town. The *Windhuk* would have been their last opportunity to leave what was to become a war-torn Europe.

'I told you, we should have gone on the *Windhuk* when we could,' Ursula said to her husband.

'I know, I know,' he grumbled, and she knew he regretted that he had, yet again, let his father determine the course of his life.

Soon the war began taking its toll and young men were sent to the front lines. At the Villa Eschenburg though, the consensus was still that 'this mess' would be over quickly and that Wolfgang and Roland, the two sons who had been called up, would be back in no time. Ursula was utterly relieved that her husband was not eligible to fight in the German army since he had become a South African citizen.

Weeks went by and the situation did not improve. Possibilities were discussed as to what to do with the young South African family.

'What would you say if I sent you to Juchow?' Grandfather Eschenburg asked one day, after he had called Ursula and Hermann into his Herrenzimmer.

A vast estate in Eastern Pomerania, Juchow belonged to the Eschenburgs' second cousins, the Dennigs.

'Heinz-Jürgen Dennig has been called up, and so has Uncle Boli,' the patriarch continued. 'That leaves his wife Erica on her own there. I think you should all go to Juchow until this trouble is over, or at least until the ships are sailing again. In the meantime you can help Erica manage the estate.'

So it happened that in autumn 1939 Hermann, Ursula and their three children boarded a train instead of a ship and travelled east instead of south. Again, they admired the passing landscape through the train's windows. Their journey took them through the flat and fertile lands of northern Germany. They passed wheat fields that had been harvested, immense forests in their astonishing autumn colours, and small and large towns, many of them set next to deep blue lakes.

The further east they got, the more sparsely populated the land became. Pomerania, and particularly its eastern parts where Juchow was situated, was still an inherently rural area.

Again during this journey, Hermann Eschenburg explained to his young family what they saw, and where they were going.

'Did you know, boys,' he began, for Elsa was too young to understand, 'all these lakes we are passing are remnants of the past ice ages. Folklore has it that once there were giants living here, and we can still see their graves in the forest.'

'Really, Dad? Giants?' Hermann was a little sceptical, but Walter listened with big eyes.

'Tell us more, tell us more!' he pleaded.

And so their father launched into an extensive account of the region's past. He explained that Pomerania had a mottled history of people coming and going, and of many battles fought. It was a land of harvests and sowing, of potatoes, wheat, cattle and geese; a land of hard work, steeped in tradition, ancient folklore and superstitions.

Once the last ice age had retreated, leaving an abundance of interconnected lakes, moraines and boulders behind, the area was populated by Stone Age hunters and gatherers. They shared the land with the ancestors of bison, reindeer and wild horses. Over the next millennia, they developed their tool making skills and began to settle.

Remainders of these early settlements could be found in the megalithic graves; large boulders were used as building blocks for burial sites, the giants' graves Hermann had referred to. Many of these were still unchanged, bearing witness to long gone and mysterious times.

'About two thousand years ago, northern Germanic tribes settled in the area,' Hermann explained. 'They continued their journey south some five hundred years later and the all but empty lands were subsequently populated by Slavic tribes moving west.'

Around the beginning of the ninth century the large and intricate migration of peoples that had characterised European history during the previous four centuries had come to an end and the situation stabilised. The west-Slavic people living in the north of Pomerania soon became known as *Pomorani*, 'those who live by the sea', as opposed to the east Slavic tribes who had settled further to the south and were called *Polani*. The following centuries were tumultuous for Pomerania, as Scandinavian, Danish, Wendish, Polish and German duchies vied for control of the area. The country was Christianised, and at the end of the twelfth century, the Duchy of Pomerania became part of the Holy Roman Empire under the German king Frederick Barbarossa. At the time, the area was still very sparsely populated, and the gentry, the current rulers of the land, encouraged the migration of farmers, tradesmen and merchants from the western parts of Germany to settle there.

When they crossed the river Oder, the children had long nodded off and even Ursula struggled to keep her eyes open; these names all meant nothing to her, and it was a long journey. Yet her husband continued his history lesson unperturbed. He told them that Pomerania began to prosper, that cities were founded and that, after more battles had been fought, the region became part of Prussia. It was the King of Prussia, Frederick the Great, who introduced the potato to Pomerania. Ironically, he virtually had to force this new crop onto his subjects, and it was not until well into the nineteenth century that potatoes found widespread acceptance. A hundred years later, when the young Eschenburg family arrived in Pomerania, *Kartoffeln* had become the mainstay of the local economy.

They had to change trains a number of times in ever smaller towns, until they reached a village called Eulenburg. It consisted of not more than a few houses, a post office and a railway station, where Erica Dennig was waiting for them on the one and only platform. She received the Eschenburgs with open arms and a broad smile.

Tante Erica to the children, she was a small and gracious woman, radiating energy and was, as they would soon learn, not scared of hard work. She had been a city girl, working in Hamburg as a secretary, when Heinz-Jürgen Dennig had proposed to her. Yet it hadn't taken her long to adjust to life in the country. With her husband having been called up, she now managed the vast estate of Juchow single-handedly.

To Walter's delight, Tante Erica had come in a horse-drawn carriage. She steered the two chestnut warmbloods effortlessly through the dense beech forest along the narrow and winding cobbled road that linked Eulenburg to Juchow.

When they arrived at what was commonly known as 'the castle', Walter couldn't believe his eyes. Grandfather Eschenburg's house in Lübeck had already surprised him with its size and grandeur, because he had always believed that their farmhouse at Uhlenhorst, with its *stoep* that surrounded it on three sides, was rather large. In fact, he'd thought that's what houses looked like.

Juchow, 1930s

MY HOME IS MY CASTLE

The carriage had come to a halt in front of the castle's main entrance with its sweeping stairs. Walter gazed at the magnificent red brick façade that rose before him. The two rows of large windows above the front door were flanked by symmetrical, tall and slender towers, wind vanes glinting in the afternoon sun atop their pointy roofs.

To the left was the new wing, not quite as elegant as the main façade, but if anything more imposing and majestic. To the right, completing the third arm of the u-shaped complex stood a double storey house with a large red tiled roof. It housed the pantry and store rooms and was home to the butler and his family. The dimensions of this building, the so-called *Hauswirtschaftsgebäude* were so big they could have fitted their house at Uhlenhorst into it several times.

And the trees! All around and behind the palace were the largest, proudest, most colourful trees Walter had ever seen. Across the cobbled street, which led from the castle to the village, he could make out something blue shining through the branches, Juchow Lake. A little further on stood a building with a high chimney, resembling a factory. It was the distillery, he'd later learn, where mere potatoes were turned into schnapps. Adjacent to it was the large farmyard surrounded by a barn, and stables for the cows, horses and pigs.

Beyond, closer to the village itself rose the spire of the *Marienkirche*, the church of St Mary, elegant and slim. Built from red brick, she looked surprisingly like her older, grander sister in Lübeck.

The houses in the village were, although modest, neat and tidy. The foundations and walls had been partly built of round boulders found in the surrounding fields, with brick structures on top. The windows were small and the eaves of the roofs hung low, some were covered with reeds, others with red tiles. Each house was surrounded by a little garden, separated from the neighbour's plot and the main street by painted, hip-high picket fences.

Tante Erica and her husband Heinz-Jürgen Dennig inhabited the new wing of the castle together with their six children, while the Eschenburgs were assigned three rooms on the second floor, behind the towers.

The next few weeks were paradise for Walter and his brother Hermann. Together with their cousins and the other children living in the castle, they explored every room and corner. Every day, they discovered something new; the *Schlosshalle*, the big hall with its collection of hunting trophies; the play room with its toy cupboard full of treasures; the library, famous, because it was the second largest in the region; the *Jagdstube*, the hunting room, with its gun cabinet; the cellar and the attic.

Walter felt it would take him forever to discover every secret this castle kept. It seemed huge, with an endless number of rooms. Shortly after their arrival, he attempted to count them all, but eventually had to give up. There were just too many.

'Hey, Hermann,' he said to his brother, 'I think it has at least ninety-nine rooms. If not more!'

The young Eschenburgs found out about the history of the castle and explored its surroundings.

The estate, they learned, included Juchow Lake, the village, extensive forests and vast cornfields. It had been bought by Karl August Dennig in 1874 together with the surrounding country estates from the von Kleists, a family of ancient nobility, settled here since the early thirteenth century.

For Karl August Dennig, himself the son of a successful family of trades- and businessmen in Baden, in south-western Germany, this was a prestigious project. Landholdings of the dimensions that could be acquired in Pomerania were not available where he came from and owning a country estate in these eastern regions had become the 'thing to do' and a somewhat romantic idea. The ground was fertile, and the endless forests lent themselves to forestry businesses and hunting. At the same time, one could rub shoulders with some noble families.

On the foundations of the eighteenth century manor house of the von Kleists, the Dennigs built a palace that was unique in Pomerania. It was singular in its eclectic style and surrounded by a large park, with a variety of indigenous and exotic trees.

In 1882, at the age of thirty-three, Karl August's son Georg Dennig, who had taken over the estate, decided the time had come to get married. In Berlin, he met the sixteen year old Ina Eschenburg from Lübeck, with whom he immediately and irrevocably fell in love. Georg soon found out that Ina was the daughter of the first family of the Hanseatic town. It took him ten months before he found access to the reserved Lübeck society, before her father, Walter's great grandfather, would see him. After a magnificent wedding in 1890, befitting the social standing of both families, Ina moved to Juchow.

Now, in 1939, the Dennigs were well established in the area. Their castle was famous and the once small settlement of Juchow had grown into a village with a population of nearly five hundred people, most of them gainfully employed by the Dennigs.

The Eschenburgs were not the only family that had found refuge at the castle. Relatives from all over the country had come to stay or had sent their children to this safe haven, far away from the cruelties of the war. At meal times, some twenty boys and girls were gathered around the children's table. They were strictly educated, Prussian style, as was custom in the manor houses of Pomerania. In the castle, they were seen, but not heard. The boys had to click their heels and bow when greeting an adult and the girls had to curtsy, behaviour patterns that were practised to perfection.

Soon Walter adapted to the routines of castle life, made friends with his cousins and learnt who was who. He realised quickly that it paid to be friendly with the *Mamsell*, who was not only in charge of the kitchen, but the queen of the household.

In her late fifties, she soon developed a soft spot for the shy, little blond boy who was always hungry. Walter only had to appear at the kitchen door and greet her politely to be slipped a slice of her homemade sausage, a piece of bread or, on special occasions, a taste of cake.

Mamsell was not to be confused with *Mademoiselle*, the children's governess and French teacher, employed to ensure their future worldliness. Both women, the large and feisty Mamsell, as well as the elegant, slim and gentle Mademoiselle, would get terribly upset when addressed by the wrong title.

In her efforts to provide the castle children with a more sophisticated education than the village school provided, Mademoiselle Jacqueline was joined by *Herr* Petzold, the tutor. There was also *Fräulein* Russ, another governess, and Tony Friedrich the nanny.

Tony was a distant relative of the Dennigs. She had been taken in after she was orphaned, her mother euthanized by the Nazis because she was blind. Also orphaned was Hänschen Bautz, the grandson of the castle's butler. The same age as Walter, the two boys quickly became close friends.

Outside the castle, Walter made acquaintance with Kuhnert, the chauffeur, and sometimes would help him polish the black Ford that was housed in the garage right next to the dog kennels, where the hunting dogs, mostly pointers and Weimaraners, were kept. Although in the later years of the war there was no petrol available to drive the car, Kuhnert would polish it each and every day. It was his pride and joy. Second in place was his moustache, a masterpiece of face hair that he looked after almost as thoroughly as the car. The ends were twisted and looked to the children somewhat polished, too.

'Mammie, why does Kuhnert have this stuff crawling out of his nose?' Elsa asked one day, much to the delight of her older brothers.

Teggerts, the coachman, was in charge of the stables and only too happy to teach the curious boys how to harness and drive the horses. And Herr Dummke was the forester, in whose footsteps Walter wanted to follow when he grew up. He loved it when Herr Dummke took him for a walk in the forest, pointing out spoors of deer and wild boar, the different calls of the forest birds and of course the edible wild fruit and mushrooms. He was only beaten in popularity by Old Bohm, the stockman, who enchanted the children with his little flutes and windmills before he was killed by a raging bull.

Walter and Herrmann also met the other cattlemen, stable hands and the blacksmith; the secretaries, kitchen and chambermaids and laundresses; the permanent employees, the seasonal labourers, and over time, most of the village people.

Life and fabric of this rural society hadn't changed much since the times of Kaiser William II. The revolution of 1918 and the Weimar Republic had not shown much effect on this part of Germany. Land was owned in large swathes by the upper class, many of noble birth, and the formerly feudal structures had not changed bar in name. Although life in bondage had been abolished more than a hundred years previously, there was a clear dependency between the masters of the manor houses and the peasants.

Employees of the castle had a comparatively high position in the village. They were given free accommodation and a small piece of land, on which they could cultivate potatoes and fodder beet. They were paid mostly in kind, receiving an exactly determined part of the estate's produce; potatoes, cereal and firewood. One cow and a calf per employee were allowed to graze on the estate's pastures, and the geese roamed the stubble fields after the harvest to put on the last grams of fat before slaughtering.

Only a handful of village families owned land in their own right, but all had their livestock. Cows, pigs and geese were part of every household. In general, villagers led a mostly self-sufficient life, and they could earn a little extra cash by selling milk and butter from their cows. Pigs were slaughtered and the meat preserved, and children contributed to family life by collecting blueberries and mushrooms in the forest. Every man, woman and child had their place in this society and nothing much ever changed.

Soon after their arrival it was decided that Walter and his brother needed to go to school too, just like all the other castle and village children. The school-teachers had all gone to war, and so it was their mother who took over this position. Known in the village as the 'English Lady', Ursula taught the children to read and write, and introduced them to maths, history and poetry.

The villagers were delighted to have a teacher passionate about the education of their children, yet the authorities had their doubts. In these times of racial hygiene, when the countryside was purged of foreigners, could the so-called English Lady impart the right values to the next generation of German children?

An inquisition was held and Walter felt the atmosphere in the castle was tense. Tante Erica and his father apparently had heard that government officials had been discussing the possibility of deporting his mother. But some strings were pulled, a pig donated and eventually the storm blew over.

Ursula was allowed to stay and continue teaching, but not without being advised to include more of the correct political education.

A couple of weeks after their arrival, the autumn storms passed over Pomerania, and the trees lost their last leaves. Their first European winter greeted the South African children with icy, biting easterly winds from the Siberian steppes, bringing cold air and unusual amounts of snow, which of course they had never seen before.

Juchow Lake froze over, and it was the first time in their lives that they experienced real cold. The chill of a Highveld winter morning in South Africa, when there was perhaps a little frost on the grass, could not compare. This was a totally different experience. They learned to skate and discovered the joys of skiing, tobogganing, and being pulled through the snow by an old veteran horse called *Vater*.

Country life at Juchow was determined by the idiosyncrasies of each distinct season and the associated rituals, ceremonies and festivals. Some were Christian, others pagan, most of them a combination of both. Some culminated in huge feasts, and others meant hard work. Something they all had in common was their connection to the land and its produce, and that they had been celebrated in one form or another for centuries.

For Walter, the first year at Juchow seemed to swing from one exciting celebration to the next. There were of course those he knew, Christmas, New Year and Easter, but also some others he had not really even heard of before.

SEASONS AND RITUALS

Pfingsten was celebrated in May. Winter was long forgotten, all the trees were coming into leaf, and everything was green and fresh and so intense, it never ceased to amaze me.

'Tomorrow is Pfingsten,' we were told.

Pentecost had never really featured on our calendar back home in South Africa.

'Tomorrow is Pfingsten and we all have to get up early. But remember, you are not allowed to utter a word until you have collected the *Pfingstwasser*,' we were told.

The Pentecostal water, Tante Erica explained, had to be fetched at first light from the little stream in the park behind the castle. This water had some magical properties. It was believed that it would bring good luck and make all the girls beautiful - but only if it was fetched in silence. As if that wasn't a hard enough task in itself, some of the older, naughty boys had fun trying to break the spell by making us laugh or giving us a fright. What it was really about, I'm not too sure, but it was serious.

Once we all had washed in the magic water and dressed in our finest Sunday attire, a span of horses arrived with a hay cart to take us into the bright green birch forest. Armed with little choppers, saws and axes, we each cut down a couple of young trees and loaded them onto the cart until it was piled high. Driving down the village street, we then offloaded two trees at each house and placed them next to the front door, until there were only six or eight trees left, which we put around the castle.

Every building thus adorned with this symbol of spring, it was time for church. During the annual Pentecostal service at the church of St Mary, we, the Eschenburgs and the Dennigs, sat in our dedicated pews right in front, with the village people behind us.

The highlight for us boys was that on this occasion we were allowed to ring the church bells. We took turns pulling the ropes and the large bells began to chime in rhythmic waves, the sound reverberating through our entire bodies. It was a magical experience!

After the service, celebrations continued in the castle hall, which was decorated with flowers, green branches and all the joys of spring. The big wooden table was set and I will always remember this as the first real feast I ever participated in. I ate and drank until I could no more and then I struggled to keep my eyes open. There were processions around the hall, poems were recited and a lot of singing and dancing that continued until late into the evening.

Also in May, my father and I would go out into the forest at the end of the lake for another magic experience. We'd observe the deer in their mating rituals, and there was one specific roebuck that we looked out for every year. He always came out onto the same clearing and each year he was bigger and stronger.

My father knew how to imitate the doe's call. With pursed lips he'd make a squeaky noise and after a few attempts, the buck would eventually appear. He'd jump out and bounce on his feet, like a springbok *pronking*, drinking in the wind, as they say here in South Africa. If a roebuck did that, jump straight up and down on stiff legs, he was called a 'May-Buck', because he'd only show this behaviour in May, during breeding time.

Summer was all about swimming in the lake. A sandy footpath sheltered by fragrant, lush green vegetation led down to the best swimming spot, which incidentally couldn't be overseen from the castle.

Castle and village youth mingled happily on the shore and what mattered was only how far one could swim. We were meant to wear swimsuits, while the village children just unashamedly swam naked. But as soon as the adults were out of sight, bathing suits were ditched by all of us.

The swimming spot was ideal for getting in and out of the water, with grass sloping right down to the water's edge, but we had even more fun a little further on, at a place called *Hechtlaiche*. It was a rather muddy area, where the pike were said to lay their eggs. The mud there was pitch black and one of our best games was to roll in it and smear it all over us until we were covered from head to toe.

Later in the summer, the swimming examination loomed. It was a ritual that had been practised for years and the result determined whether we were considered still small, half-small or big. Juchow Lake was more than five kilometres long, but close to the village it was only about two to three hundred metres wide. Tradition stipulated that in order to pass the exam we had to cross the lake from the swimming spot to the watering place for the cattle on the other side, and back.

It was a scary venture. The lake was very deep, and there were rumours that a dragon lived in the depths below. During the previous winter I had seen with my own eyes how part of the lake never froze, even if temperatures fell well below zero and the entire landscape was covered in snow.

'That's because of the dragon,' I was told, 'it breathes fire.'

Some years later it would dawn on me, that what kept the lake from freezing was actually the warm water, the effluent from our potato distillery, but one couldn't be too sure.

I was certainly quite wary of that dragon when I lined up to do the swimming test for the first time, but I was determined to pass. I was so determined that I very nearly drowned. I had learned to swim by then, but I was still considered to be small, if not very small, and I really wanted to change that. So I swam and swam and swam, and somehow I missed the watering place on the other side. I ended up a little further along the shore, in an area that was covered in reeds. They were so dense that I couldn't see how to get to the shore. Then I found an aisle. It had been cut to allow the hunters to shoot duck. I didn't know though, that the reeds were cut only just below the surface, so once I got into this aisle, I was properly stuck. The reed stumps seemed to be holding onto my legs from below and made me think of the dragon.

Fortunately, Hermann had been keeping an eye on his little brother, as usual, and he came to my rescue.

Despite this little incident, I passed the swimming test and my status was elevated to half-small.

In autumn we celebrated *Erntedank*, the equivalent to Thanksgiving. Every year, at the end of the season, the villagers gathered for a great procession, and each and every person carried little bits of their harvest as gifts. Some had bunches of rye, wheat or oats, others bundles of garden vegetables. These were put around the big castle hall which, on this one day of the year, was open to everybody.

The most senior village person then handed the harvest crown to the head of the castle. Normally it would have been Uncle Heinz-Jürgen, but because he was away fighting in the war, Tante Erica took his place. The crown was made from straw and would later find a place of honour in the castle, where it would remain until the following year.

Thanks were given to each other and then in a loud chorus to God, before a noisy feast ensued. Amongst the revellers were people dressed up as symbols of good luck. There was a bear, who danced with his chain, and a chimney-sweep, who carried a ladder and, with a big ball on a rope, chased after the girls trying to mark them with some soot. There was the *Glücksschwein*, a fat, pink and happily grinning pig, and the *Klapperstorch*, who according to local belief delivered the babies. He was also after the girls with his long, sharp and bright red beak. If he pecked a girl, it was said, she'd have a baby the following year.

It was a noisy and happy feast, with plenty of beer and schnapps for the men, and coffee and cake for the women.

Later in autumn, it was time to dig up potatoes, by far the most important crop in the region. Potatoes grew exceptionally well in the sandy soils of Eastern Pomerania and were exported all over the country.

But people didn't only eat potatoes, they also drank them. *Kartoffelschnaps* was part of daily life, and from the manor houses to the poorest peasant's hut a glass of schnapps was enjoyed by everybody. It was so popular, that most estates had their own distilleries.

The gathering of potatoes was the last harvest effort of the season, and it was really hard work. The fields were vast, each potato had to be picked by hand, and all hands were needed. The mechanical potato harvester was drawn by three horses, unearthing a couple of rows of potatoes at a time, with everybody following behind.

It was great fun. Instead of going to school, we collected potatoes. And what we liked best about it was that we got paid for it, just like the villagers. We filled baskets and panniers and for every full receptacle we were handed differently shaped discs. At the end of the harvest we were paid according to the amount of potatoes, or rather discs, we had collected.

In the early mornings it was quite cold already, so we quickly learned to make a potato fire. The leaves and stalks were dry at this time of year, and we'd make a heap and light it. We'd do some work, and once a basket was full, we'd warm our fingers at the fire before rushing off again. If we were lucky, there were some tiny potatoes left at the end of the plants and they roasted slowly in the fire. When we came back with our full baskets, we'd look out for these almost burnt little things. They were most delicious, with a taste all of their own. In a way, that was an even better reward than the money we received.

Winter would come again, and round Christmas time, when the snow was high and the nights long, the whole family would go out on Sundays to feed the deer. Vater, the old horse, was harnessed to a large sleigh full of hay, and we went for a drive into the forest. I loved this winter adventure, not least because of the can of piping hot soup that was taken along. Mugs of it were handed out once the hay had been laid out for the deer and we all agreed that pea soup had never tasted as good as on those icy winter days.

Throughout the year we had a lot of fun. We never got bored or lacked company because there were so many of us. We were mostly left to our own devices, the older children looking after the younger ones. My brother Hermann got me out of trouble more than once, and I always looked after Elsa, our little sister. She was still very small and her feet often hurt from walking on the cobbled stones, so I'd carry her around on my back a lot. We were mostly cousins from different branches of the family and all grew up like brothers and sisters. But there were friendships that went beyond that and some very special bonds developed, usually between cousins of a similar age.

Christa Dennig and I were two who soon became inseparable. We were good, bad and only sometimes indifferent, and we were always up to something. We loved nothing more than discovering what nature had on offer and soon we were *au fait* with most of the fauna and flora surrounding Juchow.

It was a world full of adventures. Often, when we got home in the evening, dirty and tired but happy and excitedly chatting about our latest escapade, we got into trouble. Christa more so than I, because she was a girl and she did boys' things; I less so, because I was the little homeless boy and the adults felt sorry for me. For no real reason. Despite the circumstances, I had the time of my life.

BULLFIGHT

On a memorable afternoon in May 1942, Christa and Walter skipped along the track that led over the *Kaninchenberg*, the Rabbit Hill, and on to the paddocks on the lake's shore where the villagers' cows were taken to graze.

The beech and oak trees were resplendent in their new green foliage and the meadows bursting with fresh, nutritious grass. The birds were twittering as if to make up for lost time and the long winter's silence, and along the path, the edges lined with a myriad of spring flowers, butterflies and bumblebees were plying their trade.

'Christa, how come you call this little hill Kaninchenberg?' Walter asked his cousin and best friend. More reserved and thoughtful than the other boys, he preferred her company to the rough and tough war games played by his older brother Hermann and his friends.

Christa had to ponder the question for a second. She had never thought about it, had just picked up the name from her older siblings. But Walter wanted to know everything, he never stopped asking questions.

'Don't know, Walter, maybe there are a lot of rabbits up here?' she replied, shrugging her shoulders which sent her blond pigtails whipping while she skipped along the path.

Passing the modest houses of the Gochowanzeks, the Falks and some of the other families who all worked on the estate, they cheerfully greeted the many children they met along the way.

They were looking for Old Bohm, the stockman, hoping to persuade him to make them *Weidenflöten*, little flutes fashioned from the young branches of willow trees that grew around the lake. They found him together with his cows at the *Gänseweide*.

Amongst the children Old Bohm was extremely popular. He spent his days herding the villagers' cattle, and he had done so all his life. He had learned the trade and inherited the position from his father, who had followed in the footsteps of his grandfather. One day, his oldest son, young Bohm, would take over.

He must have been tall when he was younger, but years of hard work had taken their toll. Nobody knew exactly how old he was, but his dark eyes sparkled in a wizened face, wrinkled by seasons spent outdoors. The last few strands of grey hair were hidden under a felt hat that Old Bohm never parted with, except in church. He always wore long, grey trousers held up by braces and a dark green felt jacket, the buttons of which he had carved from stag horn.

Beneath these clothes, now hanging loose on the old man's thin frame, remained a surprising strength. No one else in the village was quite as strong as Old Bohm, the rumours went. The stick he invariably carried, intricately carved from oak wood, was a sign of his trade. He was a man of few words, but knew how to win the children's hearts.

'Herr Bohm, Herr Bohm, please, can you make us a Weidenflöte! Please Herr Bohm!' Walter and Christa pleaded, addressing the old man respectfully. His willow flutes were amongst the most prized possessions the children could have.

'Not today,' he shook his head with a sad smile. 'It's late already and I have to take the cows back home. It's nearly time for milking. Look, they are getting impatient. Come back tomorrow.'

Walter and Christa nodded. They watched how Old Bohm rounded up the cattle and slowly led them back towards the village. They knew there was no point in trying to force the old man, but tomorrow they'd come back.

Slowly, they wandered along the lake, back to the castle. Christa picked some flowers and Walter practised whistling on long blades of grass. They looked for flat stones and let them skip over the water. Suddenly, Walter grabbed Christa's arm.

'*Shhh*,' he said, holding his finger up to his lips. He pointed to the edge of the forest.

In front of a bramble thicket stood a lonely fox, his red coat glinting in the afternoon sun. With his beady eyes he scrutinised the cousins, now motionless, holding their breaths. After what seemed an eternity, he turned and casually loped away, disappearing into the forest.

For another moment, the children stood still, savouring the magic of the moment. When they eventually turned to resume their way home, both of them smiled.

'You know, Christa, this was very, very special,' Walter whispered, with a seriousness beyond his years.

'Yes, it was beautiful. And we shall never forget it,' Christa replied, and quietly, each lost in their own thoughts, they continued along their way.

As they got closer to the castle, they noticed that people were rushing towards the farmyard and heard loud shouting.

'Come on, let's check what's happening there,' Christa nudged Walter, and they started running. What they saw when they arrived scared them both.

The bull was loose, running wild in the yard. The scene resembled a Spanish bullfight, with Old Bohm the most unlikely torero. Armed only with his big stick, he tried to get the beast back into the stable.

The bull would have nothing of it. Despite his size, he was surprisingly quick on his feet and evaded Old Bohm and his stick time and time again.

The entire village had now gathered at the entrance to the farmyard, watching the spectacle from a safe distance. They all had a healthy respect for this large, black and white animal. The atmosphere became more and more agitated, and the bull, as well as Old Bohm, more and more angry.

'This is not going to end well,' one of the villagers standing close to the children mumbled, shaking his head.

'*Ach* no man, Old Bohm knows what he's doing. If anyone can get that beast back into the stable, than it's him,' another bystander said.

With bated breath they saw now how Bohm managed to hit the bull hard with his stick, and indeed, the animal moved a few steps towards the stable. A sigh of relief could be heard from the crowd. Too soon.

The bull, now really angry, turned on his heel. He stood for a second breathing heavily, and then he charged. He went straight for the stockman. Before he had time to react, the old man was thrown into the air, fell to the ground and the beast was over him.

Some women screamed, Christa covered her face with her hands, just peering through the spread fingers, and Walter watched with wide eyes.

Some of the men now took action. Not wanting to get too close to the angry animal, they aimed a hay wagon at the bull, attempting to push him off the old man with the wagon shaft.

'Michel, Michel, come quickly!' somebody shouted. Michel was the village policeman and, attracted by the noise resounding through the village, he had walked over to the farmyard.

'Police! Get out of the way!' he shouted. He took in the scene, thought for a second, and then drew his gun.

After about the fifth shot, followed by an eerie silence, the bull left his victim. He looked up at the crowd, bellowed once and then walked slowly but steadily towards the water's edge.

The crowd was quiet now, shocked, as it watched the bull walk into the lake.

With water up to his knees, he turned and looked once more at the gathering of people, dropped his head and blew into the water. A large, bright red bubble rose in front of his nose. Then he collapsed and died.

Not only the children were intrigued by the drama and it took time before somebody arrived with a span of oxen and hauled the bull out of the lake and off to be slaughtered. Slowly, the crowd dispersed.

For old stockman Bohm, nothing could be done. He died in the yard, trampled by the bull he had known and tended all his life.

Not surprisingly, this tragic episode was talked about in the village for months, if not years, until far more dramatic events engulfed Juchow. But until then, it was Michel, the policeman, who had to bear the brunt of the villagers' teasing.

'*Der Michel, der Michel, der kann ja nicht schiessen. Der hat sieben Schüsse gebraucht um den Bullen zu erschiessen!* – Michel doesn't know how to shoot. It took him seven shots to kill the bull!'

THE GEESE

The years we spent at Juchow really left some profound memories and one of my fondest is of the geese. All the people in the village had geese which, during spring and summer, were sent to graze on the Gänseweide, a paddock on the other side of the lake.

In the mornings, each of the young village women carried a basket full of little goslings and the adult geese would walk behind. At dusk, they had to be brought back home to safety, otherwise the fox or the marten would come and get them. As the goslings grew bigger, they started to swim back in the evenings.

Just imagine, hundreds of fowl swimming across the lake on their way home to the village, bright white birds against the soft, late afternoon light.

We used to run to the shore calling excitedly, '*Die Gänse kommen*, the geese are coming!'

It was a spectacular sight! And we were always amazed when we observed how they came ashore, walked down the village street and then turned into their respective homes, all knowing exactly where they lived.

Once the wheat had been brought in, the villagers' geese were fattened on the estate's stubble fields and in return every seventh goose belonged to the castle. Closer to Christmas, when the lake started to freeze over and the first snow covered the grazing, it was time for the *Gänseschlachtfest*, a feast dedicated to the slaughtering of the geese.

The village women and the maids from the castle did the killing and plucking together. It was a jolly event, with lots of coffee and cake, singing and gossiping.

Feathers and down were separated; the finer feathers were collected and stored in big sacks, while the down was used to stuff *plumeaus*. I couldn't believe my luck the first time I slept under such a fine down blanket; it weighed next to nothing, covered my entire bed and although it was freezing outside, I felt as warm as toast.

With so many geese slaughtered at the same time, their meat had to be preserved. Some parts were smoked, others salted or bottled. The innards were cooked into patés or certain types of sausage. Two specific meals were inevitably linked to this occasion. One was called *Gänse-schwarz-sauer*, which consisted of goose blood cooked with vinegar, and was eaten with cranberries and mashed potatoes.

The real delicacy though was *Gänseköpfe*, goose heads. The beaks were cut off and the heads cooked and served with a sour sauce. They were usually put on a bed of mashed potatoes and eaten with two special knives with sharp points. It was quite a feat to cut them open and get to the brains, but it was well worth it; they were fantastic!

A HARD-WORKING WALKING STICK

For Walter there was no doubt. The most interesting room in the castle was the Jagdstube, the hunting chamber. It was full of mystery, saturated by the smells of mothballs, gunpowder and oil. Situated upstairs in the older part of the castle, it was at the end of a long, dark passage, and the curtains were always drawn.

What made this gloomy room most intriguing was the fact that it was strictly forbidden territory for the children. It was used by the adult hunters only. There was an odd collection of old trophies on the walls, a pool table, some antique chairs and a gun cabinet.

The latter, always locked, proved to be interesting beyond measure. Only once or twice had Walter got a glimpse of its contents, and over time he had developed a burning desire to investigate what treasures lay hidden behind its locked doors. Quietly he hatched a plan.

One wintry afternoon he was waiting impatiently for Hänschen Bautz. The two boys often played together; both were terribly interested in guns, a fascination that Christa didn't share.

'Hänschen, finally! I thought you'd never come!' Walter could hardly stand still, he was so excited. 'I must show you something! Guess what I've got here?'

'Looks like the key for your toy cupboard,' Hänschen said.

Ja, and guess where it fits?'

Hänschen just shrugged his shoulders. He wasn't sure where all this was leading.

'Come with me, I'll show you!'

Walter turned around and ran up the stairs. Making sure that nobody was watching, he led the way along the dark passage and into the hunting room.

'Man, Walter, you know we are not allowed in here!' Hänschen was nervously looking over his shoulder. If anybody saw him, he'd be in big trouble indeed.

'I know, I know, but I just have to show you something,' Walter insisted and tip-toed through the room, around the pool table and to the old gun cabinet.

Hänschen just stared as Walter inserted the key into the cabinet's keyhole. It turned and, with a loud creak, the doors opened.

For a moment the boys held their breaths, but nobody seemed to have heard the noise. Inside the cabinet, they found rifles, pistols and ammunition. Forgotten now was the fear that somebody might come and discover them here on forbidden ground, too fascinating was the treasure they had unearthed. They took out the guns carefully, stroked them longingly and imagined all sorts of adventures.

The most exciting piece was a twelve millimetre rifle.

'Wow, look at this thing!'

The boys were astounded.

'*Sjoe*! This is so big, you could stick your bum into its opening!'

'I've got an idea!' Walter suddenly grinned.

'Why don't we go and try it out. Nobody will ever know. Imagine shooting with that thing!'

The problem was, though, that there was no ammunition for this rifle in the cabinet. But quickly, Walter found a solution.

'Hänschen, you know, when I went hunting with father, he used that *drilling* gun. Maybe one of those bullets will fit.'

'But aren't they much smaller?'

'*Ja*, they have a smaller calibre, but they have rims around the ends and, maybe, they could fit.'

There was no holding them back now. Into the castle's new wing they went, to borrow a bullet from the new hunting room and then back to the old gun cabinet to fetch the rifle. Once outdoors, they walked along the *Buchengang*, a kilometre-long alleyway fringed by the grey, elephantine trunks of majestic beech trees, leading away from the castle and up a little hill.

Suddenly, the boys stopped in their tracks.

'Look there!' Walter whispered.

'A rabbit!' Hänschen replied.

'Shoot it, shoot it!' Walter had a bee in his bonnet now.

'But we are not allowed to!'

'Let's just shoot it! Come on!'

They put the bullet into the rifle, and Walter leant against the tree and pulled the trigger. But instead of the expected loud bang, they heard a rather strange, whooping sound.

The rabbit was still sitting there, a little further down the beech corridor. It licked its paws, cleaned its long ears and every now and again shot the boys a curious glance.

This was not what they had expected at all. It had been a true misfire. They found that the cartridge, or what was left of it, was stuck awkwardly inside the barrel. Even more nervous now that they would be found out, the two boys carried the rifle back to the castle, and it took them a long time and even more perseverance to remove the trapped bullet. Somewhat sheepishly, they cleaned the gun thoroughly and put it back into its place without anybody seeing them.

They were not caught, but they certainly had got a taste for this type of adventure. Some months later, Walter got hold his father's old drilling; it was a triple-barrelled gun, shotgun and rifle in one.

Walter and Hänschen picked up the shotgun cartridges they had found some weeks earlier and stored away for an occasion just like this, and they ventured out into the park. Nobody else was around when they walked past the pond and the idea struck.

'Hey! Why don't we try and shoot a carp?'

The shot rang out and the noise was much louder than they'd thought was possible. They never found out if they'd actually hit a carp, because while their ears were still ringing, grandfather Bautz came running out of the castle.

He didn't say anything to anybody other than to the two boys, and to them he talked with a very hard-working stick. His walking stick did overtime that afternoon, and Hänschen and Walter never, ever attempted to shoot carp again.

HEROES AND HUNTERS

At times, I think, I was actually quite naughty. Very naughty in fact. I remember once thinking they were going to send me to jail. Seriously! It all had to do with my fascination for guns.

Keeping Grandfather Bautz's walking stick in mind, Hänschen and I shifted our focus for a little while from guns and shooting to other pastimes, but temptation loomed everywhere. And when I found a small case of army ammunition I just couldn't resist. There were about five hundred rounds in this box, and we were going to see if we could do something with it. In the meantime I hid the box in what I thought was a safe place.

When the police came to the castle, I knew I was in trouble. And it wasn't Michel, the village policeman who knocked on the door, but military police. They were really, really scary. I was sent upstairs, but I could see on my parents' and Tante Erica's faces that this was serious. The son of the 'English Lady' had stolen bullets.

During the war years, whenever somebody was meant to be really warned or, probably more to the point, threatened, he was told,

'Du kommst ins KZ – you'll be sent to the concentration camp', and that was what I feared now. It was terrible. I passed weeks and weeks in huge fear. I don't know how my father and Tante Erica placated the policemen, but the whole story was hushed up and never spoken about again.

I don't think I ever experienced the same sort of fear again in my life. But that my father wasn't sent to prison was probably more to the point. Only much later did I realize that he was the one who was really in danger.

Still, I had an unquenchable fascination for guns and hunting and my big hero at the time was our Uncle Bogislav, Boli for short. A somewhat eccentric man, he always seemed to think a little differently to the majority of people. Uncle Boli owned the farm bordering Juchow and was the estate manager at Juchow before he had to go to war.

He didn't seem to take it too seriously though, because whenever it was time for the annual deer hunt, Uncle Boli was there. For inexplicable reasons, he developed some or other infectious childhood disease every year shortly before the hunting season began. One year it was measles and the next season it was mumps or chicken pox that struck him down. He was promptly sent home, so the infection wouldn't spread, or that's what we believed. Miraculously, his condition always improved dramatically in time for the great stag hunt.

Bit by bit, I pieced together my favourite uncle's story. Also part of the large Eschenburg family, Boli's father had owned a vast estate and Boli had studied agriculture. When his father sold the estate in the 1920s Boli was terribly upset at first, but then he decided to take his inheritance and emigrate. While he was still making plans, the Great Depression and the first wave of inflation hit Germany during the Weimar Republic, and literally overnight the inheritance, now hard cash instead of vast swathes of land, became worthless. Boli was stuck and not quite sure what to do, when to the rescue came Heinz-Jürgen Dennig. He employed his distant cousin as a farm manager and provided him with a credit with which he was able to buy his own land.

To go hunting with Uncle Boli was one of my greatest pleasures. In autumn, soon after the Gänseschlachtfest, it was time for the *Schnepfenstrich*, the annual snipe hunt. Although my father was not really a passionate hunter, he organised it and Uncle Boli was there, every year.

We usually set off about an hour before sunset and went into the *Auenbruch*, a swampy clearing deep within the Juchow forest. There we sat quietly, waiting for the snipe to fly over, and I learned to identify the birds by their evening songs.

The last one to sing before it got dark was the *Amsel*, the blackbird, with a beautiful melody. Then silence descended. Now was the time for the snipe.

They always flew over the clearing in a certain direction, but only when it was very dark already. Although one could hear them coming and identify them by their unique sound, a deep *'gnawk, gnawk'*, I realized quickly that only a very skilled hunter would be able to shoot them. And one year my father shot two!

During another year's snipe hunt, father and Uncle Boli shot one each. On their way home, the two men carried the birds on what was known as a *Hühnergalgen*, an arrangement of hooks and leather straps that the hunter carried on his belt and onto which the dead birds were hung.

That night, Uncle Boli led the procession home, father followed behind and I brought up the rear. Boli was walking at a brisk pace, the snipe dangling from his belt. Suddenly, my father turned around with a naughty smile on his face. He held his finger to his lips, signalling me to be quiet. Then he sped up a little so that he was walking directly behind Uncle Boli. Amazed I watched as he drew his hunting knife and furtively held it to the neck of Boli's snipe. Through the dangling motion it was cut in no time, the bird fell to the ground and father picked it up without changing the rhythm of his step. He put it into his hunting bag and Uncle Boli didn't notice a thing. Only when we got back to the castle and he wanted to show off his snipe, did he realise that there was only the bird's head still attached to his belt. He was terribly disappointed.

The next morning I anticipated the traditional hunters' breakfast with particular excitement. Uncle Boli was not his usual cheerful and boisterous self and I almost felt sorry for him. Sheepishly he received his plate with just the snipe's head, while father very generously distributed pieces of his bird to us boys. Yet Boli's expression changed when another plate was served to his hunting partner with a second, headless snipe on it. Within seconds he was chasing my father around the breakfast table, both men laughing madly.

When I turned ten, I was allowed to use a small calibre rifle. I'd get three bullets for it, and could go out and shoot rabbits or squirrels. That was easier said than done.

My brother Hermann was a brilliant shot, but I was no damn good. To be honest, I was completely useless. Sometimes I let Hermann use the gun, and when he shot a squirrel, we skinned it very carefully and then tanned it the same way we had seen the Afrikaners back in South Africa do their raw hide tanning. We made the most beautiful squirrel carpet for our little sister Elsa's dolls house. It only stank a little bit.

During that time, I made friends with Jean Pierre, a French prisoner of war who was working for the Dennigs. He was my hero, and I became his big pal. Today I think that maybe he only became my mate because he wanted to shoot something with that gun I was allowed to carry around. Who knows?

As the war progressed it became increasingly difficult to find labour to work the large estates. By now most men had been drafted and many had died. In a last desperate effort to mobilise forces, even boys from as young an age as fifteen, old men, and others who up to then had been deemed not suitable, were stuck into uniforms. Our father was one of them, it didn't matter anymore that he had a South African passport. Luckily though, he was given an administrative job in Neustettin, a small town close by. In the villages and on the farms, there were only women and children left, as well as the really old, injured and sick men. The women, although used to hard work, could not cope alone. Since the area was important for food production, so-called 'foreign workers', who were really forced labourers and prisoners of war, were allocated to each estate. On Juchow alone, there were at least two hundred of them, some French and others Polish.

Jean Pierre was a man of many talents. Back home, in his French village, he had been the pastor. In the French army he was a tank driver, and because times were hard, he had become an expert poacher. He showed me how to set snares and taught me, eventually, how to shoot.

We were perhaps an unlikely pair, but we often went out together hunting rabbits. Jean Pierre was desperate for me to let him have a shot while I so dearly wanted to shoot my first rabbit.

'Please, man, you can have the rabbit, just let me shoot it. You'll miss anyway,' Jean Pierre tried to convince me.

'No, no, no. I can't,' I replied. 'You are a prisoner of war and I'll go to jail if I give you the gun.'

I really didn't want to get into trouble again; the incident with the army ammunition was not yet forgotten.

'Come on, nobody will ever know.' Jean Pierre didn't give up easily.

'No, I really can't. I'm not allowed to.'

And so we carried on until we reached the asparagus fields.

In summer, after the asparagus had been cut, it was heaped and a few shoots were allowed to grow. They sprouted into large ferns, some nearly as tall as I was in those days. We were quietly walking amongst these asparagus whisks, when Jean Pierre whispered,

'There it is!'

I looked around but couldn't see it, whatever it was.

'There, there is the rabbit, give me the gun!'

'No, I can't! Where is it?'

Without a further word, Jean Pierre then took a flying dive over two rows of asparagus, and when I saw him again, he was standing in the middle of the field with a rabbit in his hand. There was blood everywhere and I realised that he had chopped off the creature's head with the side of his hand.

From that moment on my admiration for Jean Pierre knew no bounds. He could do nothing wrong. And when we saw another rabbit, I let him shoot it.

He gave me the dead animal to take home, because if I used up my three bullets without being able to prove I had shot anything, then I'd have to go for three weeks without. But if I brought back my spoils, I was given another three bullets.

So eventually we had a nice deal going. Jean Pierre would shoot two rabbits, one for me and another one for himself that he would take home to eat.

There was one place we avoided, and that was the forest of Kuchorow. We knew it was haunted. I had been there on occasion hunting with my father, just the two of us. At dusk, this forest became very eerie. It was dead quiet, just the owl was calling, and it sounded seriously ominous. It sent shivers down my spine. Quite how scared I was, I tried to hide, because my father maintained that there was no reason for it. But everybody knew that the forest of Kuchorow was haunted.

And couple of years into our stay at Juchow, we were warned that under no circumstances were we allowed to go into the forest. It transpired that one of the forced labourers had allegedly raped a young village girl, and in an attempt at community justice, the villagers had strung him up in the forest of Kuchorow.

'Raped?' I asked my father, 'What is that?'

'Ja,' he replied, 'that is very, very bad behaviour.'

He made sure that we didn't see the man hanging in the tree, and I don't think we ever ventured back into that forest.

A NARROW ESCAPE

For some time, the war had remained a distant reality for Walter and the other children at Juchow. Although most of the families had lost some of their men, daily life seemed to run more or less its normal course. People were spared from the terror of falling bombs that ravaged the cities, and the front lines appeared far away. Refugees who had lost their homes in the cities had found shelter with relatives in this sparsely populated countryside, and children from the industrial regions were sent here to be safe.

The children and most of the rural people accepted the reality of the war, just as they accepted a drought or a hard winter. What else could they do? Times were tough, but they had lived through tough times before, had survived the First World War and what followed afterwards. Surely, it couldn't be that much worse?

Far removed from world politics, life in the villages carried on. Cows had to be milked, wood cut, pigs slaughtered. Wheat and potatoes had to be harvested and geese and cattle needed herding. Children were born and people died. News of deaths on the battlefields were taken in their stride. The men had gone for some time; life was hard, but it had to go on.

Walter and his siblings hadn't known life in Germany before the war. They had, however, in South Africa, experienced life in a society where not all people were regarded as equal. There were many new things to explore, a whole new life to be discovered. What did it matter that there was a war on?

They had obviously heard of France and England, but Germany had fought wars against those two countries before, they had been told at school. They knew how to speak English and, since being able to converse in French was still seen as a sign of being cultured, they had a dedicated French teacher living with them in the castle.

Stories of the war with Russia sounded slightly more worrying. The children knew Russia was enormous; and it was full of communists, they had been told. What a communist was, they had no idea; they had only heard it was a bad thing.

And as for America, it was even further away than South Africa. Red Indians fought there against cowboys in the Wild West, hardly an image to spread serious worries. And quite a few people of Pomerania - there were some known in each village - had actually immigrated to America in search of a better life.

Food was scarce at times, the meals not as sumptuous as they used to be, but there was no hunger. The agricultural production had been adapted to produce crops that were needed to feed the country during wartime, a certain amount of which had to be handed over to the authorities. School children helped with the potato and grain harvests and beechnuts were collected for the production of oil, while geese and pigs provided meat. There was milk to make butter; wild fruit, blueberries and mushrooms were gathered in the extensive forests, and rabbits and deer hunted.

But perceptions of a more or less normal life were deceiving, and as the war advanced, its gruesome realities became more and more apparent, even to the children.

When the Eschenburgs had arrived at Juchow, all but one Polish family had been deported already. For a few months, Teresa and Alwin had been Walter's classmates in the village school and they'd become friends - until they disappeared, their fate not spoken about. There was always the underlying threat that Walter's mother, the 'English Lady' might not be German enough. There was talk of concentration camps, of deportations, of executions without trial, and illegal shootings of Polish and Jewish people, gypsies and dissidents. And the fact that Tony's mother had been killed because she was blind.

There were the von Ludenow boys, distant cousins of the Eschenburgs', who arrived on leave from the front. They went hunting together with the boys and shot a stag to great jubilation, before they had to go back. Shortly afterwards Walter heard that one of them had been killed. Not much later, another three died, until there was only one cousin left.

News arrived one day that Heinz-Jürgen Dennig had died in Russia, leaving Tante Erica widowed and their six children fatherless.

The military had requisitioned one wing of the castle for their officers to stay in during the four years of Germany's Eastern Campaign, which would become the largest and most lethal military operation in human history. Characterised by unprecedented atrocities, mass deportations, starvation, diseases and massacres, it left more than thirty million people, soldiers and civilians, dead.

Only a few kilometres to the south of Juchow, the German army maintained a military training area and an infamous prisoner of war camp, where twelve thousand people found their death during the war years.

After the battle of Stalingrad was lost and the eastern front began moving westwards, when the first waves of refugees from Eastern Prussia passed through Pomerania, it became clear that the reality of the war was going to demand more sacrifices.

In early January 1945 Ursula Eschenburg walked with Elsa through the large hall on the ground floor of the castle, its walls adorned by the most prized trophies of the annual stag hunts.

Elsa, now six years old, held on tight to her mother's hand. She had always regarded the antlers with some suspicion, but what really scared her were the stuffed heads of the grandest stags shot in better times, their glassy eyes seemingly observing every movement in the hall. Suddenly, she stopped in her tracks.

'Mammie, Mammie, did you hear that?'

Ursula's thoughts had been miles away, wondering, as so often, when they could go back home to South Africa. They had been at Juchow for so long now that she sometimes lost all hope. If only this wretched war was over. It was little things that would cause the Heimweh to flare up.

Like when she saw Kuhnert polish the black Ford every day without fail, although for years now there had been no petrol. It made her think of her own car, a black Model T Ford, which she hoped was still parked at Uhlenhorst.

Sometimes, only sometimes, did she allow herself to dream; she would pack her family into the black car and just start driving south. All the way through Europe, across the Mediterranean in Italy and then further on, until they'd arrive in South Africa. She missed her country with every fibre of her body, although she tried not to show it. What point was there in showing it? They had to stay in Germany until this wretched war was over.

What made matters worse was the fact that, despite everything, her husband Hermann seemed to love his life here. By a twist of fate, his biggest childhood dream, managing an estate in Pomerania, had come true. Ursula had realised it when the devastating news had reached them that Uncle Heinz-Jürgen would not be coming back home. In an effort to comfort his nieces and nephews, Hermann had said to little Christa who was curled up in his lap, 'Don't worry, I am your father now, I will look after you.' Yes, Hermann seemed to entertain thoughts of staying at Juchow.

'But Mammie, didn't you hear?'

Elsa's distressed voice called Ursula back to the present.

'Mammie, that one stag over there, he is talking to us.'

'Shush, Elsa! You know these things are dead. And in any case, stags can't talk.' Ursula picked up her daughter, the only one of her children that was still with her at the castle and whose presence made life bearable. Walter and Hermann had long since been sent to boarding school in Kolberg, a town far away, on the coast of the Baltic Sea. She missed them dearly.

'There, again! Mammie...'

Ursula turned around as she heard a deep voice, apparently emanating from one of the stuffed heads on the wall. Not believing her ears, she pretended there was nothing.

'Be careful!' the deep voice resounded in the castle's hall now.

'Watch out, otherwise the Russians will come and eat you!'

Attempting not to show her confusion, but somewhat perturbed, Ursula looked around. Her eyes fell onto a group of officers barely suppressing their grins, and she understood. She shot an angry look across the hall. What did these guys think, scaring her little girl?

'Don't worry, Elsa, it's just the soldiers over there,' she said. 'One of them must be a ventriloquist.'

It would turn out that the stag's predictions were not too far off the mark. It was only a few weeks later when one of the officers called Tante Erica aside and warned her of the imminent arrival of the Russians. That things were not good, they had all seen with their own eyes, bearing witness to the streams of refugees moving through the area. At first it had been people from Eastern Prussia only, but now it was an endless trek of carts and horses, oxen and tractors, of people living not that far away anymore. With them came the stories of the atrocities committed by the Red Army, taking retribution for their suffering during the German eastern offensive.

'Lady, I never said this to you,' the officer took Erica into his confidence. 'It is time for you all to leave now too. Things are not looking good.'

'But the mayor says there is no reason to worry,' Erica frowned. 'In fact, when I asked yesterday, I was told we wouldn't be allowed to go.'

'That's all propaganda. By party orders, they can't admit defeat. They also want to keep the roads clear for the retreating troops. But I am telling you, if you don't go now, you might not be able to leave at all. And we all know what will happen once the Russians get here.'

Erica made up her mind quickly. She trusted this man and the quiet urgency that lay in his voice. And she was not blind either. Things were looking bad indeed. Quietly, she had been making plans already.

'How much time have we got?' she asked.

'Probably a day or two. Not more than two days. If you go up the hill in the east, you can see the glow of the burning villages already. Leave tonight if you can.'

Ever since the Russian Red Army had first set foot on German soil in October 1944 in a small village on the eastern border, their reputation of cruelty and terror had preceded them. There was talk of rape and murder, of looting and burning.

Most people realised that they could no longer believe the Nazi propaganda that the German army would hold up the Russians, and decided it was preferable to move west. Their chances of survival would be much better on territory occupied by the Western Allied Forces.

Right up to the end, however, the well-oiled propaganda machine caused some, loath to leave their houses and all possessions behind, to remain on their land, until they could literally hear the rumbling of tanks. When German army troops were seen on the roads, withdrawing from the frontlines, marching west, there was no doubt.

Horses and oxen were harnessed to any vehicle people thought could make the journey. In many cases, the women who now ran the large estates of Pomerania provided 'their' villagers with animals and wagons. More often than not, the whole village fled together.

Horse carts were loaded with pregnant women, little children, the injured and the old, together with whatever provisions they still had after a long and cold winter. Oxcarts were piled high with hay and oats to feed the horses; the oxen would be slaughtered later along the way to feed the people.

Not one to procrastinate, the responsibility for the castle, the children, her employees and the villagers on her shoulders alone, Erica discussed the issue with Ursula and together they decided that too much was at risk.

A meeting was called and Erica informed everybody that they all would be leaving at three o'clock the next morning. Some grave nodding of heads ensued, but some didn't agree with her.

'But *Frau* Dennig, three o'clock? We can't feed the horses that early,' one person objected.

'But Frau Dennig, they are telling us we are safe here, our soldiers will beat the Russians before they get here,' another one said.

'I can't leave my house and animals and everything behind, the Russians are going to steal it all,' a third one worried.

'Quiet please,' Erica said. She was used to giving orders by now and didn't struggle to make herself heard. She was greatly respected by her people. 'We will leave at three o'clock. I ask you to come with me. In fact, I strongly recommend that you do, but I can't force you. It is up to you,' she said.

'So, I repeat. We will be leaving at three. If you want to join us, please be ready. If not, it is your responsibility. There is nothing more I can do.'

Shortly before three the next morning, Teggerts, the trustworthy old coach man, found Erica.

'Frau Dennig, we are ready. All the horses are spanned in. We can go.'

A procession of 24 horses, two tractors, the children from the castle, all the staff and two thirds of the villagers, altogether nearly three hundred people, left Juchow in the early hours of the morning.

Amongst them were the French prisoners of war, eager to get closer to home, while most of the Polish foreign workers had chosen to stay behind.

As they left, Ursula's heart was heavy. She was worried about Walter and Hermann, so far away at boarding school. She didn't know what the situation was on the coast, but she feared the worst. And there had been no ways or means of informing her husband about their plans either. Some weeks before, he had been called away from his administrative job into the *Volkssturm*, the last effort of mobilising troops. Ursula didn't know where he was, or if he was alive.

As soon as the trek from Juchow hit the main road, they saw an endless procession of women and children, horses and wagons. There were only few roads that led west and these were covered in ice and snow and clogged with people and their carts moving slowly, the noise of Russian tanks and fear sitting in their necks.

Two days into their arduous journey, Ursula heard rumours that her husband had been seen at Juchow. While Erica continued leading their trek forward, Ursula took Elsa and started walking back. Since it was only the two of them, they could move much faster and arrived back at Juchow the same evening.

Yes, Hermann Eschenburg had been seen, she was told by some of the few remaining souls, amongst them the baker.

But he had left again. No, nobody knew where he had gone. Into the forest, they told her, and that he had taken most of the cattle with him.

Ursula would not see or hear from her husband until many months later.

Shooting could be heard in the distance and even the most reluctant villagers were beginning to scramble for their few possessions. Ursula realised that if she stayed any longer, she'd risk her life and that of her daughter. For all she knew it might be too late already.

Leaving in all haste, she lost the little bag she was carrying with all their papers, passports and some family photographs. But there was no way she could even think of turning back when she discovered the loss. It was too late.

She walked throughout the night, carrying six year old Elsa most of the way and taking short cuts through the woods; she caught up with the trek and the rest of her group again the next day.

The next few weeks were the hardest any of them had ever lived through. Along the roadside they saw dead horses and overturned wagons. There was no time to get them back onto the road. They were shot at and bombed from low-flying aircraft. Many children died along the way, temperatures of minus twenty degrees, malnutrition, and the lack of warmth, rest and sleep taking their toll. There was no time to dig graves in the frozen ground and the dead bodies were buried in the snow next to the road.

During one night, Ursula, Erica and their group found refuge in an abandoned barn. They unhitched the horses so they could rest and feed on some hay downstairs, while the women and children slept in the hayloft. Disaster struck early in the morning when one of the women got up and fell through a hatch in the floor. She landed in between the horses where she died, trampled to death.

The 'eye of the needle' for all the refugees moving west was the crossing of the river Oder. Of the few existing bridges, some had been bombed and were burning, while others had been closed and were reserved for military use only.

When the trek from Juchow approached the river they could hear shooting in the distance, although they saw neither German nor Russian troops. Their only option was to use a pontoon bridge close to the town of Wollin, but as they came closer, the entire trek was stopped by a military policeman. When Erica asked what the reason for the delay was, he told her that the bridge would be blown up shortly.

'But where do you suggest we cross the river then?' she asked.

'Perhaps there will be another bridge put up a little further north,' he replied hesitantly.

'Do you really believe that?' Erica stared at the man.

He just shrugged his shoulders and Erica returned to her people, trying not to show her desperation. She suggested they feed the horses and have something to eat themselves while they waited. She conferred with Ursula. Where should they turn to now? The shooting was coming closer, from all sides it seemed, and the roads were hopelessly choked. Turning back was impossible and it seemed doubtful, to say the least, that they would find another bridge further north.

Suddenly, the military policeman came running towards them, shouting, '*Schnell, schnell, die Sprengung ist verschoben!* - Quick, quick, the blasting has been postponed!'

They gathered their few belongings and crossed the bridge as fast as their tired horses and exhausted legs would allow. From Wollin, the trek continued to Swinemünde. The once popular seaside town was bursting at the seams. Hospital trains stood at the station and ships with refugees were moored in the harbour. Food and resources were scarce. Accommodation in Swinemünde had been prearranged with a butcher whom Tante Erica knew. They would rest for a day before continuing their journey.

What moved Erica to change her plans, she would later not be able to explain. But once at their quarters, she looked at the situation and made up her mind.

'Get the horses ready, we will carry on,' she announced.

Ursula only nodded. She understood.

Soon a discussion erupted between the weary travellers.

Coachman Teggerts was exhausted.

'Frau Dennig,' he said, 'we have found a good place. I have unharnessed the horses. We all need a rest.'

'No, Teggerts,' Erica replied in a tone of voice that did not allow dissent.

'We will carry on.'

Against his better judgement, Teggerts protested; he was tired and so were the horses.

Eventually, Ursula Eschenburg interfered.

'Teggerts,' she said, 'if Frau Dennig says we carry on, then we will carry on. If you don't harness the horses, I will.'

She turned round and began to bring the animals together.

'Bloody Englishwoman,' Teggerts mumbled, but he helped Ursula to get ready.

Some of the villagers followed their cue, while others decided to stay behind in Swinemünde and have a good night's rest before they'd continue their journey.

It was the 11th of March 1945.

On the 12th of March, just after noon, the sirens sounded. Swinemünde experienced heavy bombing. The city was razed to the ground. Thousands of people were killed, many of them civilians and refugees. Amongst them were the people from Juchow who had decided to stay behind.

HERMANN CAN DO ANYTHING

When I turned eleven I was sent to boarding school in Kolberg, just like my brother Hermann. This was the closest we would get to receiving a higher education. Before the war, children from the castles in Pomerania were usually sent to Berlin, but that of course was out of the question now; the capital was not a safe place during the war years.

Our boarding house was situated in a woodland, about a kilometre away from the school, and my favourite teacher, Doctor Schulz, was also our hostel father.

I remember it like it was yesterday. On a cold evening in January 1945 he called us remaining boys into the dining hall. There were only eight of us left. The others, who were all more local, had been sent home some time before, because the fighting on the eastern front lines was coming closer by the day.

There was great urgency in his voice and the smile had disappeared from his face. We immediately knew that things were serious. Doctor Schulz gave us strict instructions. We were to get dressed in our *Hitlerjugend* uniforms and go down to the train station immediately. We shouldn't bother packing anything but the bare necessities and one set of casual clothes. Without much further ado, he sent us on our way with three sandwiches each, all the food that was left in the boarding house's kitchen.

At the station Hermann, who was the eldest, organized a coupé. Normally meant for three, all eight of us had to fit in. The station was mayhem. There were thousands of people everywhere, all trying to flee the fast approaching Russian army.

Hermann pushed me and another little boy inside, together with the little luggage and provisions we had. In the meantime, he and the other older boys had been ordered to help the refugees board the train. We were under strict instructions to keep the doors of our compartment locked and only when Hermann and the others came onto the platform outside was I to open the window so they could climb in. The aisles were hopelessly overrun with people.

After what seemed an eternity everyone who possibly could had boarded. The train started moving slowly, heading for Stettin, which was some two hundred kilometres away. As soon as we left Kolberg, we followed our trusted teacher's instructions, changed into our casual clothes and threw the uniforms out of the window. Everything calmed down a bit and my stomach started to rumble. Curiously I took out my sandwiches, inspecting the *Wurst* and butter that was on them.

'Remember,' Herrmann said with a worried expression on his face, 'these sandwiches are all you've got to eat. We don't know how long it'll take us to get to Lübeck and we certainly don't know when we'll find any more food.'

He was right, I realised and packed the sandwich away again. I wasn't that hungry yet.

Without any major incidents the train finally arrived in Stettin, a big city on the river Oder. Hermann had been told to make sure the other boys all got onto their trains to Berlin and Cologne respectively; a task he dutifully fulfilled.

In the meantime, I sat patiently on our suitcase, waiting for my brother, who soon joined me. The train to Berlin had left, as had the train to Cologne. But there was no train in sight to Lübeck, where we had to go. That's where our grandfather was, and that's where the Eschenburg family had arranged to meet should anything untoward happen.

We sat on the station in Stettin for three full days. Every so often, the town was bombed, and we had to run and find cover under a nearby bridge. We were loath to leave the platform, because we feared that we might miss the perhaps one and only train to Lübeck.

The sandwiches slowly disappeared and we were hungry, but worst of all, we were cold. It was one of the coldest winters we had ever experienced, or maybe it only felt that way because instead of playing in front of the fireplace at Juchow, or cuddling up under one of our plumeaus, we were sitting on the icy cold station, terrified by the bombings and even more so by the thought of not ever finding a train to move on. Every now and then I got a little sniffle-nosed, having to wipe away a tear or two, but I really tried to be brave and not show any weakness in front of my older brother.

On the third day a train arrived and some German soldiers got out. They walked around the platform smoking and stretching their legs. One of them approached us.

'Whose suitcase is this?' he asked.

'It is ours, lieutenant,' Hermann had jumped up and stood to attention.

'Who is called Eschenburg?' the soldier pointed at the name tag.

'We are, Sir.'

'I see. Do you know Wolfgang Eschenburg?'

'Yes, Sir, of course, he is our uncle. Our father's brother.'

'Well, he is our commander. Where are you going?'

'To Lübeck, Sir.'

'This train is also going to Lübeck. It is full. But you can come with us.'

The train was a hospital train, fully packed with wounded soldiers, women and children. Yet our new friend found a space for me on the luggage rack; I was still quite small. Then he asked Hermann,

'Can you shoot?'

'Yes, of course,' he replied.

'Can you shoot with a machine gun?'

'Yes.'

Hermann had never in his life touched a machine gun, but I thought, 'Of course he can. Hermann can do anything. He is nearly fifteen!'

Hermann was given a thick soldier's overcoat, had a steel helmet with a chin strap put on his head and was then ordered to sit on the train's roof and shoot at enemy planes with his machine gun.

We arrived in Lübeck unharmed and now had to find our way to grandfather's house. We didn't recognise the city at all; it was all so badly burnt and destroyed.

'Oh, it's you,' grandfather said when we knocked on the door of his villa after we eventually found it.

'What do you want here?'

'Mama and Papa told us to come here.'

'Oh, I see. But you must go to Tante Trude. You can stay with her.'

His house was already full, he told us, and so Hermann and I had to walk right to the other side of town to the home of Tante Trude, the widow of our father's younger brother. When we knocked on her door she didn't seem too delighted to see us either. Her husband had been killed only recently and she had a whole brood of children of her own to feed.

'Oh it's you. What do you want here?' she asked.

'*Opa* has sent us.'

'Oh, I see. Well, come in then.'

We were the first of our family to get to Lübeck, and at that stage nobody had any news of our parents.

DIFFICULT TIMES

The war was over, yet for Ursula Eschenburg and her children life was hard. But they had been lucky; very lucky indeed. She'd never forget seeing the flames on the horizon engulfing the town of Swinemünde not even a day after they had left. There was nothing that could be done for the other people from Juchow, those that had decided to stay behind.

Ursula and Erica had continued their journey west. When they had been some thirty kilometres out of Lübeck, grandfather Eschenburg must have got notice that his son's family was amongst the refugees. He'd sent a tractor with a wood-fired engine to pick up Ursula and Elsa. Erica had not come with them to Lübeck, but had led what was left of their group further west. She had been headed for Hamburg, the city where she had grown up and where Heinz-Jürgen had proposed to her all those years ago. Their fellow travellers also had started splitting up, some heading south and others west, all trying to find shelter and food with distant family.

Ursula would never forget the joy and relief she'd felt when the tractor driver dropped her and Elsa at Tante Trude's house in the *Königer Strasse* and she'd found Walter and Hermann there. They were both painfully thin but otherwise well. They had been lucky indeed. More so than many other people she saw in the streets of the city, which was in a terrible state.

Large parts of Lübeck had been reduced to piles of rubble; the streets were full of dirt and stones, crumbling walls and collapsing houses.

The city was awash with displaced and homeless people. If they were fortunate they were taken in by relatives, but often family members too had lost their homes and possessions. The homeless occupied ruins or abandoned cellars, or built shacks from whatever materials they could find.

Ursula was grateful. At least she had a place to stay and was reunited with her two boys. At first, there was no sign of her husband. He was missing. Nobody had seen or heard of him since that day in Juchow when she had been told that he'd gone into the forest. Yet she didn't give up hope. Then, some months later, there was a knock on their door, and Ursula just knew. Hermann stood there, skin and bones, and barefoot. He had walked all the way. From where, she was not quite sure, because her husband would never speak about the experiences he'd had since leaving Juchow.

With the family reunited the lack of space at Tante Trude's became unbearable; conditions were so crammed that Trude herself had to sleep in her rocking chair. The Eschenburgs were taken in by Frau Lehnhardt, whose house was across the road, and who had some space in the basement. It was icy cold, and there was hardly any firewood or food.

How to feed her family was a continuous worry for Ursula. Elsa was covered in starvation sores, and where Walter had hurt his leg, the wound festered and would not heal. She feared that if she took him to hospital, they would amputate. The worries just didn't stop. When was this all going to end?

Like most other women, Ursula spent a lot of her time scavenging, searching for firewood and something to eat. She queued for days, trying to get hold of some of the rations the United Nations were distributing. On good days there'd be some powdered egg from which she would fabricate scrambled eggs, much to the delight of her children; a far cry from the feasts they had had not long ago at Juchow.

What worried Ursula most though was the fact that she had lost all their papers; identification documents, passports, everything. More than ever, she was determined to leave Germany behind and go back home, to South Africa. But how would they ever get back there if they couldn't even prove who they were? In an attempt to find a solution she walked across the ruined city to the Villa Eschenburg.

British troops had occupied Lübeck on the 2nd of May 1945, a few days before the end of the war. Miraculously, the Eschenburg home had remained unharmed by the bombings and had been requisitioned by the British for army personnel. Grandfather Eschenburg and his wife had been relocated to the garden cottage.

As Ursula stood outside the grand building, looking a little worse for wear, she pondered. Maybe there was somebody here, perhaps some British official, who could help her? But when she entered the house, she only saw chaos.

Some soldiers were moving out the valuable paintings grandfather Eschenburg was so proud of; others were carrying boxes of the finest Meissen porcelain down the stairs, bumping and dropping pieces.

Ursula was incensed. She knew how much her mother-in-law loved her fine crockery, but more so, it was against her strong sense of justice. The war was over and she knew that looting was not allowed. She voiced her protest in her best English.

The soldiers, who at first had not paid any attention to this woman, whom they thought was just another German in her rags, stopped in their tracks. She was proud, standing upright and glowing despite her unglamorous attire.

'These bloody Huns speak better English than we do,' one of them said, shaking his head.

Ursula was not going to be shooed away. She was furious.

Eventually, mostly to get rid of her, one of the soldiers took her to the British headquarters, where she planned to lay an official complaint.

Waiting to be seen, she heard one of the men calling to the officer in charge,

'Hey Peacock!'

Ursula looked up in surprise and asked, 'Excuse me, Sir, but may I ask you something?'

'Fire away,' he gruffly replied.

'You are not by any chance related to William Peacock?'

'William Peacock? Of course! He is my brother.'

'He didn't go to school in Johannesburg, did he?'

'He did indeed. Why? Don't tell me...'

'Yes, I know your brother, we went to school together. He was a year ahead of me,' Ursula answered.

That solved some of the problems. The looting stopped and Ursula, who had not been looking forward to the long walk home, was taken by Officer Peacock in an army jeep.

But she was devastated. Unfortunately, he'd said, as much as he'd like to, he could do nothing for her and her passport problem. She would have to go through the channels, like everybody else.

BREAD AND GAMES

We never really had hunger. Until after the war; then we did.

One day, my father came home with a small bag of oats. Where he got them from, I don't know. We didn't ask. But oats are terrible things, they have husks.

My mother sent me to the miller to have the oats rolled.

'How would you like them, young man? With or without husks?' he asked me.

I wasn't quite sure and of course I had to pay for it. 'What makes the most?' I asked.

'Well, with husks of course. But you can't eat them. You have to feed them to the horses.'

'Can't you eat them at all?'

'Well, of course you could, but they are not good. Really. Now tell me, how shall I roll them for you? With or without husks?' the miller was getting impatient.

The price was the same, and I was really, really hungry. 'With husks, please.'

I knew I had made a mistake when I got home and saw my mother's face. She looked dreadfully disappointed. The oats looked like chaff and she was clearly not amused. But she cooked them anyway, because there was nothing else, and we tried to eat them. They tasted a little like oats, but at the same time, your mouth was full of sawdust. We actually spent more time spitting than eating.

That was in Lübeck, when we stayed with Frau Lehnhart and her son Wolf in the Kőniger Strasse.

Wolf and I soon became friends and went exploring. In the next street there were only houses on one side, while on the other there was a huge empty space. The soldiers had left a lorry there with an anti-aircraft gun tied on the back. It just stood there. And of course, us being naughty boys with not much to do - there was no school yet - we had to investigate it.

It was a canon with four barrels, and when you turned one handle, the entire thing swivelled around, and when you turned another handle, it went up and down. There was also a trailer full of ammunition. Hermann, the most enterprising of us, found some empty bottles and began siphoning off all the petrol that was left in the lorry. He took it home and hid it there.

Us younger boys, we were more interested in the ammunition and playing with the canon. We spent hours turning it up and down and around, playing war. When we got bored with that we had a closer look at the rather large bullets. I discovered that when I hit them on the side with a stone the tip came off, and inside were little sacks of gunpowder. I carefully extracted and stored them in empty shoe polish tins. It was my biggest treasure, and I swore I would guard it with my life!

Sometimes we'd experiment and put a line of gunpowder on the ground, light it with a match and watch it burn. Wolf had an army of tin soldiers and we'd both line up our troops strategically, lay traps, light a match and blow up the other one's army. It was great fun! One day, Wolf and I each stole a bottle of Hermann's petrol. We laid a line of powder, lit it, flicked some petrol onto it and got very excited when it went up with a loud puff and a big flame.

Again, we had lots of fun, until we made too big a flick and somehow the fire jumped into the bottle. There I had a burning bottle in my hands and, panicking, I threw it away. Some of the petrol, and with it the fire, spat onto a little wooden garden shed which promptly went up in flames. Luckily, Hermann was not far away. I eventually stopped counting how many times my big brother had come to rescue me out of deep trouble!

Not much later there was a huge commotion. One of the older boys had found out how to load the anti-aircraft gun. Another one had worked out how to shoot it. Wolf and I had been watching them from a distance, not quite sure what they were up to.

There was a flash and a big noise, a loud *bababababa*, louder than anything I had heard before. Within minutes, the occupation troops arrived and we took to our heels as fast as we could.

When the dust had settled, and we felt it was safe to venture back, we found that 'our gun' had disappeared.

A CLOAK AND DAGGER AFFAIR

As the months passed, Walter became more and more aware that his family was in a dire situation. Although he had lots of fun and was always out and about in search of the next adventure, he knew that the grumbling in his stomach wouldn't go away, and another winter was looming. His mother was worried, he realised, and that worried him. She was talking about going back to South Africa and was desperate because of the lost passports. Walter knew she still felt a foreigner in Germany and couldn't really see a future there for her young family, living as they were under seriously restricted circumstances. Although his father didn't say much at the time, sometimes Walter wondered if he hoped that they could return to Juchow? He'd never know. It was his mother who was the driving force in wanting to change their situation.

Ursula explored all possible avenues. Eventually she heard talk of the repatriation of people displaced during the war. For the authorities, the more people that could be moved out of the destroyed cities the better, particularly as there were still thousands of refugees from the eastern territories arriving every day. People of German origin from Poland, Czechoslovakia and Hungary, from Pomerania, Eastern Prussia and Bohemia were moving into the western areas of Germany. Most were destitute and all needed a place to stay, food and clothing.

The Eschenburgs had no proof of their South African citizenship, and thus were, to Ursula's dismay, regarded as common Germans unless they could prove otherwise. There was no postal contact with South Africa yet, the queues at the offices were long, and the mills of bureaucracy were milling very slowly.

Ursula was getting impatient, desperate at times, but she never gave up. Then, one day, she came home and was very excited.

'Did you hear?' she asked her husband, 'General Smuts is coming to Hamburg!'

'Really?'

'Yes. And I will go and see him.'

'Oh, Ursula, don't get your hopes up. Why would he want to see you of all people?'

'Because I will not let this opportunity go by. I will go and see him if it's the last thing I do,' she insisted.

'Well, do what you got to do, but you are wasting your time, I think.' Walter's father shrugged his shoulders.

Jan Smuts was Prime Minister of South Africa and Field Marshall of the British Army at the time. Family talk had it that he had fought together with Ursula's father in the Boer War, although it was probably more to the point that Adolf Wilhelmi had been part of Jan Smuts' party.

Not one to give up easily, Ursula managed to organise a permit to travel to Hamburg and, with a few pennies she had scraped together, she boarded the train. Her disappointment was great when she found out on arrival that Jan Smuts had cut his visit short and left Hamburg earlier the same morning. He had flown back to London.

Ursula was devastated. She sat on the platform at the station, and for once she cried. Her despair didn't last long, however, and soon she pulled herself together. She managed to scrounge some paper and an envelope and began to write a letter.

To
His Excellency,
Field Marshall,
Sir J.C. Smuts,
South Africa House
London

A group of British officers was at the station at the same time. They had been observing Ursula first crying and then, with what seemed utter determination, writing something. When one of the men walked over and tried to console her, she replied in her very clean and clear King's English.

Surprised, the young man turned round to his friends and laughed, 'These bloody Huns speak better English than we do!'

'Not again,' Ursula thought. She'd heard this sentence more than once. 'I am not a bloody Hun,' she retorted, 'I am a South African displaced person.'

'Oh,' the officer said, ever so slightly embarrassed. 'Maybe we can help you somehow?'

'Well, I need to have this letter posted to England,' she said, 'and I don't know how.'

'That's easy enough! Just give it to me. I'm going to London tonight; I'll post it for you there. It will get to wherever it needs much quicker.'

What followed were days of anxious waiting. Apparently the young officer had kept his promise and posted the letter. It reached General Smuts before he left England. Reportedly, he gave his secretary orders to reply and tell Ursula that he was taking her cause under his wing.

Within a week the Eschenburgs received a letter from South Africa House in London. They were told to be at a specific pier in Hamburg harbour at half past ten in the evening on a certain day.

A little sceptical, but laden with the few possessions they had, they waited at the arranged meeting point. Right on time, they were met by a colonel of the British forces, who accompanied them to Cuxhaven. There they were transferred onto a British minesweeper headed for the port of Hull.

For Walter, this second ship journey of his life felt like a real adventure again, a true cloak and dagger affair. Because his family didn't have the right papers they had to be smuggled out of the country. It was all a little bit spooky though, he thought, as he walked on board and quietly took in the troops everywhere on the ship and wondered about the sandbags that were piled up under the gunwales. Nobody really paid any attention to them, but they had been given strict instructions.

Under no circumstances were they to go on deck until they reached the port of Hull.

On arrival they were met by an official who gave Walter's father some instructions and train tickets to London. After having waited for so long, everything seemed to happen very quickly now.

The Eschenburgs reported to South Africa House, were put up in a little hotel at Piccadilly Circus for twenty-four hours and then had to board the *Flying Scotsman*, the train to Glasgow. There, they were loaded onto the back of a truck together with a lot of other people and taken to a small village. It reminded Walter of Juchow, in that it only had one street, and he wondered where they could possibly stay, when he saw the large barracks at the southern end. It was the camp for displaced people, he was told, and that's where they would wait until a passage on a ship to South Africa would become available.

Uneventful months passed and Walter got used to the new routines in his life. The queuing at mealtimes, the way the melted butter was smeared onto the large slices of bread with a paintbrush and the never changing flavour of the daily soup. He quickly made friends with another South African boy about his age called Paul, with whom he stole out of the camp to explore the heathery hills. He even managed to get himself into trouble again, this time with some local boys who had set out to beat up the 'bloody foreigners'.

Then, after months of waiting, things again happened very quickly. When Walter returned one afternoon from one of his excursions with Paul, he heard that finally it was their turn to go home.

They took the train to London and then on to Southampton, before they, together with Paul, his mother and another South African family, boarded the *SS Carnarvon Castle*.

It was May 1947.

THE OWLS' NEST

THE OWLS' NEST

The *SS Carnarvon Castle* disgorged her charges in Cape Town, and the Eschenburgs caught the train to Johannesburg where Ursula's overjoyed family was awaiting them at Park Station. They arrived on the 10th of June, Ursula and Hermann's wedding anniversary.

After resting for a couple of days at Driefontein, the farm where Ursula had grown up, she and Hermann were ready to go back to Uhlenhorst. It had been such a long time. They wanted to get home and feel at home for the first time in years. And they hoped they could pick up their life on the farm more or less where they had left off, growing flowers for the market and producing high quality milk from their herd of Simmental cows. During the long journey they had often spoken about their plans, what they would do and how, as soon as they got back to the farm. It had kept them going, the prospect of a more comfortable, fulfilled, if hard working life.

They had been warned, but nothing could have prepared them for what they saw when they finally drove up the long, tree-lined access road to their farmhouse.

Uhlenhorst was in shambles. The Van Veterens, whom Ursula had never really trusted, had lived up to her expectations in the worst possible way. What was left of the house, which once had been their home, was a mere ruin. The windows were smashed, the doors missing, the floorboards eaten by termites. Sand had blown into the house and, except for a few pieces of furniture, it was empty. All their crockery and cutlery, their books and clothes had vanished; there was nothing left.

Believing that their boss and his family wouldn't come back, that they had been swallowed up by the confusion the war had caused all over Europe, the farm manager and his wife had taken what they could.

The lands didn't look much better. The flower fields lay barren and the orchard was overgrown. The wells had caved in and the cattle had vanished together with the tractor and the panel van. Ursula sat down on the only chair left in the house, a rickety wooden piece that had obviously not been good enough to find its way somewhere else, and she cried.

She had been strong all along, but this was just too much. What had kept her going, given her strength during their ordeal, had evaporated into thin air. She could deal with the fact that they had lost their material possessions, but what really got to her was the loss of her personal things; her wedding dress, her diaries and the old family bible, which she had hidden in a secret spot behind the wardrobe in her bedroom. And the photographs. She had treasured the pictures of her family. 'Why did they take them?' she wondered.

'Mammie, Mammie, look what Walter has found!' Elsa came running into the empty house.

'How she has changed,' Ursula thought. 'When we left, she could only just sit up and now she is ready for school.' She shook her head.

'Mammie, Mammie, please don't cry. Look what we've got!'

When Ursula looked up she saw Elsa and Walter standing in the middle of the empty room that was once the lounge. Walter was holding something in each hand.

'Mammie, you won't believe it! Remember how Hermann and I buried our toys before we left? Because we didn't want the Van Veteren boys to play with them? We found them, can you believe it! Hermann's red digger and my green panel van.'

'Walter has found his toys, Walter has found his toys!' Elsa was singing now, skipping in a circle around her mother, instinctively trying to cheer her up.

'Come on, Elsa, Walter called his sister. 'Let's see, maybe we find something else!'

He stormed outside again, his sister close at his heels.

Ursula had to laugh. Despite all the hardship they had been through, her children's spirits were clearly unbroken.

'I should learn from them,' she said to herself and got up. 'Better make a plan, if we want to stay here.'

She was about to go outside to find her husband whom she presumed was assessing the state of the orchards together with their oldest son Hermann, when Walter and Elsa came running in again.

'Mammie, Mammie, now look what we found in the old shed!' Elsa's voice was squeaky with excitement.

'Close your eyes.'

Ursula obliged. What would she do without these two?

'Ok, now open again!'

Right in front of her nose, she saw grubby little fingers holding a black and white photograph showing Walter as a three year old standing in the middle of a field of white chrysanthemums. The little boy in the picture was smiling, and with his white, curly hair he could almost be mistaken for another blossom. Just tall enough for his head to show above the vast sea of flowers and both arms raised, he pointed with his short index fingers towards an exceptionally beautiful flower head.

This picture of Walter would become one of Ursula Eschenburg's most treasured possessions. In a narrow silver frame, it would soon take pride of place on the mantelpiece in the lounge of their farmhouse.

A few years later, Uhlenhorst offered a different picture. Hermann and Ursula, eager to forget what lay behind them, had thrown themselves into their work and built up the farm again. They didn't really have a choice; this was all they had left. Somehow they had to make it work. And they did. Now there were endless fields of larkspurs, gladiolas, narcissus, daffodils, freesias, delphiniums, anemones, pansies, violets, lilies of the valley and, of course, the much loved chrysanthemums again.

The peach orchard was flourishing. Different types of trees had been planted, and the fruit of Early Dawns were the first to ripen, followed by the other varieties until the grand finale of the Transvaal Yellow Cling peaches, which were used for canning.

Walter had been given a dairy cow for his birthday, the year they'd left for Germany. He'd left her in Aunty Freya's care on Driefontein, and this cow now formed the ground stock of the Eschenburgs' blossoming dairy farm.

The whole family worked hard. They started at four in the morning with milking the cows and in summer they didn't finish before midnight, after the last trip to the market with peaches. While Ursula stayed at home seeing to the dairy cows, the household and supervising the ever-growing team of Zulu and Malawian staff, her husband did trip after trip to the Johannesburg florists and fruit sellers.

Fields of tomatoes were added and lucerne, as well as cow peas and Eragrostis grass as fodder for the cattle. The herd grew and Hermann worked continuously to improve productivity and milk content.

He imported Simmental cows from Germany and was involved with the breeding of Bonsmara cattle, a relatively new South African breed. He introduced overhead irrigation to his adopted country and tried his luck importing tulip bulbs from Holland which, unfortunately, didn't like the South African climate.

In the early years after the war, when the demand for cut flowers was not great, he'd send Walter and Hermann during their school holidays to sell milk, butter, cream and cheese by the side of the road.

Hardly had the Eschenburgs arrived back at Uhlenhorst, when the children were sent to school. Hermann and Walter went straight into an English high school in Johannesburg, while Elsa had to attend an Afrikaans primary school close by. They all did well from the start. Somehow they had managed to become proficient in all the languages they needed; English and Afrikaans for school, German at home, Zulu and Chichewa to speak to the staff on the farm.

Her linguistic abilities got Elsa into trouble, when she was accused of swearing, after inadvertently using an Afrikaans expression she had picked up somewhere.

'*Nou gaan Meneer julle donner,*' she had shouted at the top of her voice when some rowdy boys had teased her, completely unaware that this phrase was considered highly unacceptable.

Walter and Hermann raised eyebrows for other reasons - for being, also inadvertently, too well behaved. When introduced to their new headmaster they both bowed and clicked their heels when they shook hands with him, just as they had been taught in Germany. The headmaster, a middle aged Englishman, was shocked. To him this was indoctrination at its worst. In his eyes, the Nazis had left their mark even in the behaviour of these young boys.

Hermann and Walter didn't really understand. It was good, upper class manners and they had spent hours practising, until the click of the heels and the bow were perfectly synchronised. Manners had been drilled into them in Germany, no doubt. But the two boys weren't angels, and although they both excelled academically, they were apprehended for being naughty more than once. Having to catch the so-called 'Pretoria bus' every morning, they'd been given bicycles to ride the four kilometres to the road where they'd meet it, and they got into serious trouble when their father caught them bunking one day. Driving along the same road, he saw the bicycles that should have been securely stored at a friend's farm parked only partially hidden behind a big rock in the veld. He stopped to have a closer look and found his two sons sleeping in the shade of a large fig tree.

From the early days it had become apparent that the boys' interests and talents lay at opposite ends of the spectrum. While Hermann was attracted to anything technical or mechanical and knew how to fix things, Walter's realm was everything that had to do with animals. Walter loved nothing more than riding horses, while Hermann preferred fixing and driving old cars and tractors. And the other way around; anything mechanical broke when Walter used it, whereas Hermann was accident prone when it came to animals.

Both their abilities were much appreciated in running the farm, and they each had their territory. Walter was intimately connected with everything that had to do with the cows; calving, milking, dipping, checking for ticks under the tail, making sure that none had mastitis, and if they did, that it was treated immediately. He also developed a special relationship with some of them. His favourite, Alma, would only let her milk down when Walter milked her. Other cows had taken a liking to Abius, a Malawian cattle man, and a close friendship developed between Abius and young Walter, based on their love of the animals.

While Hermann kept an eye on the technical side and Walter on the health of the animals, Hermann Eschenburg Senior was the sales person. Returning from his daily trips to the market, when the pressure was off, he'd have time to enjoy the odd movie, read the newspaper or visit friends. He was a sociable man and eventually became a founding member of the Orange Grove Rotary Club.

Ursula on the other hand stayed at home most of the time and wouldn't have wanted it any other way. She was the heart and soul of the farming operation, keeping meticulous records of everything that happened in the stables and on the land; balancing milk yield with peach harvests, and numbers of tomato boxes sold with bunches of chrysanthemums.

But Ursula also knew how to throw a good party and make people feel welcome. It didn't take her long to turn their ruined house into a presentable home, where friends and family would gather and stay over for weekends.

Guests would congregate on Uhlenhorst's wide, red stoep that was always polished to a perfect shine. The kitchen had been added only later to the house and had no ceiling, just a roof made from corrugated iron. It was pitch black from the smoke of the old wood-stove which was continuously burning, and from which Ursula produced the most mouth-watering dishes. She tried hard to encourage Elsa to learn some of her skills, always reminding her that the way to a man's heart was through his stomach.

During these weekend gatherings, the adults would discuss the latest happenings in their adopted country, for most of them were German in origin. The children, now nearly grown up, passed the time riding horses and practising stunts on the lawn.

Walter had been given a black stallion called Prince, with whom he jumped over the hedges separating the lawn from his mother's little park where she grew some select shrubs and trees. He made him rear up in front of the stoep and practised how to canter while standing on the horse's back.

He also had a little mare called Comtesse, and with her he tried his luck in breeding horses. When the first foal was born snow-white, a genetic defect that would leave her dead within a couple of weeks, he was devastated. For the rest of his life, luck would elude him in breeding horses, despite frequent trying.

One summer's afternoon, Elsa wanted nothing more than get away from the hullabaloo her older brothers and their friends were causing. Although she knew they were not malicious, she was tired of being teased by them. She wondered where she could hide away to read her book, a romantic novel that kept her glued to the pages.

The long-drop toilet, which was attached to the far wall of the garage, was hardly ever used and seemed the perfect hideaway for the moment; right out of everyone's sight. Deeply ensconced in her book she sat and read, completely oblivious to her surroundings. Until, during a particularly dramatic section, she looked up. 'Would the heroine's desires be fulfilled? Would her knight in shining armour ever kneel in front of her?' Elsa looked down at her feet and with a scream that betrayed her hiding place she jumped up onto the wide wooden seat of the long-drop.

The *rinkhals* that had slithered through the opening under the wooden door stopped in its tracks. It lifted its head, looked up at Elsa seemingly surprised, and then decided quickly to take its leave. It vanished down a crack at the bottom of the wooden seat.

Walter and Hermann had heard their little sister's blood curdling scream and a second later they opened the door to find her standing on the toilet's lid. The boys were delighted. Elsa had just given them the perfect excuse to try out their father's brand new Willys Jeep. After much argie-bargie about who was allowed to drive, they parked it next to the outhouse, attached a hose to the exhaust and fed the fumes through a hole, intending to kill the snake.

Christmas and New Year were celebrated in a particular way at Uhlenhorst. The festivities fell right into the most industrious time at the farm. Peaches were ripe and needed picking, packing and taking to the market, as did the tomatoes and flowers. And the cows of course didn't take a break around the Christmas season either.

Nevertheless, Ursula took great pride in preparing and celebrating a 'proper Christmas', as she liked to call it. She followed old German traditions as much as the hot weather would allow. Every year she made 'Marzipan Potatoes', baked tons of biscuits, decorated the tree, and made sure there were presents for everybody.

The main celebration was on Christmas Eve and the family had to wait for Hermann Eschenburg to come home from his last trip to town. Every year, they had rice and herring salad for supper before unwrapping their presents, which had all been laid out under the Christmas tree. The wax candles which Ursula insisted on having would bend in the midsummer heat and drip wax onto the carpet. Sometimes, to the great excitement of the boys, the tree would catch alight, but even that was planned for. A bucket of water was always nearby.

A week later it was time for a grand New Year's party and again, every year Ursula pulled out all the stops. She prepared *Bowle*, the German version of a punch bowl, and *Kullerpfirsich*, a drink that was made by pricking the skin of a ripe peach and then dropping it into a large brandy glass full of champagne.

They played shadow movies behind a sheet illuminated with a paraffin lamp. Walter's favourite roll was that of the surgeon who, armed with a huge saw, would appear to cut open somebody else's abdomen and pull out a long string of sausages. They played table tennis on the lawn, musical chairs and charades. Midnight came and after greeting the New Year, it was time to predict the future by doing *Bleigiessen*.

A little piece of lead was melted over a candle on a teaspoon and then dropped into a basin of cold water. The lead immediately solidified and the resulting shape would give clues about the future.

The years went by and Uhlenhorst grew and prospered. So did the young Eschenburgs, and the time came for them to fly the nest. Hermann was first and married Betty, whom he had met in his last year at school. He became a mining engineer, they moved to Bloemfontein, and together they had six children. Walter went to Pretoria University, where he shared digs with a young man called Karl August Sartorius von Lindenau, and then to Onderstepoort, South Africa's only veterinary university. Predictably, Elsa was the last to leave Uhlenhorst, but before she set off on her path of becoming a teacher and later on a nurse, she and Walter undertook a memorable journey together.

Elsa, Walter and Comtesse

ADVENTURES

Walter and Karl August Sartorius von Lindenau, the young man with the grand name, quickly became close friends. Karl August hailed from *South-West Africa*, where his family owned various large farms and his father was a Member of Parliament. While studying in Pretoria, he spent most weekends and short holidays with the Eschenburgs at Uhlenhorst and soon became part of the family.

Walter and Karl August travelled to the Kruger Park together and to Swaziland; they rode horses, went hunting and invited the young women of their circle of friends out to dances.

Elsa was still at school when Karl August first came to Uhlenhorst and she became like a little sister to him, a target for merciless yet friendly teasing. More often than not, she was allowed to accompany the two young men on their adventures, but she had to behave. Since Walter had always had a soft spot for his little sister, it was Karl August who put her in her place when she became just too annoying, like only a little sister can. Despite, or possibly because of it, Elsa had developed an overwhelming crush on Karl August; a passion that she knew how to hide, and that nobody else was ever aware of.

For Karl August, she was just the little sister and later on became a good friend. Once he had completed his degree in agricultural science, he moved back to his home country, which at the time was administered by the South African Parliament as a de facto fifth province and often just called *'South-West'*.

Walter completed his studies at Onderstepoort a year after Karl August, and he decided that it was time to reward himself with a journey he had long wanted to do.

Elsa soon got wind of Walter's plans to take his first car, a brand new Morris Minor, to the former German colony. When he announced one evening that he'd be setting off as soon as the graduation ceremony was over and the New Year had started, Elsa didn't waste any time.

'Please, Walter, can I come with you?' she asked.

Walter pretended he didn't hear.

'*Ag* please, it would be so great to go on a trip with you.'

Walter looked at his younger sister. She had just passed her matric and he knew that she was not quite sure what to do next, whether to become a teacher or a nurse. Some time to make up her mind would do her good, Walter thought, and a road trip was just the right thing. But before he agreed, he just had to tease her a little longer.

'Actually, I had hoped for some peace and quiet,' he said.

'I promise, I won't say a word during the whole trip. I'll even cook for you, every day, I promise!' Elsa replied eagerly.

Now Walter had to laugh. He knew full well that his little sister hated nothing more than cooking.

'Oh dear, now that is a threat,' he smiled. 'Let's put it that way. If you promise not to cook, you can come with me.' He had actually hoped that she'd want to join him. She was good company, and they always had been very close. Now that he was soon to leave home and start work at the Veterinary Hospital in Johannesburg, he'd enjoy spending some time with her. He was at his happiest when he had somebody to share his passion for nature, and when he could pass on some of his knowledge.

'Are you serious? I promise whatever you want!' Elsa cried and slung her arms around her brother's neck.

Finally, the New Year arrived. 1957. After one of Ma Eschenburg's legendary Old Year's Eve parties, Walter and Elsa set off in the little grey Morris Minor 800 cc. Since they both felt a little worse for wear, they decided to stop over at Daniel's, a friend's farm that was only a couple of hours' drive away.

They rested for a while, but once darkness fell Walter and Daniel decided it was time to have some fun, and with Elsa tagging along, they set out to hunt springhares.

Elsa sat quietly in the back of the Morris Minor and watched in dismay how the little creatures she thought of as rather cute were mesmerised by the headlights. When the two young men leapt out of the car and tried to club them over the head, she closed her eyes and held her breath. To her relief, this method of hunting required a good deal of skill and speed, and after the previous night's party, it seemed, Walter and Daniel were lacking both. In the end, they returned with just one dead springhare, which was promptly skinned, gutted and hung, to be eaten soon.

The next day, Walter and Elsa left at first light and covered seemingly endless distances on sandy dirt roads until they reached the southernmost parts of the Kalahari Desert. It was hot, the glare and the heat of the sun reflecting off the sand, the air heavy.

'Where are we going to sleep tonight?' Elsa asked.

It was the first time in hours that either of them had spoken.

'We'll just stop somewhere next to the road.'

'Isn't that dangerous?'

'Dangerous?' Walter laughed. 'I don't think so. Look around you, Elsa, there is nothing and nobody out here.'

Just before sunset Walter pulled over. He was worried they'd get stuck in the sand if they ventured further off the road, and anyway, what difference did it make? He took out their *kaross*, a fur blanket made from many rectangles of pelt that had once belonged to African Civets, and placed it on the ground close to the car. Next to it, he arranged his water bottle, a torch and a little sheathed axe.

'Wake me up if there is a problem.' Within seconds he was snoring.

Elsa looked at her brother and shook her head, amazed at his ability to fall asleep anytime, anywhere. She watched the stars for some time, magnificent in the desert night sky, before she too closed her eyes.

A bright beam of light appeared in the desert night. Still half asleep, Walter leapt to his feet, grabbed his sister's hand, pulled her up and started running.

'Walter, what are you doing?'

'Quick, quick, we must get off the road, there is a car coming!' he shouted.

'But Walter, we are not on the road!'

'Yes we are! Now get up, otherwise it will hit us.'

By the time they had stumbled away, the car had long passed and Walter had woken up. He realised that Elsa had been right, admitted as much, lay down again and was snoring within seconds. Some hours passed, before he was woken by an ear-piercing scream.

'What's it now?' he asked.

Elsa pointed the torch at a large, pitch-black scorpion that was headed towards her side of the kaross. With its pincers stretched out ahead and the tail with the poison gland bent up and forward, ready to strike, it offered a rather scary sight, Walter had to admit.

'Don't worry, this one is not so bad,' he tried to calm his sister. 'You see, he's got a relatively small tail. That means he relies more on the pincers than on his poison for defence and to catch his prey. The ones you must watch out for are those with a fat tail and small pincers. They are normally seriously poisonous.'

Despite the fact that he had advertised the harmlessness of the creature, he picked up the axe and started hitting the scorpion.

'Walter, you still have the sheath on the axe.'

Ja, ja,' he replied. 'No problem.' He seemed to be asleep before his head hit the pillow again.

Elsa retreated to the back seat of their little car where she'd spend the few remaining hours of the desert night. She had no intentions of sleeping out in the open again.

'Did you know that in South-West you can't see a herd of sheep crossing the road?' Walter asked.

'Why is that?'

'Because the corrugations are so bad!'

They had followed the dry bed of the Auob River through the *Kalahari Gemsbok National Park*, until they had reached Mata Mata and crossed the border. Indeed, the road surface had changed from deep sand to hard baked dirt with deep corrugations that shook them and rattled the car.

'You have to go over them fast!' Walter said with a sparkle in his eyes. He loved driving fast. As far as he was concerned they had been going slowly for long enough, driving through the National Park.

But what a wonderful drive it had been! Their animal sightings had been amazing. Vast herds of springbok and gemsbok, all gathering around the waterholes in the otherwise dry riverbed; wildebeest and ostriches; some black backed jackals sniffing out a relatively recent lion kill, and a family of cheetahs. He wished they could have stayed longer, but there was no accommodation in the park and Elsa had refused point blank to spend another night under the stars, especially not in an area where they knew lions were roaming.

He laughed as he remembered her face when she tried to have a look at the dead scorpion in the morning. It had vanished. He had probably just pushed it into the sand with the sheathed axe. The same had happened to the bright yellow Cape Cobra that had slithered across the road right in front of them. He didn't have the slightest chance to stop in time. Running over snakes was never a good idea as they could whip up, travel somehow underneath the car and then come out when one least expected it. Or so the story went. But when they'd stopped and looked back they saw the snake moving along as if nothing had happened.

'You know what I think was the most beautiful sight, Walter?' Elsa asked as they moved higher up onto the escarpment, where it was a little cooler and they both felt more energetic.

'No, but I'm sure you are going to tell me.'

'Yes, you know, that early morning in the Kalahari? The red sand dune in the morning light. It was covered with those little yellow flowers, strung together by thin green tendrils, and the herd of fat shiny impala right in there…'

'Are you sure?' Walter interrupted her.

'Yes, of course, didn't you see it? Oh, I wish I could paint, it would make the most beautiful picture!'

'But Elsa, we were in the Kalahari! You don't get impala in the Kalahari! Well, apparently you do, but they are very, very rare. They don't really belong there. And we didn't see any. And certainly not a whole herd.'

'Man, springbok I mean, of course. But tell me, since you are so clever, what were those yellow flowers? Do you know?'

'Of course, don't you?' Walter loved teasing his little sister. 'It's the *dubbeltje*, or Devil's thorn; its Latin name is *tribulus zeyheri*. This creeper appears after a good rain with loads of yellow flowers. And springbok, ostriches and even the little ground squirrels all love this little devil.'

100

Slowly they made their way north, enjoying the sights of this country that seemed, compared to South Africa, so deserted. For miles and miles they raced along dirt roads without seeing a soul. The landscape was dry, bizarre at times. They saw the largest termite mound ever and admired the nests of the sociable weavers, which were precariously perched on telephone posts. When they passed through a settlement called Uhlenhorst, they stopped, just for sentimental reasons, because it bore the same name as their home.

Eventually they reached Windhoek, where they got in touch with Walter Gilbert, a renowned local artist and Walter's godfather. To their absolute delight, he introduced them to Henno Martin, author of '*The Sheltering Desert*', a book they both treasured.

Together with a friend, Henno Martin had spent two years living in the Namib Desert during the Second World War to avoid being interned. He told them about some of his adventures; how he and his friend had managed to survive in the extreme conditions of the desert, and the idiosyncrasies they had developed after living in such isolation for two years.

Apparently they had learned quickly that it was not only their bodies that needed feeding, but also their minds, and so they began studying their environment and its biodiversity in great detail. They made friends with a large gecko, whom they called Phillip, and were good neighbours with a snake, who lived under a rock nearby. This friendship faltered when the snake ate Phillip. Beside himself, Henno Martin's friend, who had observed this act of violence, killed the snake, cut it open and retrieved the gecko, which, after having the snake's digestive juices washed off its back, lived a long and happy life ever after.

Walter and Elsa were delighted.

Bergfontein, the von Lindenaus' farm was vast, even by Namibian standards. The modern house, built on a precipice with a breath-taking view, was dark and cool inside. Walter and Elsa settled in quickly, and together with Karl August and his brother Ernst Rudolph they explored their surroundings.

The von Lindenaus didn't only own Bergfontein and before long, they took Walter and Elsa to the north of the country. They showed them Etosha, one of the largest game reserves in Southern Africa, with a vast salt pan desert at its centre.

They stayed on a farm nearby, which belonged to Mrs von Lindenau's sister. There they rode horses and suddenly found themselves in the middle of a herd of elephants, an experience neither of them would ever forget.

Another farm owned by the von Lindenaus was Kakatswa. It bordered the Kaokoveld, a vast and wild area, only sparsely populated by the Himba people. The farm teemed with wildlife, including elephant, rhino, lion and anything else Walter had ever wished for.

Mrs von Lindenau joined them on their trip to Kakatswa; evidently she loved the bush and the wilderness and knew a lot about it. Also part of their small group was another guest of the von Lindenaus', a German artist by the name of Fritz Kempe. He was what Walter imagined a typical Berliner to be - loud and bombastic.

It was full moon and Mrs von Lindenau decided to take her visitors to the Kakatswa *Schlucht*, a long gorge that ran across the farm. They would spend the night on the rocks above a waterhole, and just wait and see.

At first they all stayed awake and just enjoyed the moon lit evening, but later on they took turns to keep watch, waking the others whenever something interesting approached the waterhole.

At about two o'clock in the morning two black rhino appeared and immediately Walter was wide awake. He observed how the animals came closer and closer until they stood right below the little group's vantage point. Then they stopped. In awe, Walter took in their beauty as they stood still for what felt like hours without as much as batting an eyelid. He had a quick glance at his companions. They were as fascinated as he was. Nobody dared move. Nobody, except Fritz Kempe. He apparently couldn't sit still any longer.

'Frau von Lindenau,' Walter heard him whisper, 'Frau von Lindenau, I'm going down there now to have a closer look.'

And Mrs von Lindenau, who must have known, that there was no stopping him, replied,

'Do what you've got to do, but you do it on your own head. And make sure you don't get run over.'

Walter nudged Elsa and shook his head as they kept an eye on Fritz Kempe climbing down the rocks and getting closer to the rhinos, which still hadn't moved. He hid behind a bush, not more than ten feet away from the animals. Suddenly Walter sat up straighter. He couldn't believe his eyes. Without any of them noticing, Fritz Kempe had taken one of the glass cylinders of the paraffin lamps with him and now put it to his mouth. Using this prop, he made a loud, trumpeting sound, imitating what he must have thought was a rhino call.

They both flew around and came for him without any hesitation. One charged past in front of Kempe, who stood stock still, as if frozen to the spot, and the other right behind him. He could have touched them both.

Walter and the others listened to their huffing and snorting for a good while, as the two black rhinos disappeared down the gorge. About ten minutes later the bombastic Berliner came quietly back to the camp.

'*Donnerwetter*, these things move like a steam train!' he whispered.

A few days later, during a sunset stroll, Walter and Elsa ended up in the middle of a herd of zebra. In the distance, against the summer clouds tinged red by the setting sun, they could make out the silhouettes of a small group of giraffe and close by, some warthogs were on their way home to their borrow.

'This must be close to paradise,' Walter thought.

Nobody spoke, as if uttering a word would spoil the magic of the evening.

The little grey Morris Minor had proved to be a tireless companion. It had covered endless miles on corrugated dirt roads, crossed through dry river beds, as well as raging rivers after the rain. It seemed to be able to fly over aardvark holes and could duck under the lower branches of the camel thorn trees; it climbed mountains and dived down steep gorges. But when the end of Walter and Elsa's journey arrived, their trusted companion had had enough. The car was kaput. They barely managed to drive it back to Windhoek, where they loaded it on a train and sent it home.

Sitting in the little aeroplane that would take them back to Johannesburg, they peered down onto a dramatic landscape. Walter and Elsa were both a little sad. It had been a wonderful trip and they had cherished every moment of it. It was as if they knew that this was their last long journey together. Life would take them along different roads from now on.

Elsa would go to Wits University, and then to Teachers Training College. Nearly twenty years later, she'd change the course of her life and become a nurse. She'd get married, have two children and move to the coastal town of East London.

Their parents, Ursula and Herrmann Eschenburg, would continue their busy farm lives at Uhlenhorst until they'd eventually retire to Edenvale, a suburb of Johannesburg.

Walter would start work as a junior surgeon at the Veterinary Hospital in Johannesburg.

They both closed their eyes, recalling some special moments.

For Elsa, it was Karl August's face that kept appearing amongst the pictures of galloping zebras and beautiful flowers. She had made peace with the fact that this was probably the last occasion she would've spent in his company. It was sad, but that was life. She sighed.

Walter on the other hand smiled, remembering how he had made a fool of himself.

FOOLS AND LIONS

When we returned from Kakatswa, that's when I made a real fool of myself.

We were back on Bergfontein, and they all knew I was dying to shoot something, anything, really. I'd loved hunting and everything related to it ever since those days in Juchow, when I shot my first rabbit with the help of Jean Pierre, the prisoner of war. But I hadn't done a huge amount of hunting since and I was bloody raw.

They sent me out to shoot a kudu. On my own. I walked for what felt like an eternity and saw nothing. Eventually I spotted some gemsbok in the distance, but soon they saw me and disappeared over the horizon. I was getting tired and the sun was setting. Not long and it would be dark.

Suddenly, just as I passed a little hill, I heard this noise. My heart nearly stopped. It sounded just like the lion we had heard at Kakatswa, only a lot closer. There it was again. Now I was convinced it was a lion. I stood still for a long time before I gathered all my courage and decided to climb the *koppie*, so that at least I could see.

As I was on my way up, I heard another sound. This time, it resembled hoof beats in quick succession, something like '*dufdufdufduf*'.

'Oh my God,' I thought, 'now there is something following me.'

I carried on, just because I didn't know what else to do, and eventually I realized it was my own heartbeat. Sjoe!

Once I got to the top, I still couldn't see anything. I climbed a camel thorn tree that stood right at the edge and peered down the other side and now I understood what the fuss was all about. Just below was a big cock ostrich courting a hen.

He was dancing around her with his wings spread and every now and then, he blew up his neck and made this lion-like sound.

The ostrich hen seemed very impressed indeed, and I was so relieved that I didn't even take a shot at them. Instead I decided it was time to go home.

When I got back to the von Lindenaus and sort of told them the story, they were polite enough not to laugh out loud. They just smiled, but they must have known I was scared absolutely rotten.

A VET'S LIFE

A VET'S LIFE

I became a vet almost by default. As a young boy, when we lived at Juchow, I'd dreamed of becoming a *Förster*, a forester, just like Herr Dummke. But soon after we returned from Germany, I realised that there was no such profession in South Africa. The closest one could come here to a forester was a hunter. And yes, of course I'd always enjoyed hunting and for some time it was part of my life, but I didn't want to make it a profession. Shooting for the pot, I felt, was fine, but I knew I'd prefer to deal with live animals.

As I grew up, I enjoyed biology, and with my father being a dairy farmer, there were always lots of animals around, so it just seemed natural that I'd become a vet.

The first couple of years at university I struggled a little with physics and chemistry. But the professor for chemistry was also German, and one day we got into a more private conversation. I told him about Juchow and then introduced him to my father. The two men realised quickly that they knew the same people back in Germany. Thus the problem with chemistry disappeared.

For the good marks in physics, I had to work a little harder. My professor coached the university's rugby team, and after I joined it – I was a lot taller and stronger in those days – the physics problem had been solved as well.

Botany and zoology were a different story altogether. I just loved both of those subjects and never really had to study.

Once I had passed my final exams some of the professors asked me to stay on; they were talking about an academic career. But by the time I graduated, I'd had enough of theory. I just wanted to get out into the real world. And the real world, real life, with all its ups and downs, its tragedies and comedies, well, that's what I got. There have been difficult times, hard times, yes, but I wouldn't have had it any other way. I loved every minute of it.

THE OX BEFORE THE GOLDEN GATE

The first time Walter was called out at midnight to do a calving on a Friesland cow, he felt that he stood in front, or rather behind, that animal like the proverbial *Ox before the Golden Gate*.

He had been working at the Veterinary Hospital in Johannesburg for a couple of months and was slowly finding his feet. He was taught a lot in those days, particularly by his mentor Dr Wallander. Each day brought new experiences and slowly he learned to convert all the theoretical knowledge he had accumulated during the years at Onderstepoort into practice.

Being the youngest, a bachelor and somewhat the new kid on the block, he did a lot of night shifts at the hospital. The little room, where he could rest once he had done the last round, was linked to the stables and kennels by an intercom, so that he would be alerted to any commotion there. More often than not it was a just some or other little dog crying for attention and company. Quickly Walter worked out that if it didn't sound like anything serious, he could just bark through the intercom a loud, 'Shut up!', and they'd listen and be quiet for a little while, long enough for him to check his eyelids for cracks.

There was always another, more experienced vet on duty as well, whom he could alert if necessary, and normally it was that vet on duty, who would go out and see to patients on the farms and smallholdings if there was an emergency.

One evening, Dr Wallander called Walter aside. 'Eschenburg,' he said, 'you'll be on your own tonight. I have been watching you, and I know you are ready. There are only a few patients here and you know how to handle them. If there is a call-out you just go and do what's necessary.'

Walter was surprised. Sure, he'd never had to call the more experienced vet on duty, and he'd done the rounds with Dr Wallander or one of his colleagues a hundred times, but to be left completely to his own devices was a different story.

'Ok, Doc,' he said, putting on a brave face.

'You'll be fine. And if there is really an emergency, you've got my home number. Call me anytime.'

'Don't worry, Doc,' Walter replied. 'I'll manage.'

Dr Wallander didn't have any doubts. Many a young vet had passed through his hands at one of the foremost veterinary hospitals in the Johannesburg area, but he had never come across a young man with a deeper understanding of animals than Walter. He had passed all the exams at Onderstepoort with flying colours, got an award for surgery at his graduation and what he lacked in practical experience, he made up with an intuition the older vet had rarely witnessed - not only in young graduates, but in anybody. At the same time, he knew that Walter was aware of his limitations and that, should he reach them, he would not hesitate to call for help rather than jeopardise the life of one of his valued clients' animals. In short, he knew, the young vet was ready.

As predicted by Dr Wallander, the evening was quiet and after making sure all patients were settled for the night, Walter decided to lie down and get some sleep. No sooner had he closed his eyes than the phone rang. It was midnight exactly and immediately he was wide awake. On the line was Johann Botha, a good client, who had a small herd of Friesland cows on a smallholding north of Johannesburg.

'Doc, sorry to bother you in the middle of the night' he began, 'but you'd better come. Doris, my best cow, is having trouble calving. She has been at it all evening and the calf is just not coming. There must be a problem somewhere.'

'No worries, I'll be with you as soon as I can,' Walter said and put the phone down.

'I must make sure I don't forget anything,' he thought. He had been expecting, and at the same time dreading, this midnight call. If he was really honest, he had to admit that he was a little nervous. 'Don't be stupid,' he encouraged himself. 'How many calvings have I done at Uhlenhorst? More than I can count.' And with this he grabbed his medicine bag and raced off through the cold and dark Highveld night.

When Walter arrived at the Botha's stables, he was shocked. Doris was the biggest cow he had ever seen, and he had seen a few, having grown up on a dairy farm.

'Oh well,' he thought, 'just as well I am not small and that I have long arms, otherwise I don't know what I'd do.'

He took off his shirt, lathered his arms with Lifebuoy soap and washed with icy cold water from a black bucket. He examined the cow, with the farmer hovering about.

The man was worried about his prized animal and seemed a little concerned that the young vet had come on his own, but graciously, he didn't comment on it. He had met Walter before, when doing the rounds together with his mentor.

At first Walter couldn't feel anything other than that all life was squeezed out of his arm. It seemed far too short, the cow too big. He tried again.

'Just relax and concentrate,' he said to himself and tried a little harder, stretching his arm as far as he could. Eventually, he found what he was looking for. 'The calf is alive, but its head is turned back.'

He looked at Mr Botha, who only nodded. He knew what that meant. The calf had to be pushed back and its head turned forward so that it would come to lie on its front legs. Only then would the cow be able to push it out.

In theory it seemed easy. But Walter found that no matter how hard he tried, he could do nothing. Absolutely nothing. He tried to get a hold on the head somehow; he stood on his toes and stretched as far as he could, but to no avail. His arms were just that little bit too short. To make matters worse, he could see the worry on the farmer's face. And Walter understood. He literally had the life of his best cow in his hands.

Eventually, he gave up and phoned Dr Wallander. 'Doc, you'd better come. I need your help here. I have struck the absolute impossible calving.'

'Maybe we'll have to do a caesarean section,' Walter thought while sitting on a bale of lucerne in the stable, head in hands, looking at the cow and waiting. Yes, a *caesar* would be the only way to get this calf out, and that he couldn't do on his own. If they waited for too long, the calf would eventually die and then they'd have to cut it up with an *embryotome*, lest they'd risk the life of the mother too. He imagined all possible and impossible scenarios, feeling more and more dejected.

It seemed to take forever, but eventually Dr Wallander arrived. Relieved, Walter greeted his mentor, who was in his late fifties, a short little man, with short little arms. He took one look at the cow and examined her quickly.

'But Walter, you've nearly got this calf out,' he said.

Walter just stared at him.

'Ja, man. It is nearly out. Just give me a hand.' The older vet guided Walter's hand inside the cow and pressed his fingers over the calf's nose. 'Just hold there.' Then he pushed the calf back on its chest, its neck came straight, the cow made one last effort at pushing and the calf popped out. It was all done.

The farmer breathed a sigh of relief and so did Walter. Yet he still couldn't believe what he had just seen. Not even three minutes it had taken this short little man, while he had been standing there, digging in the poor cow for two hours, thinking he had struck the impossible calving. He had literally stood there like the *Ox before the Golden Gate*.

'But you've got it out,' Dr Wallander smiled. This was just the sort of experience his understudy needed. While he was washing with the cold water from the black bucket he asked, 'Why didn't you just carry on for another minute?'

Graduation

Getting married

WEDDING BELLS

What Dr Wallander taught me that day, when I stood behind that cow like that proverbial 'Ox', was one of the most important lessons I've learned. Ever. Whenever I'd encounter a problem, in the many years to come that I practised as a vet, I would remember Dr Wallander with his short arms and the large cow, and I knew it could be done. I hardly ever had a serious problem anymore. And you know what? The solution is in your head, it's got nothing to do with your strength or the length of your arms. Absolutely nothing.

Not long after this incident, some time in 1958, I was called out to attend to another sick cow on a small farm in Bryanston. Buoyed with new confidence I arrived, only to encounter a very different challenge.

Over the back of that sick cow I met Topsy Graham, and she was the most beautiful girl I had ever laid my eyes upon. She had just qualified from Agricultural College and it was her first job as farm manager. She was brilliant. Single-handedly she looked after a small herd of about forty dairy cows, some six or seven horses which were used for hunting, a flock of ducks and all the other animals her boss kept on his *plaas*. He was a high-powered businessman in the city, yet he still wanted to live nowhere else but on a farm.

Topsy clearly knew what it was all about. Having grown up near *Naboomspruit*, her father had given her a little dairy herd when she was little, and she'd always thought that one day she might take over the family farm. But, as I was to learn some time later, Topsy didn't really get on terribly well with her mother. As she had got older, their relationship had deteriorated and when she turned twenty-one, after another huge row, Topsy had had enough.

She told her father that she thought it was better for her to leave home. She was sad to leave, but it was time, and she really enjoyed the sense of freedom that living and working on the dairy farm in Johannesburg gave her. At last, she was independent.

I realised immediately that we had a lot in common, and I made sure I had to come back and see my patient again the following day. She seemed to be pleased to see me too, and so I gathered all my courage.

'Do you have a day off here?' I asked her.

'Yes, on Saturdays,' she replied with a smile, looking a bit shy all of a sudden.

'Well, I have to work on Saturday, but if you don't mind, I mean, if you want to, you could join me on my rounds.' I took a deep breath.

'Yes, I'd love to do that,' Topsy said, and I was the happiest man in the world.

From then on I picked her up every Saturday. Instead of having romantic dinners or going out to dances, which neither of us could afford, we did the rounds, visiting sick cows and horses - and we both loved it.

After a couple of months, I invited Topsy to Uhlenhorst for Sunday lunch. She was a little apprehensive at first, because my parents were rather very 'German', and somehow she'd got it into her head that they didn't like her. She always thought that they'd had another lady for me in mind, a daughter of a friend of theirs and a good business connection. She was wrong, but no matter how hard I tried to convince her otherwise, she never really believed me.

But I'm getting ahead of myself here. We got engaged about six months after we met and then married a year later. My parents had an engagement party for us at Uhlenhorst, and unfortunately the only one from Topsy's side who could come was her sister. Naboomspruit, where her parents lived, was just too far away; it took about a day and a half to drive from there to Johannesburg in those days. We had a great party though with lots and lots of delicious food that my Mom produced on that funny old woodstove in her little smoke-blackened kitchen. How she did that I'll never know. She was just amazing like that.

The wedding was in March 1960 on Weltevreden, Topsy's parents' farm, and everybody arrived a couple of days prior to the big day.

Only, I nearly didn't make it to our wedding. And it wasn't my fault. I wanted nothing more than get married to Topsy. Ever since I had met her, over the back of that sick cow, I was smitten. Completely and utterly smitten. This tall, blonde, beautiful girl got my heart racing every time I looked at her. I can't even tell you how delighted I was when she agreed to come and do the rounds with me on Saturdays. We not only had a lot in common, but I also felt that we complemented each other very nicely. I desperately needed her to bring some sort of organisation into my life. Although I knew all that, it took me quite some time to pluck up the courage to actually propose to her. I don't think I have ever been so nervous in my life before – or after. But I managed, thank goodness.

When I arrived in Naboomspruit, Topsy's parents, who were really lovely people, put me up in one of their rondavels, which I shared with our friend Adrian Boshier.

Bogey, that's what we called him, wasn't just your normal guy. He wasn't what you'd call a normal guy at all, but he was a great friend of ours. Although there is a lot more to his story, suffice to say for now that one of his more unusual character traits was that he was an enthusiastic snake catcher. He was always catching snakes, and he always had snakes. You could write a whole book about his snake-catching stories.

Unbeknown to me, he had caught a couple of shield-nosed snakes on the farm that day, and he kept them in an earthenware pot that stood on a shelf in our rondavel.

That evening we had a festive dinner with Topsy's family, ate lots of good food and drank copious amounts of red wine. Midnight came and went and eventually I couldn't keep my eyes open any longer. I excused myself and got up, ready to 'hit the sack'.

'I'll come with you; I want to show you something.' Bogey said, and together we walked across the lawn to our little round hut.

There, he headed straight for that earthenware pot that I had presumed was just decoration. With a twinkle in his eye he peered into it, then looked at me and, barely suppressing a giggle, for he had also had his share of wine, he said,

'Oh no, it's gone!'

I feared the worst. I sat down on the bed, actually quite tired after a day out on the farm, driving around, hunting, the wedding preparations and of course all the wine.

'The snake,' he said, 'the snake, she's gone!' Feverishly he began searching the room.

We looked everywhere, but we couldn't find that bloody thing.

Then, for some reason, I lifted up my pillow. And there it was, raising its head in defence pose, ready to strike. Slowly, I backed off.

'Now that would have been a nice surprise! Glad you found it!'

Bogey grabbed the snake by its tail and deposited it back into its dark prison.

I'll take it out into the veld tomorrow morning. You don't mind if it sleeps here in the room with us, do you?'

'Well, I'd sleep better if you made sure it couldn't escape another time. Topsy will not be amused if we have to cancel our wedding because the bridegroom has been bitten by a snake.'

As far as I know these snakes are venomous, but not deadly. In any case, I didn't fancy sharing my bed with it. I didn't sleep particularly well that night, but this time the snake stayed put and we did get married. I only told Topsy about this little episode much, much later.

We spent our honeymoon at the Beacon Isle Hotel in Plettenberg Bay, then a small seaside town on the Southern Cape coast.

Topsy just loved the sea and sometimes I thought that if it was for her, she could have moved there in a flash. We never really spoke about it, but she knew how much I loved the bush and that I would have found it very difficult to live anywhere else but in the bush.

For the first year after we got married we stayed in Johannesburg and lived in Topsy's little cottage on the farm where she worked. I continued my apprentice years at the Veterinary Hospital in Johannesburg, but we were both keen to move out of the city. The time came when I felt I was grown-up enough to start my own practice.

CIRCUS

'The circus is in town, did you see?' Topsy was very excited.

Walter's Peugeot station wagon, not quite new and a little battered around the edges, had just pulled up outside the Eschenburgs' veterinary practice in Voortrekkerstraat in Potgietersrus.

'Oh ja, I saw a big commotion at the station,' Walter replied as he got out of his car.

Knowing that Topsy loved the circus as much as he did, he suggested, 'Why don't we see if we can get some tickets for tonight's show?'

'Yes, but they actually want to see you! The lion tamer wants to see you. As soon as possible.'

'Oh well, let's go then. Are you coming?'

'Stupid question!' Topsy mumbled as she jumped into the car.

Potgietersrus was a small town. Established by the Voortrekkers, the first Afrikaner settlers, in the 1800s and named after their leader Piet Potgieter, it served as an economic hub for the agriculturally rich area between the Waterberg and the Springbok Flats. Farmers produced wheat, tobacco, maize, citrus and, above all, beef. Vast herds of Afrikaner and Bonsmara cattle were bred and roamed the lands, which originally had belonged to the Ndebele people, whose once great leader, Mokopane, would half a century later lend his name to the town.

In the early 1960s, it was these large herds of cattle as much as the surrounding bushveld that had attracted the young Eschenburgs.

After having worked and learned for some years at the Veterinary Hospital in Johannesburg, Walter felt it was time to get out of the city, to live somewhere closer to the bush, to be independent, and finally, to set up his own practice. His mentor, Dr Wallander, and his boss, Dr Jeremy Zander, had only encouraged him. They would have loved to keep him working at the hospital as they had assured him many a time, yet they also understood his desire to move on. There was not much more, the two experienced vets felt, they could teach this young and talented man. It was time he stood on his own feet.

By the time the circus arrived in town, Walter and Topsy had been living in Potgietersrus for a good six months. They had settled in, and the practice Walter had taken over from an older colleague was going well. He could be busier, he felt sometimes, but as Topsy had pointed out only recently, small-town people took their time to warm to a new vet on the block.

In the meantime, there was so much to learn about the environment they were living in now. Walter was no stranger to the bushveld, but he was amazed that every day, when out doing his rounds, he'd discover something new; see a tree he hadn't noticed before or hear a bird whose call he wasn't yet familiar with. There were new roads to be explored, which he loved doing at high speed in the Peugeot, and new people to meet.

Life was quiet, as one would expect from a small town in the bushveld, and sometimes Walter wondered if it was not a little too quiet for Topsy. She was of course used to country life, but Walter was also aware how much she loved going out, and if he was honest, he himself was not averse to having some fun. To have the circus in town was a great change to their normal routine, and the famous Zander's Circus was the most splendid and spectacular establishment that plied the streets of South Africa in the 1960s. Its director, Zacharias Zander, was no stranger to the Eschenburgs.

'I wonder what the lion tamer wants,' Walter thought aloud while driving through town.

'They didn't say,' Topsy replied, 'but do you have any lion experience?'

'Some, but not too much. A couple of years ago we had twelve young lions in at the hospital. They also belonged to the Zander's Circus and of course Zacharias Zander wouldn't take them anywhere else to be spayed other than into his brother Jeremy's hospital.'

'And?' Topsy asked.

'Well, those lions were actually very, very nice. We could even stroke them. I think they were about seven or eight months old, and we kept them in the big dog run at the back of the hospital. Every day we spayed a couple. But we didn't take any chances. Although they were friendly we'd put them into a squeeze cage and only then did we give them their intravenous injections. A lion is a lion after all!'

They had arrived at the circus grounds and Walter immediately recognised Zacharias Zander. He looked par for the course in his red jacket, black trousers, polished shoes and a most impressive top hat. After they'd exchanged greetings and pleasantries, he directed Walter and Topsy to the local pub in town. That's where they most likely would find the lion tamer.

Walter had been to *Die Uitspan* before and knew Josef Fischer, the barman, quite well. When he explained why he had come, Josef pointed to the corner of the bar.

Leaning against the counter, as if in desperate need of some support, was a short, somewhat thick-set, middle-aged man. His thin black hair was in disarray and he was frowning, the thick, jet-black brows hovering above half closed eyes. Unshaven, he was dressed in a black jersey and trousers that had seen better and cleaner days. He was staring into his drink.

'Hi, I'm Doctor Eschenburg. Are you perhaps the lion tamer?'

'Tak,' the man answered.

'You got a sick lion?'

'Tak,' came the reply.

He must be Polish, Walter thought. He remembered some of the language, the basics of which he had picked up during his youth in Pomerania.

'You want to see me?'

'Tak.' He looked Walter up and down. 'You are the vet?'

'Yes, I am the vet.'

'Tak. I want to see you. You come.' He threw some coins onto the counter, emptied his glass in one quick move and headed outside, where Topsy had been waiting; women were not yet allowed into pubs.

The lion tamer walked straight up to her and asked, 'this your man?' pointing with a grubby finger at Walter.

'Yes, indeed. This is my man.'

'Ok. I bring you his clothes.'

Walter wasn't sure how to reply to the questioning look he got from Topsy, or what to make of this comment. Did he mean he was going to be eaten by the lions? He shrugged.

'This your car?'

'Yes. I'll take my wife home and then I'll come and see your lion.'

'Oh. I come,' the lion tamer said and jumped into the car with them.

Topsy looked at Walter, pulling up her nose a little.

'He smells,' she whispered, 'of booze and of lion!'

After they had dropped Topsy at home, the two men drove up to the station, where the circus train stood on a side line, the wagons and tents all painted in cheerful colours. The lion tamer directed Walter to the last coach. It was closed up and resembled a cattle wagon.

'He in there.'

'All right. Can I see him?'

'You come.'

The lion tamer showed Walter to the back of the wagon, where rickety steps led up to a small door. 'He in there.'

Walter stuck his head through the narrow gap. Quickly he turned around and looked at the lion tamer questioningly. There was not one lion in the wagon, but sixteen fully grown animals. They all looked at him with great interest.

'Well, where is he?'

'There.' The man pointed towards the other end of the wagon.

'Can you perhaps bring him nearer by?'

'No. You come.'

'In there?' Walter asked, trying not to show his surprise.

'You scared?'

'No, no. No. I am not scared.'

'You come.'

As they stepped into the lion cage Walter grasped his black medicine bag tighter, holding it in front of his body as if it were a lifesaver. He stayed as close as possible to the lion tamer who strode down the middle of the wagon where an aisle had formed, framed by lions on either side.

All sitting up, the animals followed the two men with their eyes and, just in time for their passing, lifted up a paw each in greeting. As if it was a well-studied performance, the lion tamer tapped each lion on the paw, saying, 'down, down', and they all took their hands down and edged a little further back, until the two men reached the far end of the wagon.

'There. He sick.'

The lion did indeed not look well. His ears were hanging, his eyes drooping and matt, his glorious mane a sad frame to a tired face. Looking at the sick animal, Walter forgot about the other lions and let his vet instinct take over. He took the thermometer out of his bag.

Slightly alarmed, the lion tamer asked, 'What you do?'

'I want to take his temperature,' Walter answered matter-of-factly.

'No. He bite.'

'Oh. I see.' Looking at the sick lion lying at his feet he said, 'ok. Well, I can see he has a fever. I'll just give him the injection straight away.'

'No. He bite. No injection.'

Walter scratched his head. Then he had an idea. 'Can you open his mouth?'

'Tak.' The lion tamer picked up the lion by its nose and pulled its mouth open.

'Ah, now I can see. His throat is bright red.'

The lion answered with a growl that made the wagon shudder.

'Ok, just wait a second.' Walter tried to ignore the noise the lion was making, took a bottle of antibiotic powder out of his black medicine bag and poured a good amount into his hand. 'Open now!' he said and threw the medicine down the animal's throat.

The lion growled again, licked his lips and swallowed.

'Ok, we go,' the lion tamer turned around.

On the way out, Walter felt so much better and braver that he didn't stick quite as closely to his guide's heels as before and quietly imitated him, pointing at the lions' noses, mumbling, 'down, down, down…'.

Once in the fresh air again, the lion tamer asked Walter, 'you want to see circus?'

'Yes! Very much.'

The man nodded and gave Walter a handful of tickets.

By sunset, Walter, Topsy and a couple of their friends were back at the circus. For some time they wandered around outside the large tent, eating candy floss and observing the activities there. Clowns were entertaining children, acrobats milled about on stilts, and jugglers did their thing to the cheers of an excited crowd. Eventually it was time to occupy their ringside seats. A cage had been erected, the bars so close to Walter and Topsy, they could have touched them.

'It must be the lion act first!' Topsy whispered.

The fanfare began and after a little while it died down. It was silent under the big top now, the air thick with the spectators' expectations. Then the fanfare went again. The drums rolled. Silence again.

A resplendent looking Zacharias Zander entered the arena to loud applause.

'Ladies and gentleman! Welcome to Zander's Circus!'

Again, there was loud applause.

'Ladies and gentlemen, I regret to have to announce that due to an unfortunate incident our lion tamer cannot appear tonight.'

A whisper went through the crowd before it was distracted by clowns and music, while mechanics took down the lion cage.

'Very strange,' Walter thought and looked around.

On the far side of the ring he saw a familiar figure, thick set and dressed in black, leaning against a pole.

'Topsy,' he whispered, 'I bet the lion tamer is just too drunk to do his act!'

The next morning, a Sunday, Walter and Topsy got into their car. The circus had moved on already. In small towns like Potgietersrus it normally only stayed for one performance. No sooner had the last audience left than the workers began taking down the big top. Everything was stowed in the wagons and off the caravan went. Walter knew that he would find it in Pietersburg. He wanted to check up on his patient and also, just maybe, impress Topsy a little with his treatment of the lions.

When they arrived at the Pietersburg train station, the circus grounds offered a very different scene to the previous day. On this Sunday morning circus life seemed a lot less glamorous. The colourful, happy acrobats of last night were nowhere to be found.

They asked around to find the lion tamer.

'His coach is over there. But he's asleep.'

Once they had woken him, Topsy noticed immediately that the man was still dressed in the same filthy black jersey and trousers, now emanating a smell not only of lions and booze, but of vomit as well. She decided to stand back a step.

'How is your lion?' Walter asked by way of greeting.

'Better.'

'Can we go and see him?'

'Tak.'

Excited and full of anticipation of how impressed Topsy would be about his newly acquired lion-taming skills, Walter headed towards the stairs at the back of the wagon.

'What you make?' the lion tamer asked incredulously.

'I just want to see your lion. Come!'

'No,' the lion tamer said shaking his head.

'No, no.' He eyed Walter suspiciously. 'No, no, NO!'

Walter looked at the man. 'What's the matter with you? Yesterday you made me go in there and now you don't want to go?'

'No. No. No. No!' The lion tamer walked around the wagon and pushed one of the sliding gates on the side open. There, behind some heavy bars, sat the lion.

'He looks much better today. But he needs another dose. Let's go in and give it to him,' Walter insisted.

'No. No. No. No.' The lion tamer shook his head vehemently.

'Nobody. Never. Nobody never, never ever go inside my lions.'

'But...'

'No. Never. *Nigdy.*'

Walter realised that there was no way they would repeat yesterday's procedure. When he saw how the sick lion got up and moved towards a water bowl that stood close to the bars, he alerted the lion tamer who immediately reacted.

He took the bowl, held it for Walter to pour some antibiotic powder into the water and then pushed it back into the cage. The lion, clearly thirsty, drank some.

'Oh well, that'll have to do.'

They stood quietly for a moment, observing the lions.

'You?' the lion tamer looked at Walter again and shook his head. 'You in there?'

'Yes, man. Of course. Can't you remember?'

'No. No. No. Doctor, please. Never, never, ever you tell Doctor Jeremy. Please.'

Topsy, who had retreated to the Peugeot, just smiled.

127

Walter kept his promise, for a while anyway. But when he did tell Dr Jeremy Zander his story, he learned that indeed nobody ever had gone into the lion cage before. He thought about this for a while before shaking his head.

'But you know,' he said to his former employer, 'a couple of weeks after that lion story I was called out again to the circus. They were in Vaalwater by then. I had to stitch up a horse, a pretty little black and white cross breed. Their most talented horse in the arena, they told me. But let me tell you, he was seriously vicious. He kicked, like you have never seen a horse kick before. He was dangerous! Much worse than these lions!'

ENCOUNTERS

The circus moved on and Potgietersrus returned to its own sleepy ways. Instead of lions, Walter dealt with some dogs, cats and horses, but mostly cattle. They were his bread and butter. Pregnancy diagnostics, vaccinations, calvings and the odd emergency kept him occupied most days.

He started to find his way around the many farms in the area until his car just about knew the way on its own, bumping at high speed over unmarked dirt roads. Every day came with its own surprises, and he gathered invaluable experience. He came to understand that life didn't always go according to plan and that some of his theoretical knowledge needed to be adapted to different circumstances. He learned how to make a plan and to improvise, lessons he would draw on for the rest of his life.

Walter also realised quickly that the people living on farms, in the middle of nowhere, were in general real characters and that their hospitality, like in most parts of rural South Africa, was legendary. He delighted in meeting all kinds of different folks. Some became good friends, others made him laugh; some were interesting or eccentric and others outright strange, but he knew he could learn something or other from each and everyone.

Walter had never met Josef *Goue Bad* du Plessis before, but rumour had it that he was a very wealthy and successful businessman in Pretoria. His riches were so great, people in Potgietersrus gossiped, that he had installed golden taps in his mansion in the capital.

Although Walter never met anybody who could verify that, the nickname stuck; the farmer was only ever known as Goue Bad du Plessis, the one with the golden bath.

On his farm, he had one of the most formidable herds of Afrikaner cattle Walter had ever seen. They were descendants of the *Sanga* cattle, the original, indigenous South African breed of bovines, and the Khoikhoi as well as the early Afrikaner people had used them for beef and milk for centuries. The latter then had optimised the breed for use as draft animals. It had been spans of Afrikaner oxen that had pulled the wagons of the Voortrekkers from the Cape to the northern regions of South Africa.

A proud Afrikaner himself, to Mr du Plessis his herd was his pride and joy, and he came to his farm for weekends and holidays, whenever he could. He was renowned in farmers' circles for being an excellent cattle breeder and it was said that he knew his beasts well.

Quite how well he knew them, Walter was about to learn when Du Plessis' farm manager called him to immunise this herd of Afrikaners against heartwater disease. Every single animal, all deep red in colour, had to be caught and then injected intravenously with a syringe containing infected sheep blood; a standard procedure. In order to do that the animals were all herded first into the kraal and from there into the cattle crush, also a standard procedure. What was not standard, however, were the large, sideways spreading horns the specimens of this herd had – due to the fact that Mr du Plessis didn't believe in dehorning his animals.

Walter was a little weary. He knew that Afrikaner cattle were famous for their temperament, which meant they wouldn't accept this procedure without complaint. A quick stab with one of their long, curved horns, full of indignation, hit his hand holding the syringe more than once and was a lot more painful than the needle prick the animal had to suffer in its neck. Nonetheless, the job had to be done. Together with the farm manager and a handful of cattlemen Walter continued amongst a lot of swearing and cursing, relieved as each batch of animals left the enclosure successfully immunised.

While working, Walter noticed that the two formidable stud bulls cunningly evaded being herded into the crush. They seemed to prefer watching the proceedings from a safe distance.

'This is no good,' he thought, anticipating trouble, and admonished his helpers not to leave the two males until last. He told them in a friendly tone and later on more insistently, yet to no avail.

This was exactly what the two bulls had intended and, outsmarting Walter and his crew, they succeeded. Once alone in the kraal, they changed their behaviour. Throwing themselves into their most impressive postures, heads held high and nostrils flared, they threatened each and every person who even appeared to want to come close to them.

'And now what?' Walter wondered, at a loss as what to do next.

He was still pondering possible solutions, the bulls not showing any sign of wanting to relent, when he saw a large American Buick appear in the yard. It was driven by an even larger man, who introduced himself as Josef du Plessis, owner of the herd, and of course the farm they were working on.

Before Walter had gathered his wits to try and explain the situation, the man asked,

'You must be Doc Eschenburg? I have heard lots about you.'

They shook hands.

'Seems to me, you have a little problem here?'

'Well, yes. These magnificent bulls of yours are not playing the game,' Walter replied.

'I see that. But *wag'n bietjie, ek maak hulle vir jou mak*! – hang on, wait a little, I'll make them tame for you!' he said leisurely.

Without any further ado, he stepped into the kraal to his two bulls, who by now were huffing and puffing dangerously, threatening him and following each of his steps with their keen eyes.

'Oh dear, here comes trouble,' Walter thought.

But Josef du Plessis knew his animals well. He just stood tall, stuck out his rather large stomach towards the older animal and waited. After a few seconds the chief of the herd, slowly, step by step, approached his owner, head held high and breathing heavily. Du Plessis stood still. He waited, not averting his eyes. Eventually the animal stood right in front of him and, after seemingly taking a deep breath, snorted into Du Plessis' face. Very slowly, he lowered his head until his breath blew up the dust around his owner's shoes.

Absolute silence had descended on the yard; everybody was watching with bated breath. After what seemed an eternity, Du Plessis slowly lifted his right hand, pointed his index finger and casually slipped it into the bull's nose ring. The animal seemed frozen. There wasn't a muscle twitching, and his eyes were firmly fixed on his master.

'Doc, come and inject him. He is now *mak*,' Du Plessis said calmly.

Walter was so impressed that without any hesitation he stepped into the kraal, found the jugular vein, stopped its flow, tapped it, inserted the needle and gave the bull his injection.

He had been holding his breath the whole time, he realised now, but before he even dared to exhale, Du Plessis whispered, 'Now get out of here. Quickly!'

Calm, but by no means slowly, Walter reversed out of the enclosure and Du Plessis led the bull, with still only one finger holding the nose ring, into the cattle crush.

After having observed the spectacle from a distance, the second bull followed without any hesitation and was immunised before they were both reunited with their herd. Without another word, Mr du Plessis got back into his long, black American Buick and drove off.

'I don't know about you, Doc, but I need a coffee now. Come,' the farm manager said and led Walter into the farm house.

No golden taps here, he concluded quickly.

'Oh well,' he said over his steaming cup, 'the people are right. He does know his animals well, your boss!'

PARAFFIN AND FLYING MACHINE

We left Potgietersrus and moved back to Topsy's parents' farm Weltevreden after her father had passed away in 1963. Her sisters both lived in the Cape, so it was decided that we should stay on the family farm. We didn't object and I moved my practice to Naboomspruit; it was not far from Potgietersrus and most of my clientele was spread out right across the Springbok Flats and the Waterberg anyway.

It was Topsy's grandfather who had bought Weltevreden and settled there. But initially, her family came from the Eastern Cape. One of Topsy's ancestors, Colonel John Graham, of Scottish origin, had founded Grahamstown as a military outpost to defend the eastern boundary of what the British regarded as their territory against the Xhosa people. His grandson, Topsy's grandfather, was Sir Thomas Graham.

He became judge president of the eastern districts and, if I remember correctly, was at one stage acting prime minister. His two sons, Topsy's father Gavin and his brother Robert, both attended St. Andrews College in Grahamstown before they went to Cambridge University.

When the First World War broke out, both of them became pilots and signed up with the Royal Flying Corps. Soon they were flying aces, highly decorated aviators.

Topsy's father survived the war, but his brother didn't.

As a result, the boys' mother decided she needed to protect her only remaining son with all means possible.

'You will get my son as far away from aeroplanes and wars as you can get,' she instructed her husband.

In 1920, Naboomspruit was indeed very far away from the rest of the world, so they agreed to buy the farm Weltevreden from a company called Transvaal Consolidated Lands.

Although Topsy's father successfully farmed both, cattle and crops, such as watermelon, *mielies* and ground nuts, at heart he was not a farmer but a pilot. When the Second World War broke out, he signed up again, but by then he was, much to his mother's relief, too old to fly.

Naboomspruit was not as far from aeroplanes as Topsy's grandmother would have wished. The South African Air Force had established an airbase with a flying school in Pietersburg, today's Polokwane, with unforeseeable consequences.

Topsy never really found out how her older sister did it, but she was courted extensively by the young pilots, and every weekend a handful of them came visiting her on the farm. A lot of fun was had, but none of them really impressed the girl, until one day a trainee pilot crash-landed his plane in Topsy's father's mielie field, just so that he could spend the weekend with his sweetheart. He did it on purpose, Topsy had no doubts; he was so much in love.

It so happened that just at the same time a baby boy was born to one of the families working on the farm. Their house was right next to the mielie field, and having never seen an aeroplane before, let alone one crash-landing in front of their doorstep, they called the little boy 'Flying Machine'. His brother's name was 'Paraffin', because he'd drunk a bottle of lamp oil when he was little and miraculously survived.

By the time we moved back to Weltevreden with our daughter Debbie, who was born in 1961, Paraffin and Flying Machine had grown up and did most of the work on the farm. While Paraffin was particularly good with horses, Flying Machine loved anything that had an engine in it. Both men would stay with us until they retired.

We lived in the main farmhouse, together with Topsy's mother, whom Topsy had never really had got on with, but I guess that's how life works sometimes. Apart from us, everybody was a little scared of her and called her respectfully 'Mrs Graham'.

It didn't take long for an entire menagerie to become part of the family as well. There was Rosy the pig, who loved to eat out of the cake dish, and a family of guinea fowl Topsy had brought up, and whose favourite roosting spot was on the backrest of the sofa.

Katie, my Jack Russell, came with me wherever I went, and Topsy had Josephine, the first of her many whippets. There was Jason, a Great Dane, and a handful of corgis. Jason just loved Debbie and would guard her conscientiously when she was sleeping in her pram in the garden.

Of course we had lots of horses too. My favourite was Karroo, a Palomino event horse that had been given to me one day as a lost cause, but had miraculously recovered. I dabbled a bit in breeding with my thoroughbred stallion Compadre, and our little herd of mares, as well as the ponies we kept for the children to ride, ran wild in the vast flood plains of the Nyl River.

Weltevreden was a long and narrow stretch of land, two thirds of which were under water whenever the Nyl was in flood. During the rainy season, this otherwise rather meagre river would sweep over the plains, creating a wetland called the Nylsvlei, with water knee-deep.

It must have been during the rainy summer months when the first Afrikaner settlers arrived in the area. Apparently, all they saw was this seemingly huge river, and after having travelled north for months into hitherto uncharted territory they believed that they had got as far as the actual Nile River, hence the name. In the 1960s, most of this wetland, one of the largest in South Africa, was still privately owned, but over time it would become a nature reserve.

It was a difficult place to farm, but, as we often consoled ourselves, it was a great place to have a lot of fun. Over the years, weekend gatherings at Weltevreden became popular amongst friends and family, and while we rode horses, went hunting or just soaked up the gin on the stoep, for the children it was simply paradise.

Topsy always maintains that I attract children like a magnet. I don't know. But I do know that I enjoy their company very much. So it is perhaps no surprise that come weekends or holidays, we always had some or other youngster staying with us. In those early years, it was Bowen, my godson, whose father was our great friend Bogey, whom the locals called 'Rradinhogka', father of snakes.

And then there were Tokkie and Johnny de Sand who lived on Sleutelfontein, a farm close by, and whose parents Ann and Bernhard had become great friends of ours.

In the beginning, when the boys were still little and we went hunting, Johnny and Tokkie would run after the shot guinea fowls, find them in the dense bush and proudly carry the dead birds back to the hunters.

'With you guys around, I can retire my dogs!' I often joked.

Like everything else in life, this activity was not without hazard. One day I shot a couple of spur-winged geese, and young Tokkie got the fright of his life when the heavy birds, one after the other, fell straight out of the sky in front of him, missing his head by a hair's breadth. He claimed later that the ground in front of his feet had been shaking from the impact.

Once they were a little older, I showed the boys how to use a gun and look after it, and I initiated them into the secrets of hunting; I explained how to put themselves into the minds of the animals, and how important it is to respect them. I taught them how to ride and understand horses, and together we spent hours galloping across the farmlands and the flooded Nylsvlei.

Later, I explained the bees and the birds, the trees and grasses and patiently answered all their questions. I was never a great shot myself, but in a way, I guess, I became as much of a hero to them as Jean Pierre had been to me at Juchow; the sort of hero that only small boys can appreciate.

Just before mielie harvesting time, warthogs became a problem on the farm. When they got into the fields they could cause severe damage. Then, to the boys' utter delight, we'd tell them to run through the field, from one side to the other, barking like mad dogs. This would startle the warthogs and send them running off into the other direction, where we adults waited, guns at the ready to shoot them. It was quite spooky, a real adventure, because the maize plants were at least twice as tall as the children and once in, they had to be careful not to get lost. There were lots of stories of gigantic black mambas living in the fields, and the thought of actually meeting a warthog face to face was rather scary. They hoped that barking, as loud as they possibly could, would help.

The children all had their favourite horses at Weltevreden and when not hunting, we were out riding. The most talented was, without doubt, Tokkie de Sand. He seemed to be able to communicate with the horses in a different way. Topsy and I had often commented on that, so we were not surprised, when as a ten-year old, he walked up to me and said in all seriousness,

'Uncle Walter, one day I will ride in the Olympics.'

Just like that. Not 'maybe', or 'I want to', no. 'I will'. We never had any doubts that he'd succeed - and many years later, in '92, he did!

Inevitably, Monday would come; time to go back to school. Living on farms way off the beaten track, school was far away, and at the tender age of six, Debbie and the De Sand children had become weekly borders. Sometimes I think it was tougher on us parents than on them. They seemed to have a lot of fun and there were hardly ever any crocodile tears.

'Uncle Walter, Uncle Walter, please, will you drive us to school? Please, Uncle Walter!'

I remember hearing their calling early on Monday morning. How could I resist? Normally, all three of them, Johnny, Tokkie and Debbie, were sitting in the car, ready to go, long before the time.

At about seven or eight years old, the two boys had actually learned how to drive; the only problem being that neither of them was tall enough yet to reach the pedals and see over the steering wheel at the same time. That didn't stop them. Good '*boere*' sons, they knew how to make a plan. Johnny would kneel on the bakkie's bench, stretching his arms across the wide steering wheel. As he was just tall enough to see over the bonnet he was responsible for steering. In the meantime Tokkie would sit in the foot well, manoeuvring the pedals according to his brother's instructions. They even knew how to use the clutch without the car hopping away like a pronking springbok. I had taught them well!

Taking the kids to school was always a lot of fun, they were so easy to impress. Actually, I am not really sure who enjoyed it more. My old Peugeot station wagon would fly along the dirt roads that connected the farm with the rest of the world. To the children's delighted shrieks, we'd bump over potholes and swerve for the odd *skaapsteeker* who decided to cross the road at an inopportune time. Every now and then I'd throw in a handbrake turn, just for fun.

We also enjoyed the odd practical joke in those days, and I remember the day when we came across a man on his bicycle. He was pedalling hard, struggling forward slowly on the sandy, bumpy road. Johnny and Tokkie nudged each other and started grinning. They knew me by then.

'I bet you he's gonna do it!' they whispered and just as we passed the cyclist, we all heard a loud bang, just like a gunshot. And there again - bang, bang. The poor cyclist jumped, no, flew off his mount into the ditch, flattening himself against the verge attempting to take cover.

'Poor man,' Debbie said, showing a little more empathy than the rest of us. 'He probably thought we were shooting at him! Dad, don't you think it's a little bit unfair to give this poor man such a fright?' she tried hard not to giggle.

Looking back, we could see that the cyclist had got up, dusted off his clothes and was ready to get back onto his bike.

'*Ja*, maybe. But don't worry, I do it to everybody!' I replied. Just a few nights before, I had played the same trick when driving past the house of a particularly unpleasant neighbour.

'Walter, I heard DJ on the radio earlier. He was calling the commando. He said somebody was shooting,' Topsy had greeted me, when I arrived home that day. But when she saw my face, she just laughed. 'Serves him right, this stupid right winger. First he behaves in the most impossible way and then he's paranoid that people are after him,' she said. 'He probably thought the night of the long knives had come!'

The boys in particular pestered me continuously to part with the secret of this particular practical joke. I've never told them, but I'm sure they have found out by now that when driving an old *skedonk*, one only has to turn the key in the ignition while the engine is running to cause it to backfire.

THE PIMPERNEL LION

On a cool winter's morning at the beginning of August in 1972, the *paraffin phone* rang at Weltevreden. Three short rings followed by two long ones.

'Eschenburg, hello?' Topsy answered, expecting a call-out for Walter. His practice in Naboomspruit was well established by now.

But on the other end of the line was Topsy's friend Theresa Spencer, who lived with her husband Hugh on the neighbouring farm Rosslene, where the Spencers had been breeding cattle for generations. Dismissing all polite phrases, Theresa cut straight to the point.

'Have you heard of the lion?'

'Which lion?' Topsy asked.

'Which lion! The lion who's been killing our cattle! Frans Steenkamp just popped in and told us he saw fresh lion spoor on the dirt road near Bossieskraal.'

'Are you serious?'

'Yes, of course I'm serious.' Theresa was getting impatient. Her husband had gone out immediately to have a look and indeed found some fresh lion spoor, the biggest he had ever seen, she told her friend. 'And when he went to check on the cattle, he found a half-eaten carcass in the bushes.'

'I wonder if it is the same one they were talking about a few weeks ago, you know, they said he'd killed a farm worker somewhere near Letaba?' Topsy recalled an article she had read in the local paper.

Walter had overheard the conversation with pricked ears. Not losing any time, he fetched his gun. 'I'm going over there to help Hugh find that lion.'

On Rosslene the two men inspected the spoor again and then used Hugh's Land Rover to drag some branches across the dirt road so that any fresh tracks would be clearly visible later. A group of circling vultures high up in the blue winter sky gave away the location of the dead animal.

'Now what? Shall we see if we can find him?' Walter was keen to get going, but Hugh had a different plan.

'Well, I think it would be better to go into town first and inform the authorities, the commando and such, because that bugger might just move onto another farm. Also, there might be some others who want to join in the hunt.'

The reaction in Naboomspruit was not quite what the two excited men had expected. Nobody took them seriously and the shop-owner even suggested they were being hoodwinked by some of their staff who had stolen the cattle and then taken some old lion foot to make the prints.

'Do they think we are completely stupid?' Hugh was incensed.

The next morning though, a different picture emerged. Another couple of dead cattle had been found on neighbouring farms and talk of the lion was all about town.

Suddenly everybody had a story and it only took another day before an impressive hunting party gathered on Rosslene, which had been declared headquarters of the great lion hunting operation.

Most farmers were armed to the hilt with heavy calibre rifles and shotguns; adrenalin was flowing. Two so-called 'big white hunters' from Kenya had come to join the party and the South African Air Force had sent a helicopter, complete with a parachutist and a Doberman-type dog that was specialised in lion hunting.

Walter and Hugh were in the thick of it, while the women watched and commented from the periphery, discussing the events in detail.

'You know,' Topsy said to Theresa, a gin and tonic in hand, 'it's quite interesting that it is probably only sixty years ago that our fathers and grandfathers rode along here and there were lions everywhere. I am sure they didn't have to fly in big white hunters from Kenya and helicopters with machine guns to sort them out?'

'Yep, we have become rather spoilt, haven't we?'

'On a different note, guess who I bumped into in town this afternoon?'

'No idea, but I'm sure you'll tell me,' Topsy lit another cigarette.

'Bernhard de Sand.'

'Oh, ja, he is quite a good looking dude, don't you think? And makes a good figure on a horse, too. I always say to Walter that for me, Bernhard de Sand is the perfect country gentleman.'

'You are right, and a good farmer he is, too.' Theresa agreed. 'But do you know what he said when I asked him if he was going to join the hunt?

'He said he thought it would be far too dangerous with that bunch of trigger-happy shooters. And that he would bloody well make sure that he didn't go out into the bush during these couple of days. Because it wouldn't be the first time that someone gets shot accidentally by one of those big white hunters seeing something move in the bush.'

The two women laughed.

'I told you. A real country gentleman he is!'

The second day of the big lion hunt dawned and reporters stepped onto each other's toes in their quest to find the best snippets of the story. They were after a picture of the predator, which had by now been named the '*Pimpernel Lion*'.

Like the *Scarlet Pimpernel*, a popular fictional character, who led a secretive life smuggling French aristocrats across the border during the times of the French revolution, leaving a red pimpernel flower behind for his persecutors, this rogue predator proved rather elusive.

'They seek him here, they seek him there...' the press mocked the ever growing team of professional hunters and farmers.

The most breathtaking encounter with the lion was not had by the hunters or the journalists, but by Theresa and George Baloyi, one of her young cattle men.

'I am sure we came closer to the beast than any of these hunters!' she told Walter and Topsy in the evening. 'And let me tell you, he is a beautiful lion, a magnificent animal, with a huge black mane!'

'Well, I've heard that he's come across from Botswana,' Walter said. 'He was probably too old to keep his position in the pride, so he left and turned south. And then he learnt that there is easy food and no competition down here in cattle country.'

The others nodded. This explanation sounded plausible.

'But Theresa, how come you actually saw him?' Walter asked.

'George and I were on our way back from town. We thought we were quite safe, because we had seen the hunting party and the helicopter go off in the opposite direction. We stopped at the gate and George went to open it. I saw some strange spoor on the ground so I also got out. I walked a couple of steps and bent down and I remember thinking that it looked rather fresh, when I heard this almighty roar. You can't even imagine how loud it was. George froze on the spot. He didn't move, wisely so. But I jumped straight out of my shoes and was back in the bakkie before I could even blink.

'After I stopped shaking and George had somehow made his way back into the car as well, we carried on, drove through the gate, and then I made the poor man get out again and close it. In the meantime I was looking around and suddenly I saw the lion. He was sitting under a tree close to the fence. He didn't move. He just stared at us.'

'Why didn't you shoot him? Didn't you have a gun?'

'I did, and I thought about it, but I wasn't sure if the gun was powerful enough to kill him from that distance – I didn't want to wound him and then we'd have an even bigger problem.'

'Fair enough,' Walter and Topsy nodded in agreement.

For a week the hunt went on, without success. Eventually, the big white hunters, the dog squads and the helicopters had to leave, and the Pimpernel Lion remained elusive.

SURPRISES

There was excited barking and the little bell tied to the gate jingled. Somebody was coming in, and the dogs knew who it was; their voices were friendly. Walter peered through the window. He was sitting at his desk and doing some much detested admin. It was the least favourite part of his work and he never seemed to be able to get on top of it. He was desperately hoping for a distraction.

'Wonder who this is? On foot, and it's nearly sunset?' he thought.

It wasn't like their house lay along the main drag in town. Particularly since the Pimpernel Lion had been on the prowl in the area, people tended not to walk about at dusk if they could avoid it. The figure Walter saw approaching the front door now made him smile; he recognised the man's gait.

'There is only one person I know that is 'storking' like that,' he thought and got up from his desk.

The tall, thin man with the wild curly hair and the Roman nose, carrying nothing but the clothes on his body, could only be their friend Bogey. Only he, Walter thought, walked like a European stork.

'Hi, I'm back,' said the visitor and headed straight for a chair at the dining room table, gratefully accepting the glass of water Topsy handed him.

'Do you mind if I take my shoes off?' he asked after he had quenched his thirst and, not awaiting an answer, untied the laces of his brown *veldskoens*.

Just like everything else that had happened so far, this was part of the ritual. The next part though was Walter and Topsy's favourite. They'd laughed about it many a time when talking about Bogey and his adventures. For now, with the toes of the right foot he pushed at the heel of the left shoe until it flopped off and fell to the ground, revealing

143

a broad naked foot; yet from the ankles up to the knees, his legs were covered in the upper part of good old bushveld socks.

Walter remembered the first time he had observed this procedure.

'I do it to keep up appearances,' Bogey had explained. 'People look at you funny in these parts if you wander around with no socks, let alone without shoes.'

That was a bit of a strange explanation, Walter had thought, but then, nothing about Bogey was normal, really. He was, to put it mildly, an extraordinary character.

He'd just appear one day, out of the blue, walk in the gate, just like he'd done now, and stay with the Eschenburgs for some time; a week, a month, or maybe two. He'd join Walter doing his rounds, or just sit in the garden, and he'd spend a lot of time talking to Paraffin and Flying Machine. Then, just as suddenly as he'd arrived, he would leave. They'd see him put on his boots and socks and he'd say, 'I'm off to the Makgapeng,' or 'I'm off to Botswana,' and he'd start by walking down the road.

A couple of months later he'd be back, still wearing the same clothes, essentially looking the same, except the socks.

He walked their soles through in no time, he had once explained. He didn't really care; he was just as comfortable without them. But he kept the top parts, carried them around with him for months, because despite his rather unusual life style, he cared about his appearance when entering small farming communities, and that's when he put them back on again.

Bogey's family had moved from England to South Africa in 1955, when he was only sixteen years old. They lived next to Topsy's sister in Johannesburg and it wasn't long before he visited Weltevreden for the first time.

Bogey soon developed a passion for the bush and spent months exploring it. He'd leave so-called civilisation with only a pocketknife and some salt in his pockets. He learned how to survive and before long he had developed a special rapport with the rural African communities of Southern Africa. He moved like they did, on foot; he ate sorghum and bush meat, like they did; and he drank their water. He learned about their way of life, their mythology and faith. He knew the sounds of the birds, the movements of the snakes, and the spoor of the antelope. He spoke their language and the language of the animals. The people adored him and embraced him into their communities. Eventually, he followed the initiation rituals and became a *sangoma*.

Bogey found what some would later call his totem. Snakes. Shortly after arriving in South Africa he realised he not only had the ability, but also felt a compulsion to catch snakes, which was not shared by many other people. Soon he learned to make a living by catching and milking the reptiles; their venom was highly sought after for the production of antivenom.

When he was in the rural areas, his arrival at a village frequently coincided with the community having a snake problem of some sort, which he then would be able to sort out. This earned him his nickname, *Rradinhogka*, or 'father of snakes'.

His fascination with the bush and anthropology, his knowledge of African customs and myths, and not least his ability to survive in the wild led him to work for the 'Museum of Man and Science' in Johannesburg. For Professor Dart, he collected Stone Age tools, discovered ancient rock art paintings and assisted in unravelling some of the secrets of Africa's past.

Bogey lived with a foot planted firmly in two very different worlds, this dichotomy defining him and his short, extraordinary life. On the one side was his rural African life, deeply steeped in tradition and the mythological. And on the other side he lived a normal urban South African life with his wife and children.

Living in two such different worlds with barely a connection between them was not easy. Bogey suffered from epilepsy, an ailment which in the world he originated from was marked as a serious affliction; it was feared and not spoken about other than in a whisper. In the rural African world, it was embraced as a sign of the spirits, accepted as part of who he was, and as something that possibly brought him closer to the divine.

What connected Bogey and Walter was their love of the bush. Walter had not seen this deep a connection in any other European. Bogey was different, and he seemed to have a link to the surrounding world at a different level to most people.

He was also a great friend and they had known each other for a long time. At some stage he had dated Walter's sister Elsa, and it was Bogey, whose snake had scared Walter the night before his wedding.

Some years later, he'd asked Walter to be the godfather of his son Bowen, who would often spend his school holidays with Walter, Topsy, their menagerie and the many visitors at Weltevreden.

The next day, after Bogey had settled in and told Walter and Topsy about some of his experiences during his last stint in the bush, he asked Walter to take him for a drive.

'I want to show you something,' he said. 'And bring a torch if you can.'

After about half an hour, they turned onto a dirt road and a little later onto a narrow track.

'Let's walk from here,' Bogey suggested. 'It's just over there, by that koppie.'

Walter followed his friend along the game path.

'Have you ever noticed that there is a cave up there?' Bogey pointed at the little hill. 'I'll show you. You'll be surprised.'

They clambered over some boulders and the roots of a small rock fig. How these trees grew on bare rocks, with nothing but a little crack where some water could collect, always amazed Walter.

About half way up, he suddenly saw what his friend had been talking about. Hidden behind a rock was the entrance to a cave. It seemed to be a narrow gap only, but once they entered, a large room opened up. They stopped to let their eyes get used to the dim light permeating the space.

'Further on, there must be another opening, higher up,' Walter thought, noticing another source of light.

'Give me the torch,' Bogey said.

What appeared in its beam left Walter speechless. The entire cave was covered in the most exquisite rock art, or Bushman paintings, as they called them.

'This is unbelievable,' he gasped.

The longer he looked at the wall and the more his eyes got used to the light, the more he saw. Drawn in various shades of red pigment, he could make out the outlines of eland, giraffe, zebra and even an elephant.

The men stayed in the shady cool of the cave for a long time without speaking. There was no need for words. Enthralled, they gazed at the pictures the ancestors had drawn many millennia ago.

When later in the evening Walter told Topsy about it, he was still mesmerised.

'And there I am thinking that I know the Waterberg. I must have driven past this koppie thousands of times. I just had no idea, absolutely no idea.' He shook his head.

A few days later, Bogey tied his shoelaces and left Weltevreden again. He didn't know when, but there was no doubt that he would be back.

He might have been the most eccentric of their visitors, but he was by no means the only one. To the contrary, the Eschenburg household was always a haven for weary travellers, lonely souls, stray dogs and entertaining guests. Walter and Topsy never hesitated to open their homes and hearts to whoever was in need of a place to stay, of friendship, good food and company.

VISITORS

I have always enjoyed picking up strays; hitch hikers, cyclists, and whoever else came along. Both Topsy and I have always loved meeting new, different people, and it is somewhat of a family tradition. At Uhlenhorst we always had lots of guests around, friends, family or new arrivals from Germany. My mother enjoyed entertaining visitors and always used to cook up a storm. So does Topsy and I have yet to meet a person who is not completely blown away by the meals she produces.

Sometimes a simple pick-up leads to a whole lot of unintended consequences. Take Rainer, for example, who was hitchhiking through South Africa. A medical student from Berlin, we invited him to stay the night, and Topsy spoilt him as only she can. He ended up leaving after two weeks. He'd come out with me to do the rounds and I think he would have enjoyed becoming a vet, too. He was good company, very inquisitive and always comparing my veterinary practice to what he was learning about human medicine. He was one of those people who soaked up knowledge like a sponge and his questions never stopped. What's this tree? And which bird is calling now? And why is it that some grasses are more nutritious than others? This first visit was not his only one and Rainer would come back time and again, with his ever growing family in tow.

Many years later this would lead to a really unexpected surprise. But more about that later.

Young Tim was another one of our visitors and the cause of great humour. Later he'd become one of the leading figures in the South African horse riding world and we'd meet up at just about every horse show between the Limpopo and the Vaal Rivers; we became great friends.

It was some time in the seventies, and Tim had just arrived from England; he was a mere eighteen years old and a little wet behind his ears. He didn't really know about life in the bush, nor did he realise that we still had the good old paraffin phones. For some reason that now eludes me, we left Tim alone at home for an afternoon. Topsy and I just told him to relax and feel at home.

While we were away, the phone rang, and, as he said later, staying over in a vet's household, he thought every call was, by default, very important.

Very conscientiously, he recorded into a notebook the time of each call, the name of the caller and what he thought they'd said. He struggled a bit with the latter because most callers rattled away in Afrikaans. Tim, of course, didn't speak any Afrikaans.

As the afternoon unfolded, the phone rang more and more often, and after a good two hours he had filled nearly six pages.

As the calls became more frequent, so the callers seemed to become more agitated, shouting at him down the crackling line, their Afrikaans more and more unintelligible to his young English ear. Sometimes, there even seemed to be more than one person on the other end of the phone.

'Oh dear,' Tim thought, 'they must be worrying about a really, really sick animal.'

There was no way he could get hold of me; it was in the days before cell phones. He ventured outside in the hope of finding somebody, so he could relay this vital information the callers were getting so upset about. At the gate, he bumped into three irate men, who were looking for me.

With hands and even feet, the three farmers and the young *Engelsman* tried to communicate, and that's when Topsy and I arrived on the scene.

We couldn't help but burst out laughing when we heard what had happened. This, naturally, didn't help.

The farmers became more red-faced and Tim looked even more confused.

Eventually, between Topsy and I, we managed to defuse the situation. Well, I suppose it really wasn't young Tim's fault that he'd never heard of paraffin phones before, that he didn't know we were on a party line and that our ring was three long, two short, Oom Karel's two long three short and Oom Kobus's one long and four short. He'd just answered all of them.

We ended up having a great party that evening, over many beers and whiskies trying to decipher Tim's notes of that afternoon's calls.

Some of our visitors came and left. Others, the majority, became permanent features and would make appearances in our lives at regular and irregular intervals.

And then there was Nick. He came for a visit and stayed for good.

NICK

The brand new Chev Nomad came to a screeching halt. As usual, Walter had been driving rather fast along one of the rugged dirt roads of the Waterberg. So fast that Nick, although used to the driving habits of his adoptive father, was only barely managing to stop himself from bouncing around on the passenger's seat.

It turned out to be an exciting day for the fourteen year old. Walter had picked him up from school in the afternoon, but instead of heading home, they stopped at a piggery where a sow was in trouble giving birth. Nick, still dressed in his school uniform, and Walter, in his khaki shorts and a shirt that was everything but clean after a hard day's work, entered the stable.

'Ah, Doc, glad you could still come,' the farmer greeted them. 'This sow, she seems to have problems popping the young ones out. She's been at it since this morning. The first two came without problems, but now, nothing's been happening for a while.'

'Ok, Piet, no problem, let's have a look.'

Ja man, please, it's my best sow.'

Walter observed the animal lying in the straw, panting and clearly in pain.

'Seems there is one stuck in there.'

He gazed down at his hands and then at the farmer's, who was a rather large Afrikaner. He shook his head and then turned to Nick.

'You've got the right size hands,' he said and before Nick knew it, he was half kneeling, half lying behind the sow in the straw, with his arm inside the animal.

'What can you feel?'

'It's all getting squeezed and squashed.'

'That's normal. Just relax; you'll soon get the hang of it.'

Nick nodded and closed his eyes. Slowly he could start moving his fingers around a little. His face lit up.

'Now I can feel something.'

Walter and Piet, the farmer, looked at him.

'I think it's a leg and a head.'

'Ok, pull the leg, gently,' Walter instructed.

Nick pulled carefully at first, then a little harder.

'That was easy!' He looked at his hand in surprise. It held a piglet's front leg, nothing else. His eyes widened. 'Oh, I'm sorry, I didn't want this, I mean, to rip the leg off!' he stuttered.

Walter took the little leg from him and laughed.

'Don't worry, my boy, you've done nothing wrong. Looks like this little fellow has been dead for a while. It's properly *vrot*; it's just about bubbling. It happens,' he explained. 'And now, get your hand back in there and get the rest out.'

Nick hesitated a second, but Walter encouraged him.

'What's your problem? Come on! We have to get the dead piglet out and then see if there are any live ones behind it. If we don't, they'll also die because they are stuck and then the sow will probably get septicaemia, because she's got all this rotten stuff in her uterus.'

Nick took a deep breath and did as he was told.

As if she knew that the obstruction was gone now, the sow began pushing again and a further six healthy piglets were born.

'Ok, Piet,' Walter turned to the relieved farmer, 'phone me if there are any problems; but as far as I can see, this sow should be hundred per cent by tomorrow.'

'Thanks so much, Doc, *baie dankie*.'

'Don't worry. Thank this young man. Without his small hands we would have been in a spot of bother.'

'True. Thanks Nick. But Doc, tell me, how much do I owe you?'

'I don't know, can't really say now. I'll check and bring you the bill next time I come round.'

They left the farm yard, a dust cloud trailing behind the bakkie.

'Walter,' Nick asked after they had been driving for some time, 'Why didn't you take any money from Oom Piet?'

'Good question. I should have, I suppose, but we didn't really do much.'

'*Ja*, but Topsy will be cross with you again.'

'I know, but, I always feel bad charging people, especially somebody like Oom Piet. He doesn't have much money. I know he's struggling to pay his daughter's school fees and they've had bad luck with their pigs. Only last year, he nearly lost everything because the piglets were dying of some virus and then his crops were hailed out and...' he tailed off.

'But Topsy says we also don't have enough money and you should charge for your work properly,' Nick said, remembering a conversation he had overheard back home.

'Well, she's right, actually. I suppose I should make a note and really bring him an account next time I go that way,' Walter conceded.

For some time they carried on quietly. It was dark by now and Walter swerved every now and again for a nightjar resting in the middle of the road. Nick was always amazed how Walter seemed to have eyes in the back of his head. It didn't matter at what speed they raced through the bush, if there was a rare bird somewhere, a snake next to the road or some kudu, he would invariably spot them before anybody else did.

And it happened again now. Walter hit the brakes and they stopped without apparent reason.

'Check there,' Walter said, quietly. 'Have you ever seen an *aardvark* up close and personal?'

Next to the road stood the biggest ant bear Nick had ever seen. Elusive and nocturnal, they were not easy to spot, but now he had a prime view of this eccentric looking animal.

'Looks like its snout belongs to a pig, his ears to a rabbit and his tail to a kangaroo,' Nick whispered, staring through the windscreen.

'Go and catch him!' Walter gave Nick a light push at the shoulder.

Nick, without a second thought, opened the door and jumped out onto the road. Slowly, he approached the animal. The aardvark took one long look at him, as if to judge if he was any danger, before he decided to move away slowly.

'Jump on it and catch it!' Walter shouted now, leaning out of the open window barely able to suppress a wide grin.

He watched with interest the scene unfolding before his eyes. The boy eyed the aardvark, which stood nearly a metre tall, and he had a good look at the size of the animal's front paws and claws.

Nick clearly didn't think it was a good idea to do as he was told, but not wanting to admit that he was scared, he pretended to duck and dive, performing a strange dance on the road until the aardvark had managed to get through the fence and disappeared into the darkness.

'Aaah, it's too late,' he said, trying not to show his relief.

'Oh well, jump in, we really need to get home now,' Walter smiled.

'And? Did you get a good look at this fellow?' he asked, for that had really been his intention.

'Yes, I did. And *sjoe*! His claws are quite big!'

'Yes, of course they are. And do you know what he needs them for?'

'Digging?'

'You know, these ant bears are purely insectivorous. Until recently, it was thought that they only ate termites, but apparently in the dry winter months they eat real ants too. They use these big front legs to dig large holes, at an incredible speed, and normally right into the underground chambers of a termite mound. Then they stick their tongues into the holes and lick up the panicking termites before they even know what's hit them. And,' Walter continued, 'they don't only dig holes to find termites, they also live in deep, underground burrows. They can be a nuisance to us, because sometimes calves fall into them and if we don't find them in time, they die quickly.'

'I know, when riding through the bush, I always watch out that my horse doesn't step into an aardvark hole,' Nick replied.

'Right, because that could break a horse's leg easily. But of course, like everything else in nature, these holes are there for a reason.'

'Because other animals use them?'

'Snakes and all sorts of other creatures use them opportunistically, so I reckon, whoever sticks his hand into an aardvark hole is seriously stupid, because you never know what you may find in there. But it's the warthogs, who really need them. In fact, they are essential for their survival,' Walter explained.

'As you know, warthogs are diurnal, so at night, when they are sleeping, they are at serious risk from predators. What better place to hide than in an abandoned aardvark hole? They sleep in there with their primary means of defence, their tusks, pointing at the entrance, so that nobody can surprise them. Warthogs are not great diggers themselves, so they prefer moving into a finished home, possibly extending it a bit, making some renovations, so to speak.'

154

With this, they arrived at Weltevreden, where Topsy and Debbie were waiting. They all sat down around the large wooden dining room table, which Debbie had set for the evening meal. As usual, she had been looking forward to dinner time, to see her father and Nick again after a week at boarding school.

A passionate storyteller, Walter loved to entertain his daughter with funny and sometimes hair-raising accounts of his daily life as a bush vet. Nick, who over the last year had spent a lot of time with Walter, had learned quickly and, like his foster father, he could spin a good yarn. He knew not to let the truth spoil a good story, so when he told Topsy and Debbie about his encounter and how he'd very nearly caught the biggest aardvark ever seen with his bare hands, he wisely omitted the fact that he hadn't really been upset that this strange creature 'only just' had got away.

Topsy watched her charges. Debbie was glued to Nick and Walter's every word, but her eyes seemed to sparkle more when Nick was talking, and he in turn seemed to really tell the stories just for her. Sometimes Topsy wondered if there was perhaps more than just a friendship. The two of them seemed to get on much better than she'd ever hoped.

She was called out of her reverie, when Nick asked for a second helping of warthog stew. Or was it his third already? It never ceased to amaze Topsy how much this young boy with the always ruffled blond hair could eat, while at the same time staying skinny as a rake. Walter and Nick seemed to have regular eating competitions. Topsy knew food was one of the great passions in Walter's life and Nick appeared to be heading the same way.

'I think it's time for you two,' Topsy looked at Nick and Debbie, 'to go to bed.'

'Yes,' Walter said, somewhat startled. He had been nodding off already, his chin sinking slowly onto his chest.

'Because tomorrow, Nick, you can come with me to do some pregnancy diagnostics at the Babers' farm. They say they need about two hundred heifers tested.'

An hour later, quiet had descended over the Eschenburg household. Walter was sitting in his favourite armchair, reading in his new book on trees of the Waterberg. Or at least he pretended to.

'I'm sure he's actually sleeping,' Topsy thought while she sat down too with the latest Jilly Cooper novel. But her thoughts wandered back to dinner time. It was such a joy to see Nick so happy and excited. He had been with them for just over a year now and had long become part of the family.

Topsy thought back to the previous winter, when they had gone to the Pietersburg horse show, an annual event they never missed. There, they had met up with their old friend Pat, and Topsy had immediately seen that something was not right.

'It's about Nick,' Pat had said.

Topsy had never met Nick, but she knew that the boy's mother had died in a car accident some months before. She remembered how Pat had come up to her then with tears in her eyes and said, 'My friend Helen has been killed.' It was terrible.

At the Pietersburg show, Pat told her more. Nick's father had died a few years before, and, well, it was a long story.

'He can come and stay with us for the holiday,' Topsy had immediately offered.

I'm sure Walter and Debbie won't mind.'

Come to think of it, Topsy was now convinced that Pat had known exactly what she was doing when she introduced Nick to them. The Eschenburgs immediately had liked the boy and he came home with them directly from the show for the rest of the July holidays. And then he just never left, and they'd never looked back. It had all worked out really well.

Walter appreciated Nick's adventurous spirit and encouraged it. He taught him not to be scared of anything, not even of monster aardvarks, Topsy thought, remembering the dinner time tale. He also got on with Debbie like a house on fire right from day one. It wasn't long until they started squabbling about little things like only brother and sister would do.

'Ja,' Topsy thought while she had a sip of her whisky and lit another cigarette, 'things have really turned out well.'

She had no way of knowing quite how well they would turn out in the not too distant future.

THE DAY FORTUNE SMILED

It was some time in the 1970s that South Africa produced its own make of cars. It was called a Chev Nomad, and it looked like a box. It was square cut off in the front and square cut off behind and square down the windscreen, with a flat, square bonnet. It was terribly ugly. It was meant to be a bakkie, and mine was open, without a canopy. It did have four wheels, but that's about all.

I was not really happy with this new vehicle that I'd bought after I rolled my old Land Cruiser station wagon, and the somewhat patriotic excitement of driving a home-grown car soon gave way to frustration and exasperation.

Because it looked like a box, it wasn't only ugly, but it also had a very high wind resistance, which meant that it didn't go terribly fast and used a lot of petrol. And from day one it rattled. From day two, things started falling off. First was the windscreen wiper.

'I can live without that. Give it a chance,' I thought.

Then the door handles rattled off. And a few days after that, the windscreen fell out of its frame. By the time I'd had it for a month, sixteen pieces had fallen off!

So it wasn't surprising, that I became 'a little unhappy' with it, and decided this was enough. I took it to the garage where I had purchased it and made a huge fuss and with deep embarrassment they took it back and gave me a new one. Smiling again and with a certain satisfaction that I had put my foot down and wasn't going to be taken for a ride, excuse the pun, I took my new vehicle home. It was, of course, just as ugly as the old one.

The next day, while out on a call, Nick and I were driving across the veld on a farm road, when all of a sudden this brand new Nomad complained heavily by making some stuttering noises and then it stopped.

No matter how I tried, it just wouldn't start again. It seemed like it didn't have any petrol left.

'How is that possible? I just filled it up yesterday? And I couldn't have done more than twenty miles since then?' I wondered.

We got out and I began applying my doctor's knowledge. I could smell petrol everywhere, but I had to climb underneath to come to a final diagnosis. One entire sidewall of the petrol tank had fallen off. I had to get us towed out by the farmer, and had the tank welded and everything checked.

Although we couldn't find any more apparent faults, I was now seriously getting a little more than *gatvol* with this thing.

And then, fortune lifted her brow and smiled on me.

I was on my way back home from doing the morning rounds and nearing the level crossing, where our farm road met the Great North train's tracks. Katie, my Jack Russell, was sitting on the passenger's seat and the back of the bakkie was loaded with some drums of paraffin and a few bags of horse feed. I was humming a tune and every now and again chatting to Katie about how well the morning had gone and how much I was looking forward to lunch. The Nomad was making its usual array of disconcerting noises, but for now at least, everything seemed to stay in place.

Suddenly, I heard a different sound that didn't quite fit the cacophony of the usual rattles.

'What was that, Katie? Did you hear that?'

There it was again.

'Oh shit!'

I realised that the noise was a train's whistling. And I also realised I was too close to the tracks; far too close for my liking. I hit the brakes. Luckily they worked, and we stopped. And there was the train. That close!

I was a little uncomfortable, so I slammed the car in reverse, gunned the engine and let the clutch go - and I jumped forward onto the railway line, right in front of the train. Unfortunately, in the Nomad, first gear and reverse were very close together. I should have known.

The train hit the side of the car and virtually cut it off, spinning the remainder of it around in a circle. I heard the brakes screech, but it only came to a halt a little further down the track.

After the dust had settled, I started to look around. Katie was there, balancing on my shoulder, panting. The drums of paraffin were sitting on the seat next to me, and the smaller of the mielie bags was at my feet on the floor, while the other ones were lying outside.

'What the hell, how did all that stuff get here?" I asked myself and then realised that the bakkie didn't have a roof anymore.

At this, Katie and I got out and had a look around. It was a mess.

We were just about to set off on foot towards the farmhouse that was a couple of hundred yards to the right, when we saw a short little fat man running down the railway line from where the train had stopped. He was running as fast as his feet would carry him and completely out of breath.

'*Meneer*, Meneer, did you see this?' he shouted.

'*Ja*,' I said, 'I did see this.'

'And? Where is the driver?' he asked.

'The driver? I don't know. He is probably sitting in the engine.'

'No man,' the man seemed a bit exasperated and was while still trying to catch his breath. 'Not the driver of the train. That's me. Where is the driver of the car?'

'Well, I am the driver of that car.'

Clearly not believing his ears and eyes, he looked me up and down, shook his head and then asked, '*Is jy nie dood nie*? Are you not dead?'

'*Nie, Meneer, ek is nie dood nie* - I am not dead,' I replied.

Without uttering another word, the short little fat man stared at me a little longer, then shook his head again, turned around and walked back down the railway line. He must have had a shock, because after that incident he only took his train as far as Boekenhout station, about five miles away, before he booked off sick.

For me the accident didn't really have any consequences, other than that I didn't have a vehicle for a while. The Nomad was totally kaput, but as you can imagine, I wasn't really that sad about it.

A few months later, a very legal looking envelope arrived in the post.

'There is a letter here for you from the South African Railways,' Topsy said when I arrived home one day.

'It looks quite serious. What have you been up to this time?'

'I don't know,' I said while I opened it.

I found a very official looking letter; I should have framed it, it was so beautiful:

'Sir,

You are charged with wilfully or negligently causing damage to South African Railways property, specifically to engine number so-and-so of the South African Railways, and you will by return of post pay the above mentioned damages, caused to South African Railways, or else appear in court on such and such a day to defend your actions.

Total amount: Seven rand fifty cents for damages to one reflector knocked off the engine.'

It was just typical of the South African Railways of the time to write a letter of that calibre for a damage of seven rand and fifty cents. But who knows, maybe, whoever wrote this letter had a bit of a smile himself?

BULLDUST

'Topsy, I must go and fix that bull there at the Vissers' place. The one with the blocked penis sheath,' Walter announced.

'Ok, but will you please hurry up. I don't want to be late for Margie's wedding.'

'Oh, is that today? I thought…'

'How can you be so bloody forgetful? Of course it is today! And you have to give a speech. I hope you haven't forgotten about that, too?'

'No, no, I haven't. Anyway, I must go. Nick, come and bring my bag!'

'How exactly does it work with the blocked penis sheath? I mean, why does it block?' Nick asked while they were thundering along a dirt road as fast as Walter's new car would allow.

The green Nissan 1200 had replaced the Chev Nomad, and although it was a lot smaller, Walter was delighted to have a vehicle that didn't just lose vital parts along the way.

'And isn't it very painful?'

'Sure, you just imagine how painful it must be!' Walter laughed. 'What happens is that Brahmans in particular have a penis sheath that hangs down almost to the ground. Much further than the Afrikaner or Bonsmara bulls' for example.'

Ja, I've seen that. Why is that?'

'Not sure why, but the Brahmans were probably not really bred to wander around in the African bush. I presume that in India, where they come from, things look a little different? I don't know. But anyway, these sheaths hang down real low and when they are out in the veld thcy gct grass and thorns stuck in them. The sheaths swell up and then they can't pee.'

'*Eina*! That sounds really sore!' Nick was clearly not enjoying the thought.

'It is. That's why I don't want to let this poor bull wait for another day. He'll be crazy with pain. Wedding or not.'

'Maybe Topsy doesn't really understand, after all she doesn't have…' Nick tailed off because they had arrived at the Vissers' farm.

'What a beautiful animal,' Walter thought, admiring the bull, who had been driven into the crush already. He was stocky, with a large head, deep chest and a well pronounced hump above his shoulders. His short coat was glossy and mostly grey; only the hump, the dewlap and the floppy ears were shiny black. He looked the epitome of a healthy animal, but was clearly not very impressed with the fact that he was locked up, and angry because he was sore.

Walter and Nick approached the animal and had a quick look.

Walter nodded; he already had worked out in his mind the correct amount of tranquiliser he needed to inject. He wanted him seriously calm, but not totally knocked out. Over the years, he'd developed a feel for the amount he needed to give to achieve the exact desired effect.

'I'll give him the injection while you go and organise what we need,' Walter instructed.

When Nick returned with ropes and some experienced cattle handlers in tow, the bull was asleep on his feet.

'Pass me the ropes and hold on to his head,' Walter told one of the farm workers he had known since he was a youngster. 'I'll explain to you guys later how this roping works,' he said, 'but it's a special technique, and absolutely fool-proof. Now each of you must take a rope and when I say '*pull*', you must all pull, slowly and steadily.'

The pulling from four directions brought the legs of the bull together and, dosed to the hilt, he didn't put up any resistance and lay down. The ropes were adjusted and a person placed on each end to release if necessary.

Walter bent down and, after a last reassuring look into the bull's half closed eyes, he grabbed hold of the swollen sheath with a deft grip. The bull reacted with an almighty kick. His hind leg lashed out with full force and hit Walter straight and square in the face.

Nick and the cattle handlers froze. When the dust had settled, the bull was lying still again, as if nothing had happened, eyes half closed and not moving a hair. Walter was lying close to the loading ramp, the impact of the kick having propelled him a good four metres. The thud, when he hit the ground, had sounded like a bus hitting a wall. His eyes were half closed and he didn't move a hair.

After a moment of shocked silence, Nick ran up to Walter.

'Are you ok?'

'Of course I'm bloody ok,' he replied, opening his eyes. 'What the hell happened?'

'Well, the bull, he kicked you and …'

'Bloody bastard!' Carefully Walter moved his legs and arms and, realising that everything still worked, stood up. 'At least it looks like he didn't do much damage.'

Nick and the farm workers looked at each other.

'Maybe you should have a look in the mirror.'

'Why? I don't have time to look into mirrors in the middle of the day!'

'But you should, really,' Nick insisted.

Walter hardly recognised himself. His face looked like there wasn't any intact skin left, and blood was dripping onto his shirt. For a moment he remained speechless in front of the rear view mirror. When he eventually turned around, he went straight to the tailgate of his bakkie and drew up a syringe.

'What are you doing? Can we help?' Nick asked.

'No. I'm just giving this stupid bloody bull an antibiotic and then I am leaving.'

'But what about his swollen…'

'That's not my problem. If he can't behave, then he has to live with the consequences, bloody bastard. And I hope his willy is as sore as my face!'

After giving the now motionless animal the injection he addressed it directly, *Ja,* you can stay like this you stupid thing!' And barely audible, he murmured, 'I might come back tomorrow to sort you out.'

Earlier than expected they arrived back home. Nick was the first to come into the kitchen, where Topsy and Debbie were preparing a light lunch.

'Nick, what happened?' Debbie asked. 'Why are you so pale? You look like you have seen a ghost?'

Nick sat down and took a deep breath. 'Can I please have a glass of water first,' he asked, playing for time. 'You won't believe what happened!'

'Oh my God, Daddy!' Debbie ran up to Walter but stopped short, not knowing whether she should hug her father, with all the blood on his shirt and the skin scraped off his face.

Topsy, who had been preoccupied with a roast chicken, turned around and had a good look at her husband. She straightened up, took a deep breath and said, 'Fine sight you are going to be at the wedding today! Hope you haven't forgotten your speech!'

Later in the evening, when the celebrations were in full swing and after Walter had delivered his speech to much applause, Topsy's friend Barbara said,

'Walter's face looks so sore, I'm not sure, shall I laugh or cry out of sympathy.'

Topsy sighed, 'I was really cross when he came home like that. You should have seen him. He always puts his life at risk for other people's animals, and half the time he doesn't even charge them!'

'Look, Tops, now he's dancing, you'd think his body should be hurting, wouldn't you?'

'Of course it should,' said Topsy. 'Any normal person would at least be concussed or in shock or something. But no, not Walter, he just carries on as if nothing had happened.'

'Oh well, let's have another glass of wine.'

Topsy nodded and lit another cigarette. 'Did I tell you, he had another close shave last week? He was out treating cattle somewhere to hell and gone. They were in the crush, and I don't know what he was doing, but one cow got cross with him. And as you know, they are not stupid. They know exactly where to kick - sideways through the poles.' She took a sip of her wine.

'And?'

'What happened? You know these Sheriff Jeans he always wears? The cow took three buttons straight off.'

'Eina,' Barbara pulled a face. 'That must have been very, very sore.'

'No, don't worry, she didn't get him. She literally just took the buttons off.'

'Wow, that's what I call luck! He is very lucky, your husband!'

'I don't know. Close shaves like that happen to him on a weekly basis. I think he must have nine lives like a cat, or something.'

'But I remember asking him the other day if he ever got attacked by an animal, and he just said no,' Barbara said.

'Of course, he would say that.' Topsy blew out some smoke. 'In his eyes, these are not attacks, but just normal animal behaviour.'

For a moment, the two friends sat quietly, sipping their wine and puffing at their cigarettes.

'Do you remember that train accident?' Topsy turned to Barbara.

'How could I ever forget that? I still get goose bumps thinking about it.'

'Guess how I felt. He was this close that day,' Topsy indicated about an inch with her fingers. 'The train driver thought he was dead. And I was expecting some delayed shock, but there was nothing. As if it was the most normal thing in the world, like, 'Oh well, Darling, I was hit by a train today. How was your day?'

NEVER

No, I never was attacked by an animal. Never ever. I got injured, yes, but never seriously.

One day, a cow got me with her horns. I obviously didn't pay enough attention and she got me right along my jaw, from underneath. The skin split open and I was bleeding like a stuck pig. It wasn't really that the cow had knocked it through from the outside, but the jawbone is very sharp and it had cut through from the inside, one clean cut. Doc Kroon just put some stitches in and finished. I don't even have a scar!

Another time, I was holding on to a cow by its horns. She just twisted her head a little bit, basically rolling her horns in my hands, and all the skin was gone, in one movement. I clearly needed some stitches and I considered doing it myself, because the farm where it happened was a long way out and I had to do a few more calls. But that wasn't a good idea, because I realised quickly that I was not brave enough. I couldn't even give myself the local; it burns like fire! And then of course, it was the wrong hand. So back to the doctor I went.

I was never attacked by an animal, but of course I was kicked. When a cow kicks you, it really hurts. She gets you in the guts every time. For a long time, I had a healthy respect for horses and their ability to kick, but over time I've learnt, in general, horses are just as well-behaved as cows. Thoroughbreds are, anyway. Despite their reputation, they are easy going. Yet, with some of these quiet crossbreeds, you can expect an explosion! One day, I had to stitch up a cut on the neck of one of these ponies. He chopped me so that

I saw stars. It was an instantaneous affair, without any warning, and far, far quicker than any thoroughbred would do it. A thoroughbred would do it gracefully.

I was never attacked by an animal, and I was never bitten by a snake. I know what it feels like, though, to be stung by a scorpion; now that is quite an ugly thing. It usually gets you on your hand or foot. Unless you are a little child or old and fragile, a scorpion doesn't do any serious damage, but it is rather very painful, and whenever you put cold water onto the sting, it feels like an electric shock. Then, virtually to the hour, after two weeks the pain is gone. That this is true, I had the honour to experience myself.

I was lying in bed one day, because a nasty flu had got hold of me, and I felt sick as a dog.

Topsy didn't show much sympathy.

'You men,' she said, 'you are all the same. A little bit of a cold and you think you are going to die.'

She had asked Paraffin to cut the grass that morning, but for some reason he couldn't start the lawn mower. From my bed, I could hear all the failed attempts, but chose to ignore them until Topsy came in.

'Sorry, I know you are not feeling too well,' she said, 'but maybe you could quickly help Paraffin to start that machine. It looks like a jungle out there, and he just can't get it going.'

'Ok, ok, I am coming.'

I went outside barefoot and dressed in my pyjamas. I had long learned that if Topsy really wanted me to do something, I had better do it; otherwise there would be no peace and quiet. I figured it wouldn't take me long, and planned to get straight back to bed once the machine was rolling.

'What's the problem, Paraffin?' I asked.

'I don't know, Doc. I tried everything, but it just doesn't want to go,' Paraffin said.

Inwardly, I cursed Flying Machine for being on leave just when we needed him, because he actually was the one who understood machines better than any of us. With a sigh, I bent down and fiddled a bit with the lawn mower, but I couldn't find anything wrong with it. And because I really wasn't feeling too strong that morning, I decided to sit down right where I was, before having a closer look.

Next thing, I must have shouted in surprise, because I remember a strange look on Paraffin's face and Topsy came running out of the house.

'Why on earth are you jumping around like a mad man, holding your backside?' she asked.

I just shrugged. What did I know? But it was bloody sore.

Then Paraffin suddenly shouted, '*Dok, Dok, kom hierso en kyk*, come and have a look here.'

There was a scorpion, black and shiny; he had his tail raised, poison still dropping off its sting, and was clapping his pincers, as if applauding.

'Serves him right,' I heard Topsy mumble.

'Who else would go outside in bright daylight wearing only pyjamas.'

For two weeks after that scorpion had stung me, every time I sat in the bath, I got an electric shock in my backside!

FLIGHT BEHAVIOUR

Walter found Topsy in the garden, where she was feeding the family of bush babies she had adopted. The two adults and three youngsters had become quite tame. Strawberry yogurt with worms was their favourite dish and every evening, without fail, they'd be waiting for Topsy at sunset. They had conquered a place very close to her heart, and the *nagapies* had become part of the Eschenburgs' extended family with all its two- and four-legged members. Once fed, they'd take off with prodigious leaps into the night to hunt for insects.

Their ability to jump many times their height had always fascinated Walter, and often he used them as an example to illustrate what he thought was one of life's most important lessons – how one, although small and fragile, could easily leap over the most intimidating obstacles. Size didn't matter, but courage did, and the belief in one's abilities.

'Topsy, guess what?' Walter couldn't hide his excitement any longer and in supportive sympathy, the dogs started barking.

'Shh! You are frightening the bush babies with your hullabaloo.'

'Ok, ok, but guess who I just spoke to?'

'No idea. But I'm sure you are going to tell me,' Topsy said as the last of the little primates left the dish with an extravagant leap onto the lower branches of the *terminalia sericea*, the silver cluster-leaf tree. Its reddish-brown branches formed a wide spreading crown that had become one of the favourite vantage points of the bush babies, as well as that of their biggest enemy, the eagle owl.

'So?' Topsy looked at Walter questioningly.

'It was Louis Le Roux. He's asked me to dart a rhino for him tomorrow.'

Louis Le Roux was a ranger and lived together with his wife Sandra at Lapalala, a nearby game reserve. Lapalala encompassed thousands of hectares of bushveld with rugged valleys, bush covered hills and sheer cliff faces on either side of the Palala River. Since the land had not much agricultural value, it had become one of the early conservation areas in the Waterberg. Over the previous few years, it had been restocked with zebra, giraffe, various types of antelope and rhino, and the wildlife was now flourishing.

One of their rhino had somehow managed to get its hind leg tangled in what seemed to be a rather thick cable, Louis had told Walter. Where and how it had happened, he didn't know. The cable was much thicker than the wire normally used by poachers for snares, but just like a snare it had lodged itself tightly around the rhino's leg, cutting into the skin, the trailing end causing much irritation. Louis surmised that all attempts by the rhino to get rid of the cable had only resulted in it becoming more deeply embedded. Something needed to be done.

'I'll come with you,' Topsy said immediately. 'It's Saturday tomorrow anyway, and after all it's your first rhino. Can't miss that! And,' she added, 'I've wanted to pay the Le Rouxs a visit for donkey's years. They are awfully nice people.'

Topsy could see Walter was delighted. She knew darting and dealing with wild animals had become the favourite part of his practice, although it was all still quite new. He had been out darting giraffe, some antelope and the odd wild bull, but never a rhino.

Walter's friend Reuben Joubert had only recently set up a game capture business, after having spent some time in the United States where he had acquired the necessary skills. He had adapted them to the African bush and now frequently asked Walter to come along, and to be the responsible vet for the operation. The business of game capture was still in its infancy in South Africa and Reuben and Walter were amongst its pioneers.

At the time, a paradigm shift was taking place amongst the farming community in the Waterberg, which had never been a prosperous farming area because of its steep ravines, rocky fields and sour, unpalatable grass. More and more farmers were allowing marginal farmland to revert to its natural state, realising that game farming could be a profitable business.

170

Game that was indigenous to the area didn't need the same attention as livestock. The animals were much better adapted to the varieties of grass occurring in the region and more resistant to parasites and diseases. Game could either be sold for hunting or to new game farms and conservation areas for restocking. It was good business.

The change from cattle to game farming required a new set of skills for farmers and vets alike. Helicopters, vehicles, dart guns and teams of specially trained people were used for capturing game. Immobilising drugs had only just become available, and a lot was still left to improvisation.

Walter and Reuben were both aware that the greatest difficulty lay often, not in administering the right dose of medication, but more so in the handling of the immobilised animal.

Immobilon, better known as *M99*, had indeed revolutionised the veterinary wildlife practice. As opposed to tranquilising drugs, it could be used to completely immobilise the patient. Now, elephants could be knocked out without too much risk to their lives, and the same applied to rhino, giraffe or buffalo. They could be safely loaded onto trucks and transported, treated for injuries or freed from snares, and their blood could be taken and tested. In short, a whole new world had opened up. Conveniently, the equally strong antidote could revive any immobilised animal within minutes.

Topsy knew, Reuben valued Walter's presence and input, and not only for his veterinary skills, or because he was a good shot. It was, Reuben had told her only recently, the fact that Walter was compassionate.

Without anthropomorphising, he understood the animals he was darting. He knew how they would react and how scared they were. This knowledge stood him in good stead now; that and his perseverance, his ability to improvise, and the ingrained confidence that nothing was impossible, that he would not stand there like '*The Ox before the Golden Gate*'.

The rhino at Lapalala wasn't going to be captured; it just needed to be immobilised long enough for Walter to remove the cable from its leg. This, Walter had agreed with Reuben, he could do on his own, with the help of Louis Le Roux and a couple of his employees.

The dart gun prepared, the Eschenburgs and Le Rouxs set off the next afternoon in search of the handicapped rhino. With them came a

171

handful of reluctant staff members who tried to make themselves as invisible as possible on the back of the truck. Rhino were dangerous, everybody knew that.

Just as Louis had predicted, they found the animal quickly. It was nearly full-grown, but still 'traveling' with its mother; both of them were grazing peacefully amongst some bushes.

'We better get out here, otherwise we'll alert them,' Walter whispered and climbed out of the Land Cruiser.

Louis and his team followed.

'Just keep your eyes open, Sandra,' he said to his wife, who remained in the driver's seat of the open game viewing vehicle. 'If it comes for you, you know what to do. Just go! No point in being brave; these rhinos are fast!'

'Your husband seems to be a bit on edge,' Topsy said, perched on the edge of the passenger's seat, so as to not miss any of the action.

Walter and Louis approached the two white rhino from downwind. They lifted their heads and pricked their ears; they must have heard the two men, but then they continued with their grazing.

To be able to move as quietly as possible, Walter took off his shoes and gestured to Louis to stay put. He went down on his hands and knees and very slowly crept closer, the dart gun precariously stuck under his right arm. Once the distance had shrunk to some twenty odd metres, he stopped. Any closer and surely the rhinos would become aware of him. Camouflaged by some bushes, his vision was not one hundred per cent clear, as he would have wished.

'*Jirre*, I hope I'll get the right one,' he thought. 'It's quite difficult to tell who is who.'

After some deliberation he pulled the trigger.

'Ha!' he nearly said out aloud. 'That was a good one!'

In textbook fashion the dart was lodged in the muscular hindquarters of the younger rhinoceros. The young bull was not at all amused. He lifted his head, let out a couple of loud snorts and stamped his foot. Immediately, the mother was on the alert too. They stood still for a second and then, with another snort, they started charging at full speed. They came straight for Walter.

'Oh sh…' he said, not worried anymore that they'd hear him.

He dropped the gun and ran as fast as his legs would carry him. Half expecting the situation to turn out like this, he had earmarked a suitable tree beforehand and that's where he was headed now. It seemed though, that he had underestimated the speed of a charging rhino, or had he overestimated his running fitness?

Topsy and Sandra sat in the Land Cruiser and watched. Louis was fine, at a safe distance; he was standing next to a tree, ready to climb up should it become necessary. But Walter? He had just reached a dense bush, possibly thick enough to hide him, and he dived straight into it. To the two women's relief, the two rhino didn't seem to have noticed and carried on charging straight past the bush. But now they took aim at their vehicle and were coming closer at a terrifying speed.

'Start that bloody thing!' Topsy shouted. 'Let's get out of here!'

But the Land Cruiser wouldn't listen. *Njenjenjenjenje*, the starter motor sounded, but the engine didn't catch. The sound of the thundering rhino feet became deafening, followed by the thuds of the cable hitting the ground. Realising that they couldn't get away, Sandra and Topsy sank lower and lower into their seats, trying to make themselves invisible.

Within seconds it was all over. The animals had run straight past the vehicle, missing it by a couple of inches. If Topsy had stretched out her arm, she could have touched them. They veered off into the denser bush where, eventually, the medication took effect.

In hot pursuit came Walter. The last thing he wanted was to lose the two animals. Close on his heels was Louis. The two men arrived just in time to see the youngster come crashing down. Relieved, they slowly came closer, only to realise that the position the animal had chosen couldn't have been less suitable. His head rested on a rock that was wedged between two large mopane trees. Mother rhino was hovering about, getting more and more agitated; she was circling the trees and the immobilised patient. Every now and again she'd scan her surroundings, snort and mock charge in the direction of Walter and Louis.

'I'll never get to him like this, I'll have to dart the mother as well.'

Walter was prepared and had another dart in his pocket. This time it was easier. The dart hit and without further ado, the mother, wanting to stay close to her youngster, sat down only a couple of metres away. Walter and Louis removed the cable from the young animal's leg; luckily it hadn't cut too deep into the skin yet.

'So, that's done,' Walter looked up. 'But now the next question is, how are we going to bring him around so he doesn't hurt himself?'

He pointed at the two tree trunks.

'I think we'll have to cut at least one of those trees,' Louis replied. 'I've got a saw in the Cruiser.'

The tree removed and the young rhino blindfolded, Walter injected him with the antidote.

'I'll give him a low dose. That'll give us time to lead him away while we wake up his mother. But wait a minute!' He looked over to the Land Cruiser and called for Topsy to bring their camera. 'Seeing that I have never before 'shot' a rhino, let's take a 'trophy picture',' Walter joked.

He posed next to the rhinoceros with his foot perched on his shoulder, trying to keep a serious face. He noticed the two women exchanging amused looks.

'What are you girls laughing about? Never seen a 'big white hunter' before?' he grinned.

Later, the first rhino darting operation wrapped up successfully, they all sat together on Louis and Sandra's stoep, having a coffee with a good dash of brandy. Excitedly, they relived the events of the afternoon.

'*Jirre*, I was frightened!' Sandra admitted.

'So was I!' said Topsy. 'I have never been so frightened or so bloody close to a rhino in my entire life!'

'But tell me,' Walter asked, 'why didn't you just drive away?'

'Because that stupid Land Cruiser wouldn't start. That's why,' and keen to change the subject, Sandra asked, 'but Walter, have you had a look at your trousers?' and with this the two women burst into hysterical laughter.

Walter looked at them, uncomprehending.

'Women,' he thought, 'what is there to laugh about? There is nothing wrong with them, is there?'

Nonetheless, he had a look and suddenly understood.

'I was wondering why it was so nice and cool down there!' he laughed.

His long khaki trousers had split open from the left turn-up, along the entire inside of his legs all the way down to the right turn-up.

'Oh dear, and there is me thinking that I am having a presentable trophy shot taken.'

'His first rhino'

AFRO DISIAC

Ja, that first rhino we darted, that was quite a story. In those days, it was all still very new; a real challenge. Although for me it has never lost any of its excitement. Today it has become quite fashionable for young students to want to become wildlife vets; can't blame them really, because it is fascinating stuff! But a lot of them somewhat romanticise the whole idea. I've had more than one student come through my practice, telling me 'yes, a wildlife vet', that's what they want to be. Quite a few of them had never really been in the bush, let alone stood eye to eye with a rhino or an elephant. Bloody scary that is, I can tell you!

It wasn't long after our first adventure that Reuben Joubert asked me to dart some rhino for him in the Thabazimbi area. He needed to capture and relocate sixteen animals, and the whole procedure would take about five days.

A few days prior to the planned beginning of the operation, I happened to pick up two hitchhikers on the road to Pietersburg. They looked like interesting guys to me, and it turned out that they were both journalists from England. It was their first visit to Africa, and they were planning on financing it by writing a couple of freelance articles. James and Duncan were their names, if I remember correctly.

I took them home and they stayed with us for a couple of days, and as usual Topsy made it her mission to feed them up. We got on really well and it was only a matter of time before they got wind of the planned rhino capture.

Not surprisingly, because they were of the adventurous kind, they asked if they could join. They had never seen anything like it. In fact, they didn't even know you could capture rhinos and move them around. They even said they had never seen a rhino in real life.

The textbook says you are not supposed to take observers along when darting game, as they usually get in the way; but I could understand those two guys, and I felt sorry for them. They were so very keen that I thought, 'What the hell, what damage can they do, they seem to be really sensible guys?'

I phoned Reuben and he gave the all-clear. James and Duncan were very excited and I think they imagined their article and photographs on the front page of some UK magazine. They didn't have the faintest idea what they were in for and in the end, it turned out that they got more than what they had bargained for! Much more!

During this operation I was not with Reuben in the helicopter, but on the ground. We managed to find one of the cows relatively quickly and darted her. Predictably, she wasn't too impressed. Now you must know, which I did, but the two Englishmen obviously didn't, a white rhino calf always runs ahead of its mother.

Somehow, inexplicably, James got in between the two. Not a place you'd want to be. Immediately, she charged him. You should have seen his face!

Duncan, the photographer, thought this was great. I don't think he even worried about his colleague. He just took pictures. There was James, running as fast as his legs would carry him, and right on his heels an angry rhino cow.

At one stage I actually got worried. Could he keep up this speed until the M99 took effect? The cow hadn't started showing any of the symptoms associated with the immobilising agent yet. James was fast, but what if he wasn't fast enough? I had told them both that if something like this were to happen, they should climb up a tree, but James seemed to have forgotten. He was just running, running, running. Every now and again he looked over his shoulder, panic written large in his eyes, and the rhino came closer and closer.

Luckily, at this stage one of the young guys who was part of Reuben's team saw and understood what was going on. Without a word he took off and he ran between the cow and the Englishman. Immediately the rhino switched from the reporter to that youngster, who was very fast and nimble. He aimed for a tree, went around it and with one leap ended up sitting on a branch. Not quite as nimble, the rhino carried straight on at full speed until eventually the medication worked.

James and Duncan were clearly shaken, and they couldn't stop talking about their rhino capturing adventure. With every round, the rhino got faster, the trees higher and everything more dramatic. It was clearly an experience of a lifetime for them, for who in England can say they have been chased by a rhino?

A few months later, we received a letter from James. He thanked us profusely before telling us some more about the rest of their trip and so on, but what he wrote at the end of the letter made me laugh out loud:

'I will never, ever, forget the day in my life when I nearly had my ass reamed by the world's most expensive aphrodisiac – whilst it was still attached to its owner's nose.'

DANCING WITH HYENAS

Peter was one of the many a students who sought out Walter's surgery to gain some practical experience. He was a tall, bespectacled and gawky young man. His thin, dark hair was in desperate need of a cut and his round glasses could have done with a good clean. His long limbs moved hesitantly and his speech was slow, tinged by a broad Yorkshire accent.

Peter had come to South Africa as a teenager with his parents. For some peculiar reason Walter could never work out, they had settled in *Naboom*, of all places, and opened a general dealer shop. He was in his third year of veterinary science at Onderstepoort, had great marks in all the subjects and his mother had asked Walter if he could spend a couple of weeks of his holidays to learn from him. Her son's biggest dream was, she'd said, to become a wildlife vet. Walter, who knew the young men, as people tend to know each other in a small town, had accepted with a quiet sigh.

Peter had been with the Eschenburgs for a week when a farmer called, who had caught a hyena.

'So, Peter, we have to get a hyena out of a cage trap. What do you think we should take along?'

'I don't know. I have never seen a real hyena.'

'I see. Do you know anything about hyenas?'

There was silence.

'You do know that we get two types of hyenas here in South Africa, don't you?'

More silence.

Walter, a little exasperated, continued, 'What we get in the Waterberg is the brown hyena. I believe that many years ago the spotted hyena also roamed here, but it seems they have been shot out and are now largely confined to the east of the country, where you'll find them in Zululand or the Kruger National Park.

'Unfortunately, brown hyenas are also quite rare these days. They are a bit smaller than their spotted cousins, and look pretty much like a large, shaggy dog. You'll easily recognise one if you see it.'

'Are they dangerous?' Peter asked.

'No. Although some farmers will tell you a different story, claiming that they kill their sheep and calves. Brown hyenas are scavengers, and they eat eggs, insects and sometimes even crabs or other little aquatic animals. What has always fascinated me is that they can go for quite a long time without drinking. In the Kalahari, they'll eat wild melons for water.'

They walked over to the bakkie and Peter literally had to fold himself double to get into it. Dart gun, tranquilisers and other medicines loaded, they headed at high speed towards their destination. Walter shot the odd glance at Peter. He knew that in theory he was a brilliant student, but unfortunately he had proven rather slow and not the most apt when it came to thinking on his feet. He'd stand and think and always seemed to discuss all the pros and cons thoroughly in his head before taking any action, by which time the situation usually had moved on.

Walter sighed. 'So tell me, Peter, what on earth made you want to become a wildlife vet?'

Peter hesitated for a moment before he replied. 'Suppose I watched a lot of *Dactari* when I was young, back home in the UK. It looked sort of interesting.'

When he saw the uncomprehending look on Walter's face he added that it was an American TV series for children aired in the late 1960s and early '70s. Set in the East African bush, the hero was a veterinarian who ran a wildlife study centre. Then he'd read all the James Herriot books, about the charismatic vet who plied his trade in Yorkshire, Peter continued.

'Everybody said it was impossible to get into veterinary science, but when I finished school, I tried anyway, and was accepted at Onderstepoort. They even gave me a bursary. So I went.'

'Do you sometimes have any doubts?' Walter asked. He actually quite liked the guy, but a wildlife vet? That's not what he saw in the young man. Somehow he needed to get the message across.

'Well, I really quite like the scientific stuff; chemistry, physics, pharmacology and biochemistry. But I don't know; I am not sure. These animals are a lot bigger than I thought...' Peter tailed off.

Walter nodded. Maybe there was a way. 'You know,' he ventured, 'they offer some great jobs in the research departments at the university as well.'

Arriving at the farm, they were promptly shown to the cage trap that contained a snarling and clearly unhappy hyena, with what seemed to be a broken leg. Walter darted it and, once the animal was sound asleep, they put the entire cage onto the back of the bakkie and returned to the surgery. Carefully they laid the sleeping hyena on Walter's sturdy iron surgery table and proceeded with the examination.

'Shit, it looks to like a broken femur. What do you think, Peter?'

'Don't really know. But I think you are right.'

'So in your opinion, what shall we do now?' Walter couldn't help but push the young man a bit; it irked him that there was so little response.

'I don't know...'

'First thing, we actually need to have the leg x-rayed. And then it needs to be pinned, with a big and heavy Steinmann pin, otherwise it won't hold. What do you think?'

'If you say so...'

Walter took a deep breath before he explained that neither could he do x-rays, nor did he have the wherewithal to pin the fracture. Therefore the patient should be transferred to the Pretoria Zoo where they had all the necessary equipment and experience. Peter nodded.

When Walter phoned the vet department of the zoo, a young and competent colleague answered. They should bring the hyena as soon as possible, he advised, because one of their specialists was available to do the operation.

As an afterthought, the young vet asked, 'By the way, what's he under?'

'*Rompun* and *Ketavet*,' Walter gave him the brand names of the commonly used tranquiliser and anaesthetic.

'Oh,' his colleague said, 'you'd better watch out that he doesn't wake up!'

Walter casually turned around. He had been standing with his back to the surgery table while on the phone, trusting that Peter would keep an eye on the animal. When his gaze fell on his patient, he saw him flick an ear.

Ja, I see what you mean. I'd better top him up.'

Quickly, Walter filled a syringe and turned back to the surgery table when, without warning, all hell broke loose.

'Luckily, he didn't want to bite us,' Walter would tell Topsy later in the evening, 'but he certainly chased us around the surgery. Young Peter was dancing around; I was dancing around and the hyena was chasing us from corner to corner, broken leg and all. I was impressed how quickly Peter could move all of a sudden!'

For a moment Walter had been at a loss as to how to resolve this rather uncomfortable situation. He'd wished he hadn't left the dart gun in his bakkie. Instead, he'd grabbed a piece of rope he had left lying in the surgery on a previous occasion, thankful he was not always too tidy.

He'd tied a noose at one end and managed to lasso the hyena. In one quick movement he'd got to the other side of the surgery table, pulled the hyena right up against it and fastened the rope onto its sturdy legs. Feeling some serious resistance, handicapped by the broken leg and still a little dazed from the anaesthetic, the hyena had given up the fight. With the second dose of Rompun administered, he had slumped down and closed his eyes, again oblivious to the rest of the world.

The end of the story was twofold and to Walter's satisfaction. The hyena's leg was pinned successfully and once he had recovered, he was released at a wildlife sanctuary near Pretoria. And young Peter changed his plans and became a highly regarded research scientist in biochemistry.

ABLUTIONS

It was late on a Friday afternoon and Topsy decided to have a bath. She turned on the hot tap and knew it would take an eternity to fill up the large tub, what with the old, low-pressure Junker geyser and its tiny little flame. One day they would have to fix it. Tired, she sat down on the rim of the old bathtub.

They had just finished moving house. After more than twenty years Walter and Topsy had decided to leave Weltevreden and start afresh. Topsy had never thought that they would be able to sell her portion of the family farm. It had been subdivided many years previously and the Eschenburgs' section was a long, narrow stretch of land, two thirds of which were part of the Nyl floodplain. It was impossible to make it work financially, Walter and Topsy had soon realised, not, if they didn't want Walter's practice to slack off.

Walter had become a much respected vet in the area, and his rounds took him from Naboomspruit to Potgietersrus, Vaalwater and Warmbaths. Farmers and townsfolk alike valued his experience and knowledge, and they trusted him. He understood not only the animals, but also their owners. He gave advice freely, listened to their grievances and was always there when needed. He never complained when he was called out to an emergency, be it in the middle of the night or during a weekend braai, and many of his patients' owners came to regard him as a friend.

People who knew Walter accepted and loved him for who he was and wouldn't have had it any differently, but amongst newcomers to the area he became soon known as a rather unorthodox vet.

That was no surprise, Topsy thought while she watched her bathtub slowly fill up. Walter never drove a fancy car, his instruments were always in disarray, and more often than not, when he returned after a long day out he looked the worse for wear. He didn't seem to mind if his shirt was stained with blood or his shorts torn. His glasses always looked like they needed a wipe and his hair often stood on end.

He saw nothing wrong in castrating a dog or cat on the owner's kitchen table or, in the case of Topsy's friend Pamela Baker, on the chest freezer. He sometimes made use of the most unusual healing methods and often devised improvisations that seemed strange to the uninitiated eye. Many animals that had been given up by their owners or his colleagues, so-called hopeless cases, he gave another chance – and often with success.

He was open to learn from each and every person he met and would delight as much in the conversation with a farm worker or traditional healer as with the most erudite academic. He had the ability to put people at ease and make them feel comfortable, no matter who they were.

The same applied to most animals. Many of his clients swore by his sometimes uncanny ability to communicate with his patients. There was many a case when he was called out by a desperate owner who was not able to go near his animal, and Walter would just walk up to it and do what he had to do. Often the wildest beasts became tame under his hands.

Walter also had a sense of humour and Topsy now remembered how he had invited the same Pamela Baker, who then was still new in town, to Debbie and Nick's engagement party. Pamela had congratulated him and then asked, jokingly, if he approved of the groom.

'Of course I do,' Walter had laughed. 'After all, he is my son.'

'He is ... your son?'

Topsy would never forget Pamela's face. It was confusion writ large.

'Yes, he is!' Walter had said with a smirk before he'd explained, 'We adopted Nick a few years ago when he was a teenage boy.'

Topsy shook her head as she remembered. It seemed such a long time ago.

Her thoughts went back to Weltevreden. Money worries aside, they had loved their life there. The birdlife had been just spectacular and it was at Weltevreden that Walter had passed on his passion and knowledge about all things alive to Nick and Debbie, Bowen and Tokkie, and a host of other kids.

Times really flew, Topsy thought. She remembered it as if it was yesterday, yet in the meantime the children had all grown up. Nick and Debbie had been married for three years already and were expecting their first child. Bowen had become a renowned artist, making the most beautiful pencil drawings of wildlife and trees, and just like his father Bogey, he undertook long solo trips into the bush. Tokkie de Sand was somewhere in England, working with horses and coming closer to his dream of riding in the Olympics one day.

It was at Weltevreden where Walter had let Karroo, his beautiful Palomino gelding, run barefoot for a year, curing him of some ailment that would have been his death sentence. Karroo had been a successful event horse, when he suddenly went lame and none of the vets in Jo'burg could cure him. Heavy hearted, his previous owner wanted to have him put down, but Viola, an old childhood friend of Walter's interfered. She begged and pleaded with the owner until he let her have the horse so that she could give him to Walter. He took one look at the Palomino and said, 'I think we should just take his shoes off and let him run barefoot for a year. Then we'll see. Won't cost us anything.' Not that he would have cared, Topsy thought now as she remembered. They always picked up strays and lost causes anyway. So what was one more mouth to feed?

As usual, Walter had been right; it seemed he just knew these things. A year later Karroo was one hundred per cent fine. He became the only horse Walter ever competed with at the Nylvalley Horse Trials. Since they had started to organise and run this horse riding event, it had become a big part of their lives and a fixture on the South African eventing calendar. But that was a different story altogether.

When the owner of the property next to Weltevreden had offered them a good deal, because he wanted to take down the fences and turn it all into a nature conservation area, Walter and Topsy couldn't refuse. And it so happened that their dear friend Ivan Visser was looking for tenants for his farm Boekenhout at the same time. It was situated a mere twenty kilometres out of Naboomspruit, along the fringes of the Waterberg.

The old farmhouse, shaded by some large wild seringa trees, had a wide stoep all around and immediately appealed to Topsy. It was a little dilapidated, since it had been standing empty for some time, but nothing that couldn't be fixed with a few hours of good, honest work.

Apart from some minor details, they were done with the moving on this particular Friday afternoon in 1988. Paraffin and Flying Machine had retired to their new servants' quarters and Walter had headed off to see to a patient.

Still sitting on the rim of the bath and waiting for the geyser to do its thing, Topsy's gaze fell onto the toilet bowl.

'I can't believe it,' she said to herself, 'there are still rust flakes floating around in there.'

The water from the borehole had a high iron content and with the house standing empty, rust flakes had formed. 'Better get them out before it all blocks up.'

But as she stuck her hand into the bowl to clean it out, she saw a movement. Startled, she took a closer look. No, her eyes hadn't betrayed her; there was a snake following her hand. She flung the toilet lid closed and found herself standing back to the wall by the door. Just then, she heard Walter's bakkie pull up outside.

'For once he is coming at the right time,' she thought and shouted, 'Walter, Walter! Come quickly, there is a snake in the loo.'

Walter at first didn't hear, and then, to Topsy's dismay, he didn't believe her.

'Where is that snake of yours?' he asked with a grin, leaning against their bathroom's door frame.

'There!' Topsy said, pointing at the loo.

'Where?'

'There!'

'Well, I can't see anything.'

'Just open the lid and you will see.'

'Sorry, Tops, but I can't see a thing. Are you sure you really saw a snake and it wasn't just some rust moving?'

Topsy was fuming and Walter, clearly aware now that he was treading on thin ice, tried hard to placate her and suggested she get into the bath. Not really a good idea, she told him, with a snake watching.

'You can say what you want and you can do what you want, but I know this snake was there. It must have got a fright when it saw you and done a double U-turn. But I will not use this bathroom again until we find this *blerry* thing.'

Walter sighed and went to phone Oom Ticky, the snake catcher.

'Pity old Bogey is not with us any more, he would sort this out in no time,' Topsy said while they waited. Bogey had died a premature death some ten years previously. He'd understood snakes better than anybody they'd ever met.

'*Ja*, but Oom Ticky is also a good snake catcher; he'll sort this problem out for us, I'm sure.'

Oom Ticky had loved and caught snakes ever since he was a child. Over the decades, this fascination had become a real skill, and when he went into retirement he became the snake catcher in the area. For the venomous reptiles, he had a snake stick, about a metre and a half long with pincers at the one end that could be operated from the other. But unless he had to deal with a black mamba or an aggressive cobra, he didn't see too much of a problem using his hands either.

Carefully, Oom Ticky listened to Topsy's story before he entered the bathroom. He was short, had thin white hair and thick glasses, and his head moved from side to side while scanning his surrounds.

'I'm surprised, his tongue is not flickering,' Topsy marvelled, and she could see Walter was entertaining similar thoughts as he was standing in the doorway.

'*Jammer*, but I can't see anything,' Oom Ticky said a little disappointed after checking in all corners of the bathroom, even lifting the lid of the cistern.

'It was in there, I swear.' Topsy felt she was repeating herself constantly. Somewhat absentmindedly, she flushed the loo. 'Hang on, did you see that?'

'*Ja, ja, ja!*' Oom Ticky suddenly got excited.

'What?' Walter clearly had to get with the programme.

'Something just came out from under the rim. Just saw it out of the corner of my eye.'

'Serious?'

'Serious.'

The snake catcher bent down and carefully stuck his hand under the rim of the toilet bowl. As he straightened up he'd got hold of the tail of a metre-long and by now rather upset Mozambican spitting cobra.

Maintaining a respectful distance from the man who quickly moved to put the snake into a sack, Topsy couldn't help but say to Walter, 'See, I told you so. But you never believe me.'

188

Ja, ja, alright. But now we better check where this thing came from, because I've never heard of a snake climbing into a toilet.'

'Well,' said Oom Ticky, 'if it hasn't gone in through the bowl, and you are sure you saw it coming out, then maybe it came the other way. Let's have a look outside. Where is your septic tank?'

When they inspected the tank, which had just been covered with a brand new concrete slab, it dawned on them what must have happened. The old slab had been broken for some time, leaving the tank uncovered. A dark and humid hole, it became the perfect hiding place for frogs and other creatures.

'That makes sense,' Oom Ticky nodded. 'Where there are frogs, there are snakes. And with the new slab, the only way out is for the snakes to go up the pipes and through the toilet. Is there another toilet that feeds into this tank? You better check that one, too. And I suggest you be a bit careful because I bet that this fellow,' he pointed at the sack, 'isn't the only one.'

It was only a couple of weeks later that Topsy's sister and her husband came for a visit to Boekenhout. Arthur, Topsy's brother-in-law, was about 20 years her senior. He had been a fighter pilot in the Second World War and received various medals for bravery. Sunday lunch was served under the large seringa trees in the garden. The atmosphere was jolly, wine and beer flowed, there was a lot of laughter and, of course, the snake story was bandied about.

After the men had moved on to their second postprandial brandy, Arthur got up from the table and headed for the outside bathroom. Suddenly, the entire Sunday lunch party was alerted by a loud scream. The bathroom door flew open and Arthur came rushing out as fast as he could with his pants around his ankles and a terrified look on his face.

A thorough investigation of the incident, however, led to the conclusion that it was a wasp that had stung Arthur in his nether regions.

MAMBA MERCY

The story of the snake in the bathroom and Arthur's subsequent show of bravery kept us entertained for some time. But of course, there are lots and lots and lots of snake stories...

One day, I was on my way to Louis Meyer's farm. I suppose I was driving rather fast when I saw this dark band stretched across the road. Immediately, I hit the brakes. Skidding, the bakkie came to a halt about fifty metres on the other side. It turned out to be a black mamba. A shiver ran down my spine. Although I wouldn't say that I was scared of mambas, I never felt really comfortable in their company either.

Out of principle, I didn't run over snakes on the road, like many farmers still do here, but this had been a genuine accident. I contemplated the dead snake, wondering what to do with it. It was by far the biggest mamba I had ever seen, well over three metres. Somehow it seemed a waste to just leave it lying on the road, so I picked it up and threw it in the back of the bakkie.

'Maybe that was a mistake,' I mused, because as I continued down the road, the hairs on the back of my neck began to stand on end.

'Nonsense,' I said to myself, 'don't be a fool'. The snake was very dead, and the cabin was totally separated from the back of the bakkie. Yet somehow, something just didn't feel right.

The black mamba is, by the way, only very rarely black. Its colour varies from olive green to greyish brown or gunmetal grey. Large and fast and deadly, it has a coffin shaped head and black lining on the inside of its mouth, hence the name. In one of the local African languages spoken here, I think in Northern Sotho, it is called *'muriti wa lesu'*, which means as much as 'shadow of death'.

Whoever talks of black mambas can be sure to have the attention of the audience, and there is no shortage of black mamba stories. Everybody seems to know of somebody who knows somebody who had an encounter with this snake. The reason being that if you do get bitten by a black mamba, it most likely means you won't live to tell the tale; at least in this neck of the woods. There are a few exceptions, and those stories as well have been circulating and embroidered through many a conversation. Nobody really knows how much is true, or based on truth, and how much is folklore.

Anyway, not a moment too soon I arrived at the farm.

'Howzit?'

'Howzit!' I was a little excited, so I told Louis, 'Hell, I just ran over a bloody big mamba. The biggest I've ever seen.'

'Ah. Dead?' Louis Meyer was not a man of many words.

'Yes, dead. I chucked it into the back of the bakkie.'

'Let's have a look.'

We opened the canopy.

'Where is your mamba?'

'I don't know...' There was no snake. And I clearly remembered my raised hackles and ominous feelings on the drive. 'I really don't know.'

'Sure it was dead?'

'Ja, man, very dead. Do you think I would have picked it up otherwise?'

'And you sure you put it into the bakkie?'

Louis just shook his head and was about to walk off, when he looked up and froze. I followed his gaze and couldn't believe my eyes. There we saw it, the flickering tongue of a big snake; it had wedged itself up on the ledge above the canopy windows. We looked at each other and without a word stepped back. I got into the vehicle and reversed it into a bush with the canopy wide open. But I made sure that the doors and windows of the cab were closed. Properly.

'Let's go and have a look at your cattle,' I suggested.

After having done a couple of hours of work, I was in no rush to get back to my vehicle and happily accepted Mrs Meyers offer for a cup of coffee, some rusks and a good chat. Eventually though, I had to leave. Louis Meyer accompanied me, just to have a look, but the snake had vanished, this time for good.

CHRISTMAS

Walter was tidying up his surgery at Boekenhout after the last patient for the day had left. And what a patient it had been. Fred and Minnie Badenhorst, some new people in town, and a bit uptight as Topsy had observed, had brought in their Alsatian early in the afternoon to be castrated.

They had insisted on watching the operation, and Walter of course had said that he didn't mind. He never did. But this time, for some inexplicable reason, the dog had died under the anaesthetic. He hadn't even used his scalpel when he stopped breathing. There was no pulse either, nothing. He'd tried some heart massage, but without success.

The Badenhorsts of course had been distraught, and Walter had suggested they do a post-mortem to investigate the reason for the sudden demise of the animal. Then, the strangest thing had happened. As the cold metal of the scalpel touched the skin for the first incision, he had seen the chest of the dog expanding with a loud wheezing sound and the Alsatian had taken a deep breath. Minnie Badenhorst nearly had fainted and then wanted to take her dog home straight away, but he'd convinced her that they should proceed with the castration so that the animal needn't be put under anaesthetic again any time soon.

'Not sure we'll see them again,' Walter had mumbled to himself after the Badenhorsts had left. He didn't really have an explanation; sometimes one just had to accept that strange things happened.

'Walter, why didn't you charge them?' Topsy had asked.

'How can I charge them if the dog nearly died?'

'Easy, you still used all the medication and everything, and what about your time?

And I don't have to remind you, we have to pay Paraffin and Flying Machine's salaries, and, and, and…'

Walter sighed as he sterilised his instruments. Money had become a constant issue between him and Topsy. Hardly a day passed without them arguing about it. Mostly it was Topsy who voiced her gripes, and often with reason, he had to admit. He knew he often forgot to charge people, or felt sorry for them if they didn't have money. Added to that, his accounting system was in shambles. Often he'd lose the notes he'd made during a visit, and in general money wasn't really that important to him.

Only last month had he promised to 'get his act together' as Topsy called it, but he struggled.

Granted, there were some of his long-standing, trusted clients, like the De Sands, who would pay a monthly sum into his account, if he sent them a bill or not. And often, it was more than he would have charged.

'Please don't argue, Walter,' Bernhard de Sand had said when Walter had queried this once. 'I have worked with other vets before, many of them, and none of them as competent as you are. Not by any means. In fact, these other blokes were utterly useless. But they all charge me at least five times the amount you put on your bills. And I have taken animals to Onderstepoort; I know how much they take. So, I do know what I owe you and I will pay you what I owe you, because I don't like owing people money. And you can just put on your bills whatever you like; I'll pay you what is right.'

'Anyway, glad that Alsatian came round again,' Walter thought, somewhat startled when Topsy called that she'd go to town to get some more cigarettes.

He himself had stopped smoking more than fifteen years ago, went from sixty cigarettes a day to zero, something nobody believed he could do. He remembered the day he'd come home, put his packet of cigarettes onto the table in front of him and said,

'I'm stopping this now.'

'You are what?' Three faces had looked at him in surprise.

'I am giving up smoking,' he'd said and pushed the nearly full packet of *Golden Leaf* away.

'Arc you serious, Dad?' Debbie had asked with big, hopeful eyes. She hated his smoking.

'Wow,' Nick had nodded. 'But isn't that going to be difficult?' He had experimented with cigarettes himself and had felt the pull of the nicotine.

'Difficult?' Topsy had laughed. 'Difficult? No ways. It's impossible. He'll never do it. I bet you, at the latest tomorrow, he'll be lighting up again.'

He had proved her wrong, and while she still had to go to the café at all possible and impossible times, he hadn't touched a cigarette since.

'Not a big deal,' he'd say if people asked. 'Once you make up your mind, it's easy.'

As Walter wandered over to the house after he had finished tidying up his surgery, it struck him.

'Oh ja, it's Christmas Eve today, how could I forget. I better have a bath before they all arrive.'

As every year, they were expecting quite a few people to join them. Debbie and Nick would arrive later with their two daughters, Hannah and Jade. They'd bring Karin and Rainer, whom Walter had picked up when hitch-hiking through Africa many years previously.

'I wonder who else will pitch up tomorrow,' Walter pondered. It had become a tradition that any stray dog, canine or human, was welcome, and anytime really, but particularly at Christmas.

He was woken from his reverie by the sound of a bakkie. The gate squeaked. 'Must be Topsy coming back. But who is she talking to?' he wondered.

Following Topsy into the house was a middle-aged, fit looking man with short brown hair and a broad smile on his friendly face. He greeted Walter in German.

'Walter, this is Gerd,' Topsy introduced the newcomer. 'I saw this bright yellow bicycle outside the café in Naboom. Can you imagine, he's come all the way from Germany on his bike, and now he doesn't really have anywhere to stay and spend Christmas, so I thought I might as well take him home.'

'He looks like a really interesting man,' Walter thought. He'd fit in well with the rest of the crowd.

After Gerd had freshened up, he joined Walter on the stoep and told him his story. A fighter pilot in the German air force, he had retired a few years back and now travelled the world on his yellow bicycle. He'd been all over Europe, through Asia, the Near East and now Africa.

'I normally write an article or two about the trips I do,' he explained, 'and I absolutely love it. I've always had itchy feet. Maybe that's why I became a pilot. I had a great time in the air force and luckily I never had to fly in a war. But the best thing about it is that they retire you early and now I have lots of time to travel.'

Christmas Day started with a phone call. A farmer was desperate because his cow had problems calving. He apologised profusely and said he knew it was Christmas, but he thought they would have to do a caesarean section.

Walter headed straight for his bakkie. 'Ok, I'd better go. Who's coming with me?'

It was indeed an emergency. The calf was stuck the wrong way round, and all attempts at turning it had dismally failed. They had arrived not a minute too early as the cow was in serious distress, her breathing laboured and the pulse too quick and flat.

Nearly thirty years of experience and practise showed their rewards now. There was a bucket and some soap, Walter gave the cow the local anaesthetic, the farmer tied her up against a fence and Nick got the instruments ready on the bakkie's tailgate. The left flank was shaved, washed and cut open, layer after layer, and eventually the calf, which was still alive, pulled out.

'Here is your Christmas present, a beautiful heifer calf,' Walter laughed as he handed it over to the farmer. Then he stitched up the wound.

'That's it!' In the meantime, the farmer had put the new-born calf in front of her mother's nose, rubbing her dry. Even while Walter was still busy closing up the wound, the mother started licking her daughter and within minutes she struggled to her feet.

'This is just too cute!' Karin said. She had come along for the ride and now couldn't take her eyes off the little calf. 'And I thought baby foals were cute, but this is just the loveliest thing I have ever seen!'

When Walter and his entourage arrived back at Boekenhout, the Christmas party was in full swing. The table had been set under the big seringa tree and he saw Debbie looking at it approvingly. The white linen tablecloth, red serviettes and the good family silver were complemented by flowers, chocolates and nuts, Christmas hats and crackers.

Walter looked around. What a lovely, warm place this was, and what a menagerie of animals and people. There were Topsy and Carla, Nick's older sister, sitting on the stoep, soaking up a little gin and puffing away happily on their cigarettes. Nick and Debbie's toddler Jade, and Hannah, the baby, were both having a sleep under the tree.

Three whippets, a Doberman and the inevitable Jack Russell were also lying in the garden in various shady spots. The newest addition was a racing pigeon who had taken up residency in the old budgie cage. Topsy had called him Herbert when he'd arrived a couple of weeks previously, crash-landing on the stoep with a broken leg. They'd realized he was completely tame, and Walter had fixed his leg and put it in plaster. Topsy had phoned the pigeon people in Naboom, but they'd just told her not to bother.

'Wring its neck,' was what they'd said. A racing pigeon that didn't find its way home was useless to them.

'I think, once his cast is off, I'll just leave the cage door open, so he can decide himself what he wants to do. If he wants to stay here, he's welcome, but if he wants to go home and face the music there, that's also fine by me,' Walter overheard Topsy just then say to Carla. 'Maybe I should tie a little piece of paper on his leg that says: *Please don't kill me, I've been at the vet having my leg fixed.* Ja, I think that's what I'll do.'

Topsy took a sip of gin, before she turned to Debbie and asked her if she remembered Esmeralda. 'The other day I heard that she'd choked on a Sunday roast.'

'She did what?'

'Yes, Rosemary walked into the kitchen and there was Esmeralda lying stretched out on the floor, a whole leg of lamb stuck in her throat. Nobody knows how she managed to get it out of the closed oven, but she obviously did, and that was the end of her.'

'Who is this poor Esmeralda you are talking about?' Carla asked, confused.

Topsy laughed. 'Esmeralda is a tame pig that belonged to Walter's cousin Rosemary. She always claimed Esmeralda was much more intelligent than any of her dogs.'

Finally it was time for Christmas lunch.

'But wait, wait,' Debbie called, 'we need to hang the watermelon up first and everybody needs to take a sip.'

Within minutes Nick had helped her suspend the large fruit from one of the lower branches of the tree. Walter poked some holes into it with his pocket knife and stuck straws into them.

'Karin, Werner, Gerd, come and try this!' he called. 'It is… heavenly!' He took a big gulp, a grin appearing on his face. 'I think this is the best one we've ever made.'

Everybody tried the special watermelon drink and soon the atmosphere was even more jolly. When a giggling Karin asked Debbie, how one prepared something so delicious, Debbie rattled down the recipe as if memorised too many times.

'Cut off the short end of a watermelon, but keep it. Scrape out three quarters of the flesh. Fill with a mixture of gin, cane spirit, vodka and sweet white wine. Leave to stand overnight and put it into the fridge. Blend strawberries and vanilla ice cream and add to the melon. Put the 'lid' back on and place it in an orange bag tied shut at the top. Drink with straws directly from the melon, and whatever you do, don't pour it into a glass.'

'Why is that?'

'Because it looks absolutely revolting!'

Eventually, they all sat around the table, donned their Christmas hats and started enjoying the food. Melon and ham, smoked turkey and gammon, crispy roast potatoes, vegetables and lots of gravy boats full of the most delicious sauces. For dessert, there was steamed fruit pudding with good, strong brandy butter, red wine jelly and of course plenty of wine and champagne and later, brandy and whisky too.

'And I thought we ate a lot for Christmas in Germany,' Gerd said, after he had collapsed in the shade of a tree. 'Even if I wanted to, I couldn't move. I don't know how I am ever going to ride my bicycle again!'

A SERIOUS SENSE OF HUMOUR

The cow took aim. She came straight at Walter. Everybody - the owner of the cow, André van Heerden; his farm workers; Walter's friend Willem, who had come for the ride; each and every one froze. They all held their breaths. It was clear that there was no way Walter could manage to get out of the cow's path in time. Although she was sick, very sick in fact, she developed a hefty speed over the short distance, and she had some mighty forward pointing horns.

Before, they had tried to get her into the crush, but she wouldn't have any of it. Not one ever to give up, Walter had got hold of a catching pole, put a rope around the one end and had bravely entered the kraal. He'd thought that he could get close enough to put the noose around the cow's horns. His plan didn't seem to have worked out this time.

As soon as the cow got wind of it, she started charging. With no alternative and nowhere to hide, Walter dropped the pole and stood his ground. Just when everybody thought the worst, and the cow was right in front of him, he grabbed her by the horns. He jumped to the side and in one quick movement twisted her head around and pulled. Before she knew what was happening, the cow was lying on her side and Walter was half sitting, half lying on top of her head, holding her down.

'Why are you all standing around? Quickly! Come!' he shouted at his dazzled spectators. Everybody started moving again and some of the cattlemen came to hold the beast to the ground. They still couldn't believe what they had just seen.

'Like in the movies!' Willem said, shaking his head, as he passed the vet his stethoscope.

Walter examined the cow that didn't seem to know what had hit her; she didn't flinch. He listened to her heartbeat, her lungs, her stomachs and their movements, and decided his first impression had been right; the cow was suffering from *rumenitis*, or acute indigestion. The farmer had told him that she had broken into his feed room and gorged herself on grains. How much she'd eaten, he didn't know, but the results were evident. The abnormal amount of carbohydrates was fermenting, causing acidosis and indigestion, and the cow now suffered the consequences. She had stopped eating altogether, and seemed depressed as well as dehydrated.

When Walter administered the treatment, a rather painful procedure during which he stuck a tube through her nose and down her gullet, she didn't bat an eyelid. He dosed her up with vinegar and sugar, a traditional remedy he found often worked surprisingly well in such cases.

'Ok, you can let her go now,' he said to his assistants after he had removed himself from the scene of action. The cow got up and slowly trotted back to her mates, disappearing inconspicuously into the herd.

'Walter, my God, how did you do that? I thought we were going to have to pick up the pieces here,' Willem said.

'*Ag*, you know,' Walter grinned, 'when you grab the horns like that, you actually have got quite a bit of leverage.'

'Have you done this before? I mean, it looked like you were completely cold-blooded and used to doing it just about every day!'

'I didn't really have a choice, did I? But no, I've never tried that one before. I've seen it in the movies though, the cowboys do it all the time!' he laughed. 'And it's quite amazing what you can do if there is a bit of adrenalin involved!'

Willem, who always insisted on wearing very short, blue rugby shorts, no matter if it was summer or winter, was a great friend of Walter and Topsy's. He ran the garage in town and over the years had attended to more than one of Walter's vehicles, which often suffered a rather unglamorous end. Walter enjoyed Willem's company and an extra pair of hands always came in useful, so when, not long after Walter had wrestled the irate cow, he was called out to catch a couple of elephants, he asked his friend if he wanted to come along.

The two young pachyderms, who only recently had been relocated to a game farm in the Waterberg, had broken out of their boma and escaped into the surrounding hills. Walter wasn't quite sure how they had managed it, but he knew that he wanted to find them before they did any damage to themselves. Quickly, he got a good team together. He'd do the darting, Reuben was responsible for the helicopter work and Heinz Hauser, who was not only the owner of the game farm but also of a trucking business in Johannesburg, provided the flatbed trucks complete with cranes.

After a lot of searching, they eventually found the two escapees, darted them without any trouble and then loaded the elephant bull onto one of the trucks and sent it off. The young cow, she stood about three metres tall, was heaved onto the other flatbed, when Walter realised that they were short of a few metres of rope. They tied her down as best they could, and Willem jumped onto the truck with her. He sat with his feet against the side and his back under the elephant's gullet, trying to keep her from sliding back, while Walter brought up the rear in his bakkie.

He saw the grin on Willem's face and it was obvious quite how much his friend was enjoying this outing. He would have some stories to tell, because who else gets to travel on a truck with an elephant?

They had to negotiate about ten kilometres of a rough dirt road back to the boma, and the driver of the second truck was very cautious. He was perhaps a little slow for Walter's taste.

About two thirds along the way, Walter became aware that Willem's expression suddenly changed. His eyes widened, his mouth opened and then he shouted, '*Walter, Walter, die ding word wakker*! - She is waking up!' There was more than a little panic in his voice. The truck just carried on slowly, the driver completely oblivious to what was happening behind him.

From Walter's vantage point, things looked quite safe, so he leaned out of his bakkie's window and shouted back, 'Hold on Willem, it's not far now, hold tight!' hoping this would do. He didn't want to inject the cow with another dose of M99 unless it was really an emergency. To his delight and Willem's dismay, he then watched how the elephant began exploring. She didn't move anything but her trunk, but with that she began feeling Willem from top to toe. Walter couldn't believe his eyes and at that moment he really felt for his friend, because now she ventured with her trunk up Willem's leg and inside his short blue shorts.

'*Walterrrrr, sy word wakkerrrrrrr*! – she is waking up!'

Once the elephants were safely back inside their boma and the operation wrapped up, Willem recovered quickly. He was beaming.

'Thanks, Walter, this was great!' he said, 'now I have a story to tell my grandchildren, because who can say that they've been caressed by an amorous elephant?'

Walter nodded before he replied, pensively, *Ja*, you know, there is a God in heaven – and he has got a serious sense of humour!'

HOW I GOT MY MICROSCOPE

I often thought that somebody, somewhere out there, must have a serious sense of humour; it's quite obvious. Shortly after the incident with the amorous elephant, a cattle farmer near Naboom called me. I can't remember his name, call him whatever you like. This story is quite similar to the one with *'Goue Bad'* du Plessis's Afrikaner bull. This time though, the farmer wasn't an Afrikaner, he was an Engelsman. Maybe his name was Douglas Netherdale; ja, that fits. Anyway, Douglas had a herd of Brahman cattle and when he called me, he had sold part of that herd and had to move it to another farm, some hundred kilometres away.

Brahmans are much better adapted to our climatic conditions than most European breeds. The cows are famous for being extremely good mothers and the bulls' behaviour can range from being very gentle and tame, to quite vicious or outright dangerous. I've had my fair share of experiences with their kind, as you know, but in general I always took them for friendly fellows. One just had to accept that dealing with a two thousand pound animal could have its consequences.

'Tell me, Doc, can you tranquilise a bull?' Douglas asked me.

'Of course I can tranquilise a bull.' Stupid question, I thought.

'Yes, but can you do it with your dart gun?' he asked.

'I can do that too,' I replied. Now I understood. There weren't that many vets around in those days who knew how to use a dart gun.

'Ok, then can you be at my farm tomorrow morning at five, I need your help loading one of my bulls.'

'I can do that, for sure, but don't you have a loading ramp?' I couldn't help myself asking.

'Yes, of course I have; but this bull thinks he's the boss and we just can't get him near the ramp, let alone onto the truck. We've tried, believe me!'

The next morning, I arrived at Netherdale's farm. The herd was already in the kraal and Douglas greeted me with an energetic, 'Doc, there he is, shoot him!'

'But he looks very calm!'

The bull just stood there peacefully and watched us while chewing the cud. He didn't seem to be in the least perturbed by the impending voyage.

'Yes,' Douglas said, 'he was a show bull, so he is quite tame. But if you try and load him, he just jumps out.'

I thought I knew better, climbed into the kraal and slowly approached this Brahman, which, by the way, was enormous. I didn't even get close. Despite his substantial weight he jumped straight over the fence.

'You bloody fool, I told you to dart him!' Douglas rolled his eyes.

'Sorry.' I felt really stupid, but what else could I say?

The whole procedure had to start all over again. The herd of cattle had to be taken out of the kraal, and after the bull was reunited with his pals, they were all manoeuvred back in.

'Ok, let's try again,' I said and loaded my dart gun. I went to where I could see the bull's backside and shot him.

He snorted once, threw up his head and flew around amazingly quickly for an animal his size. Then he stared at me over the top of his cows. I thought I'd better wait for a couple of minutes for the medication to work, because I didn't want to upset the apple cart a second time. But then the bull, without taking his eyes of me, walked towards the fence. Step by step he came closer, his dewlap slowly swaying from side to side, until he was standing right in front of me.

'Douglas, are you sure he was a show bull?' I asked, looking at the animal.

'Yes. Hundred per cent. I bought him at the Rand Show.'

He still looked me in the face and I looked back at him. I lifted my finger and carefully placed it onto his nose ring. The bull did nothing. Absolutely nothing. He just looked at me as if he was asking 'and now what?'

Without taking my eyes off of him or the finger out of his nose ring, I slowly climbed through the fence. I led the big Brahman with one finger up the ramp and onto the truck, and there I held him while they loaded the cows. In the meantime, Douglas pulled the dart out of his backside.

'Now we just have to wait until he lies down,' I said. And we waited, and waited, but after half an hour he still stood there.

'Where is the dart?' I asked. Something was not quite right.

When Douglas handed it to me, I put a long needle into it, aspirated, and out came all the medicine that I had put in. The dart had sat all right, for sure, but it clearly hadn't discharged its content. The bull didn't have a drop of *muthi* in his bloodstream.

Douglas Netherdale was so impressed that I had taken his wild bull just by the nose ring up the ramp and into the lorry, that he gave me a Zeiss microscope as a present. It's in the surgery now.

So that's how I got my microscope – and was reminded once more, that somebody out there must have a serious sense of humour.

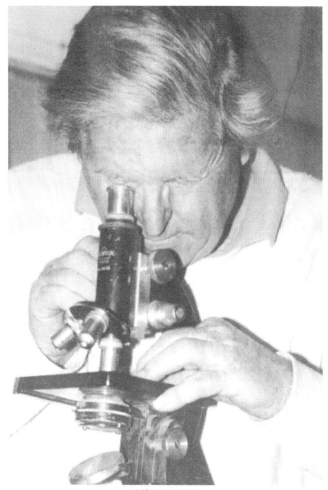

Microscope

WILD MEN AND WILDER BEASTS

Over the years, Walter might have become known as a somewhat unorthodox vet, but he was by no means the only unusual character who roamed the foothills of the Waterberg. For a long time Walter had heard rumours about Frikkie van der Merwe, and he was delighted when he eventually got to meet the man, who was regarded as a real legend in farmers' circles.

Frikkie van der Merwe was famous for two very different reasons. Firstly, everybody knew, Frikkie never, ever wore shoes. He just didn't do shoes. He even went to church without shoes. And secondly, he was known as the man who had killed a leopard with his bare hands.

The *tier*, as a leopard is called in Afrikaans, had been killing a lot of young game on the farm where Frikkie worked as the manager. And when, what he presumed was the same animal, began to kill their calves as well, he'd had enough. He set a trap.

One morning, so Walter had heard, Frikkie went to check on the trap, but everything was quiet. Perhaps too quiet, because he could feel the hair on the back of his neck bristling. He looked around, but couldn't see anything. He shrugged. As he turned to go back to the house for his morning coffee, he heard an almighty roar. The leopard was on him - where from, he would never find out.

Frikkie didn't have a chance to shoot, it happened all too quickly, but fortunately he always wore a strong leather belt, which saved him from being gutted straight away. While the leopard got his hind feet into the belt, Frikkie, fighting for his life, managed to close his hands around the animal's throat. He hung on with all his might. Slowly he felt the beast's energy wane. After what seemed an eternity, the leopard's body slackened completely.

Frikkie was very lucky that day, some people said afterwards, because he survived. He had lots of bad luck that day, others said, because he had to spend a month in hospital.

Walter actually thought that anybody who saw a leopard was lucky. Shy and elusive as they were, he believed they were the most beautiful and elegant predators. Their numbers had been decimated dramatically, and their reputation with the farmers was a lot worse than the actual damage they did.

Be that as it may, after he'd killed the leopard, Frikkie felt a real hero.

The leopard was not the only animal on the farm that gave headaches to Frikkie's employer, Jacques Burger. The other one was Bruno, who was a very nasty buffalo bull, at least according to Jacques.

'He is no good for man or beast,' Jacques would say in English – he normally conversed in Afrikaans – whenever Bruno had been up to mischief again.

Bruno was strong and powerful and had a large, wide boss. Hand-raised and relatively tame, Jacques had thought he could keep him as a mascot on the farm. Bruno didn't seem to agree. When he was in a kraal, he'd allow his head to be scratched and he acted very friendly, but if anybody was foolish enough to go into the enclosure, he would create havoc and try to kill the intruder. The biggest problem, however, was that Bruno regularly got bored, managed to break out of the kraal and then set about killing all Jacques' domestic bulls.

Eventually Jacques had had enough and decided to sell Bruno. With a buyer lined up, he called Walter. They managed to dart the buffalo, but couldn't get him loaded or even into the kraal. Despite having a good dose of medication in his system, Bruno wasn't cooperative. Never shy of making a plan, Frikkie van der Merwe stepped into action and tied the buffalo up behind the bakkie and tried to drag him along. But Bruno clearly didn't think this was a good idea. He refused to move. Frikkie, reaching the end of his tether, jumped out of the vehicle and tried to chase the buffalo on from behind. But still, Bruno wouldn't budge. Then Frikkie had another idea.

'This'll make him move!' he shouted to Walter and Jacques, before he jumped onto Bruno's back.

With a loud snort, the animal woke out of his stupor, jerked his head back and broke the rope that tied him to the back of the Land Cruiser. He started moving, and Frikkie found himself sitting on a bucking buffalo.

Jacques and Walter, dumbfounded, just stood and watched. They saw the pair charging off, and Frikkie's hat went flying. Bruno was heading for a big wild fig tree with some thick, low hanging branches. As the buffalo passed under the tree, Frikkie grabbed hold of one of the branches and pulled himself up, while the buffalo galloped on. Everybody was relieved, but only briefly. Wanting to get back to the safety of the Land Cruiser, Frikkie was just about to let himself down to the ground, when the buffalo stopped, turned and charged at full speed, coming straight for the tree and Frikkie, who didn't have a choice but to hoist himself up again.

Walter couldn't suppress a grin as he watched them play this game for a while, long enough for Jacques to go back to the farmhouse to get some more M99.

'Just give him that stuff,' he said to Walter. 'If it kills him, well, too bad.'

The second dose of the immobilizing drug did the trick, and 'Good riddance,' was all Jacques had to say, again in English, once Bruno left the farm on the back of the truck.

For Walter, the story was not over yet. Six months later, when he had all but forgotten about Bruno, he received a call from Marble Hall.

'Hello, is that Doc Eschenbach?'

'Yes, this is Doc Eschenburg.'

'Can you dart a buffalo? He is in a kraal. He does untold damage. We've sold him to the research station where they want to do semen experiments with him. Whatever, I don't really care. Just come and dart him so that we can take him away,' the man pleaded.

Walter wondered; this sounded only too familiar. When he arrived on the farm his suspicions were confirmed. The buffalo in question was no other than Bruno, and Walter was greeted by the most peculiar sight. Inside a sturdy kraal stood a tractor and what looked like a brand new car, both in a sorry state – and there was Bruno, lying down chewing the cud.

A gaunt and hollow cheeked man approached Walter.

'Doc, please, either you dart this thing now and we load him up and take him away, or I shoot him. Right here and now,' the exasperated owner of the farm, Mr Pretorius, said. 'Just look at this!' Nearly in tears, he pointed at his vehicles.

All of a sudden, as if aware that he now had spectators, Bruno jumped up and pummelled the tractor. Then he lay down again, chewing the cud. A few minutes later, he jumped up, and this time he battered the car before lying down again, as if this behaviour was the most normal thing for a buffalo to do.

Walter darted Bruno. He was loaded, this time without any complications, and Mr Pretorius took great pleasure in taking the buffalo away himself. Walter stayed behind with a clearly relieved farm manager.

'Good riddance!' he shouted, as if echoing Jacques, before inviting Walter into the farmhouse to tell him Bruno's story.

Mr Pretorius had bought the farm only recently and designed the house himself. It was quite an extravagant building with a large, thatched roof. At the corners the grass hung down right to the ground.

Walter was taken through a large glass sliding door into the lounge. It took him a moment, but once his eyes got used to the dim light, he had to suppress a gasp. From across the room a huge elephant's head stared at him, tusks and all. It was framed on either side by the stuffed heads of kudu, gemsbok, nyala, waterbuck and possibly every other animal that could be shot in this part of the world. In front of the fireplace stood a fully grown crocodile and the doorway to the kitchen was flanked on one side by what must have once been a majestic lion, and by a leopard on the other.

There were no pictures. Instead, the remaining space on the walls was covered by karosses, blankets sewed together from the skins of civets and other little creatures. Adding to the peculiar atmosphere, all the furniture was made from dark, polished railway sleepers, and Walter was relieved when he was asked to come through to the kitchen, where the manager launched into his account.

Just like at Jacques's farm, Bruno had suffered from boredom. He'd also realised that he enjoyed human company and had started hanging around relatively close to the house. They had tried to herd him into the kraal, but he refused to go and if Bruno didn't want to go, he just wouldn't go.

He seemed to have taken a liking to Mr Pretorius's new car, so they thought, 'If we can't put the buffalo into the kraal, maybe we should put the car and the tractor out of harm's way; and what better place to put them than into the kraal, the only place where Bruno didn't want to go.' Said and done.

A strong palisade fence surrounded house and garden, separating it from the rest of the farm. Probably to relieve his boredom, Bruno soon busied himself with the fence, ripped out some stakes and continued, until he had created a hole big enough for him to walk through.

He discovered the house; the thatch that came down from the roof looked edible, so he chewed it a bit, but had to spit it out. Obviously, it wasn't really for eating, and that made him cross. Bruno started horning it, until he had broken up most of the hanging thatch. Now he had free access to the stoep. When he suddenly saw another buffalo, he decided to attack. He went for his reflection and charged straight through the plate glass windows. Confused as to where this other buffalo had disappeared to, he must have stared for a moment at the elephant's head, the crocodile and all the other stuffed animals. Not enjoying what he saw, he turned on his heel and went rushing off.

He went back through the window, back through his hole in the fence and straight into the kraal, where he lay down to chew the cud as if nothing had happened. Quickly, they'd closed the gate and Bruno was quiet, as long as nobody attempted to come too close.

Everybody was relieved; it all seemed under control now. Except for the car and the tractor in the kraal. Although Bruno sat there peacefully, it was obvious that no one would be able to remove the two vehicles. And if anybody came near, he'd jump up and give the car and the tractor a serious hiding.

Walter just shook his head; this was the weirdest buffalo story he had ever heard, and he had heard a few over the years. Why Mr Pretorius hadn't just shot the buffalo himself would always remain a mystery to him.

Unfortunately for Bruno, his story didn't end at the research station. He was soon found to be sterile, and the last Walter heard, with some regret, he had to admit, because he had come to regard Bruno as a real character, was that he had been sold to a hunting outfit and had ended up as some brave 'Big White Hunter's' trophy.

TACKLING TALL HORSES

Walter and Reuben Joubert had been out capturing giraffe. Everything had gone well; the helicopter had herded the small group into the mobile boma, and Walter had tranquilised the animals, which were then transported to their new owner's farm. There they would be kept in a holding camp for a few days to allow them to acclimatise to their new surroundings and to make sure they didn't suffer any delayed side-effects from the drugs.

From the helicopter, Reuben and Walter had noticed that a young male giraffe, which was not part of the herd to be moved, had a wire snare around one of his back legs. There had been no time to attend to this giraffe bull, but Walter had decided to come back the next day to dart him, and to remove the snare before it could lead to infections and ultimately death of the animal.

This time it was Bernhard de Sand, the perfect country gentleman, who came along for the ride and, if necessary, to lend a hand. Paraffin and Flying Machine were also part of the team, travelling on the back of Walter's little green Nissan 1200 bakkie. Bernhard was by profession a lawyer, who had changed his robes for shorts, long socks and veldskoens. He had decided to follow his dream, had taken over the family farm Sleutelfontein and become a cattle farmer. The De Sands had met the Eschenburgs when Johnny and Tokkie went to the same boarding school as Debbie, and Walter enjoyed the company of his erudite friend. Bernhard on the other hand was a great admirer of Walter's skills as a vet.

It was the first time Bernhard had joined Walter capturing giraffe and he wanted to know how it all worked. Patiently, Walter explained the procedure.

'It's not rocket science, but there are a few things you have to watch out for. First of all you need to prepare the dart beforehand, because these animals don't tend to hang around, especially if they sense you are up to something. Secondly, it is important to dart the animal accurately so that the muthi is injected into the muscle. Hindquarters or shoulders will do.'

'And how do you know it is working?' Bernhard asked.

'Soon after the animal has been darted, its gait should become ataxic, uncoordinated. It starts to high-step, lifting its 'knees', like a Lipizzaner during high dressage; showing a lot of action but not actually moving forward. At the same time, it will throw back its head, pointing its nose to the sky,' Walter explained.

'Two people then need to take advantage of this near immobility to take a rope across the front of the giraffe, as high as possible. They should try to get it around its neck, and then cross it over behind. When the giraffe goes down, they should have control of its head.'

'I see, so it doesn't come crashing down?'

'That's right. After all, we don't want the giraffe to hurt itself during that procedure. Then a blindfold needs to be put over its head.'

'How do you restrain it, so it doesn't suddenly get up again? I believe they can kick quite hard, too?' Bernhard asked.

'Giraffe are really peculiar animals,' Walter continued. 'Of all land mammals, they have the biggest heart, the longest neck, the longest tail and the longest legs. And they will use those for self-defence. A good kick from an adult giraffe can break any human's skull. But their long neck, once they are on the ground, becomes their Achilles heel. If you hold it firmly to the ground, and the emphasis here is on firmly, then it is utterly impossible for it to get up, even if no other part of the body is restrained.'

They found the giraffe bull; the dart was lodged where it was meant to be, and the animal showed all the symptoms in textbook fashion. They secured a rope around his neck and he was about to come down on a relatively clear piece of bush, with hardly any rocks or trees in the way that could cause injury. But then he made a last effort to move forward, and when Walter reacted by stepping to the side to get a better grip on the rope, he put his left foot straight into an ant hole. He heard a terrible sound and immediately felt an intense pain soaring up his leg.

At the same time Bernhard de Sand, Paraffin and Flying Machine were surprised by the sudden flurry of swearing that came from the other side of the giraffe. Although they were not proficient in German, they well understood that Walter had reverted to his mother tongue to express his utter annoyance and agony.

'*Scheibenkleister, Mann.*'

'What's it, Walter? You ok?'

'*Ag*, nothing,' he said, pulling himself together. 'It's only my Achilles tendon. I think it just went. But let's carry on, we haven't got much time.'

The giraffe went down and the blindfold had to be put in place. He had folded his legs neatly underneath his body and put his head down, but as soon as the men approached, he tried to get up again.

'Bernhard, quickly, sit on his neck and hold the head down, he mustn't hurt himself!' Walter called. He realized he had slightly under-dosed the animal, but it should be fine, as long as he couldn't lift his head.

'No problem.' Or so Bernhard thought. The giraffe thought differently and nearly shook him off.

'Man, Bernhard,' Walter shouted, 'don't be so cautious, just sit on the bloody things head!'

'Ok, ok.' Bernhard now sat down squarely on the giraffe's head.

But Walter saw out of the corner of his eye that the giraffe was again attempting to stand up.

'No man! Jirre, Bernhard, can't you just hold this stupid bloody head down for five seconds?' Walter was about to lose his cool, and the aching ankle that hindered his movements dramatically didn't help. He turned around and saw Bernhard, himself not a small man, perched on the giraffe's head. He was levitating a good meter and a half above the ground, his long and thin legs, clad in khaki bushveld socks, dangling uselessly in the air. Clearly he was wondering how to get out of this somewhat undignified situation.

Walter realised he had to do something. He shouted, 'Paraffin! Flying Machine! Come and help!' before he took aim and charged. Despite his damaged ankle, he threw himself onto the giraffe's neck. Not a moment too soon. Paraffin and Flying Machine arrived a fraction of a second later, and with combined efforts and body weights they succeeded in keeping the animal's head firmly pressed to the ground.

Bernhard, relieved to have both feet on the ground again and perhaps a little contrite, shook his head and said, 'Walter, I'm impressed! This tackle would have put any *Springbok* rugby player to shame!'

'What do you know?' Walter mumbled, cursing his ankle, which now hurt even more. 'It's because I played rugby that I passed my first year physics exam at Onderstepoort. If it wasn't for rugby, I might not even be here today!'

He got the wire cutters and removed the snare from the giraffe's foot. It had cut deep into the skin and the first signs of an infection were showing. After injecting a long lasting anti-inflammatory and antibiotic, he administered the antidote and the men stepped back. While Paraffin and Flying Machine collected the ropes and other pieces of equipment, Walter and Bernhard observed the giraffe. It didn't take long and the animal stretched its long legs, got up, looked around for a moment and then loped off into the bush.

Walter's ankle did not improve over the next few days, and after much nagging from Topsy, he decided to pay his old friend Dr Kroon a visit.

'*Ja*, Doc, you see, giraffes are dangerous animals!' he laughed.

'Na Walli, it's just a bruise, we'll put it into plaster for a couple of weeks and then it'll be fine, you'll see.'

Yet a few weeks later, there was no sign of improvement.

'Oh dear,' Walter said, 'it's still flopping around like it doesn't belong to me.'

'Mr Eschenburg? It looks like both tendons are torn,' the specialist at the Sandton Clinic, where Dr Kroon had sent Walter, remarked. 'You should have come earlier. But anyway, we don't have a choice. We need to operate and stitch them back together. How did you manage to do this anyway?'

'I was running through the veld after a giraffe and I stepped into a hole.'

The doctor laughed politely. 'No, I actually need to know what really happened.'

'*Ja*, well, giraffes are dangerous animals, Walter grinned. 'How long, Doc, before I can use this blerry foot again?'

'At least three months.' The doctor shook his head. He'd had stubborn patients before.

Three months! But there was no other option. However, it would take more than a foot in plaster to stop Walter from tending to his business - and more giraffes. Within a few weeks he had become used to his plaster cast; it had taken him a day to learn how to drive with it and it didn't really hinder him when doing his rounds. The once white plaster of Paris had taken on a rather unidentifiable hue by the time Walter's friend Leon phoned up.

'Can you catch a giraffe for me?' Leon asked without much further ado.

'Well, not really. Not in my present condition,' Walter replied with some regret in his voice; he had started to miss the thrill of the wildlife practice. But looking at his foot, still in plaster from knee to toe, he shook his head.

Having retired to the Waterberg recently, Leon and his wife Juliana had bought a large farm to the east of Vaalwater. It wasn't good cattle land and too rocky to grow anything, but it would be ideal for the game farm they had planned. 'We don't want tourism, we don't even want hunting,' they had explained to Walter. 'In fact, we hate hunting. We just want a piece of land where animals can roam freely. We have dreamed of that all our lives and have decided now is the time, before we get too old to really enjoy it.'

They had erected a game fence along the perimeter of their property and taken down all the internal fences of the former cattle camps. Slowly they began introducing game, and now Leon had acquired a young giraffe. He couldn't wait to see it roaming the hills of his own farm.

'Come on,' Leon said. 'It's just a little one.' He knew how to bait his friend.

'Oh well, if it is only a little one, then I'll come and have a look anyway.' Walter was hooked. 'I have a blowgun and if we get close enough, I'll blow a dart into it.'

'Yes, yes, we'll get close enough for that; the little bugger is in a stable.'

What Walter found when he arrived at Leon's 'stable', was a very angry little giraffe. It stood about eight foot tall in a small enclosure at the end of a narrow and otherwise empty shed that was so low, that even this little giraffe had to duck his head down. He was clearly upset and kicked at the wall as soon as anybody came close.

'Seems to me he's a little cross? We'd better dart him quickly!' Walter observed. He fixed up a blow dart, aimed at the animal's upper hindquarters and blew, smack into the middle. That was clearly too much for the little fellow. With a loud snort he took off, lashed out and crashed out of his pen. Head low, he charged through the shed, galloping up and down the full length of it, his head ducking rhythmically under each of the roof beams. Then he took aim at the door, an opening secured only by two poles. Sending pieces of wood flying, he escaped into the kraal, a strong, wooden structure. But he still hadn't found freedom. Getting more and more agitated, he galloped around the perimeter.

Walter, substantially slowed by his plaster cast, hobbled along trying to catch up with the angry animal. Just as he reached the kraal, the little giraffe threw himself against the two thick cables used to close off the entrance. They didn't give way but stretched a fraction and then threw him back like a bungee cord. With a confused look, he landed on his side, right in front of Walter's feet.

'Ha, now I've got you!' he called out triumphantly, jumped onto the animal's neck and pushed the head down. There was no resistance anymore. 'It's funny,' Walter thought, 'just as if somebody's let the air out.'

In no time, Leon and his staff managed to blindfold and truss up the little giraffe like a chicken, with all four feet securely tucked in. They decided that the quickest and easiest way to move him would be on the back of Walter's vehicle. This turned many a surprised head as they drove down the road; Walter and Leon were squashed into the front, and the giraffe sat on the back of the Nissan 1200, his head resting on the cabin. Eight of Leon's team in turn sat on top of the giraffe to hold him down, just in case.

Not once did the little giraffe move during the journey, and as soon as they arrived, Leon and his assistants carefully carried him off the back of the bakkie. They had no trouble untying all the ropes and taking the blindfold off, while Walter got the antidote ready. But before he could get close enough to inject it, the giraffe lifted his head, looked around, jumped up and loped away.

'And now what? Just up and gone? How does that work?' Walter wondered aloud. Now it was his turn to look confused.

'Walter,' said Leon, 'I think you should have a look at this.'

When he saw the dart in Leon's hand, he just shook his head. 'It's still full of muthi!' he realized, just like when he'd darted the Brahman bull some years previously. 'I can't believe we loaded this little fellow onto the back of the bakkie and drove all the way here without any medication. That is absolutely unbelievable!'

The little giraffe became one of Leon and Juliana's favourites on their game farm. Wild as he was, he wouldn't let anybody near him, but often they saw him wandering past their house.

'Sometimes I wonder…,' Leon commented to Walter some time later. 'You know, we think we watch him, but …'

'*Ja*,' Walter laughed, 'you are wondering who is actually watching who?'

LUCKY

I was on my way back from doing some pregnancy diagnostics at a farm near Alma. It's a lovely area of the most beautiful sour bushveld with a huge variety of trees and shrubs. I passed some beautiful wild fig trees; there were large terminalias as well as bush willows, albizias, wild seringas and, of course, the ubiquitous mopane trees. Apparently, in some of the more remote ravines, there were even some magnificent yellowwoods. I would have to check it out one day.

It was quite late in the afternoon and the dry grass appeared golden. It was hot and I was dawdling along, not really concentrating on the road, which was more of a jeep track with a high *middelmannetjie*. I was halfway between the farmhouse and the main road and, as this was a large farm, a long way from either, when a kudu cow and her calf caught my attention. Although lacking the impressive horns of the males, they were very handsome animals. Watching them while they were browsing in the afternoon light, their coat glowing, it struck me again how lucky we were to live in this beautiful part of the world.

But then a sudden grinding sound took me back to reality and my bakkie came to a slow stop. I was in the Nissan 1200, of giraffe transporting fame. It didn't have a lot of ground clearance and I had reached a stretch of road where the middelmannetjie was particularly high; the grass growing on the middle ridge was nearly as tall as I. Perched on the ridge, the chassis was grounded solidly, and three of the four wheels were hanging in the air, unable to find traction.

'And now?' I wondered. I didn't really feel like walking back to the farm, and old Hannes Lamprecht, the farmer, was not likely to go out again so late in the afternoon. I tried to get the bakkie to move, but the wheels were just too far off the ground.

I pushed the old girl, but she just wouldn't budge. Then I started to rock her. Throwing all my weight onto the back I realised I could get the wheels to touch the ground. Again, I looked around if there wasn't perhaps somebody coming, but no, no such luck. Even the kudu had left. The sun was dipping closer and closer to the horizon, and I knew that Topsy was waiting at home.

Suddenly I had an idea. I set out to find a nice, brick-sized rock and put it onto the accelerator, pushing it about half way down. Then I wedged a stick between the steering wheel and the seat so that the wheels were slightly turned to the left. I started the engine and put the bakkie into gear. The wheels were spinning beautifully, spraying sand where they just about touched the road surface.

'Who needs help when there are rocks and sticks around,' I laughed. It took a lot of pushing and rocking and shoving, but I slowly, slowly got the old girl to move. Not enough though, because as soon as I stopped, she stopped. Then I gave her one more push and all of a sudden the wheels gripped and she started running off the middelmannetjie, heading slightly to the left off the road.

Wiping the sweat of my brow, I had to admit that when I'd made this clever plan, I hadn't thought further than to this point.

'Hey, wait for me!' I shouted as she ran away, but she didn't listen and cruised off into the bush, just a touch too fast for me to catch up with her. I did try though, not wanting to let her get away, and as so often in life, fortune smiled on me.

About half a kilometre further on, she drove straight into some thick, soft bushes, which slowed her down sufficiently for me to catch up and jump in. I reversed back onto the road and still made it home in time for supper.

THE PUDHI

It was at the time of the Nylvalley Horse Trials and Walter was utterly relieved that he'd finally got rid of the plaster cast. He had removed it himself a couple of weeks before it was due to come off, to much criticism from Topsy and old Dr Kroon, but it had just become too much of a nuisance. So far so good, the tendons seemed to have healed without further complications.

Just as well, he thought, because they had a very busy weekend ahead of them. Horsy people would come from far and wide for the show, which, as some of them said, was their highlight of the eventing season, a fact that made Walter beam from ear to ear.

He had been out all morning building the cross country course with his friend Johnny Perreira. They had become rather inventive thinking up new fences and with the help of Paraffin and Flying Machine they constructed different ones every year. They had a so-called 'Elephant Trap', 'W'- and 'Z'-fences and of course lots of water jumps. They made the competitors canter for hundreds of meters through the Nylsvlei; the going was good, soft and sandy, and the few rocks were painted bright white so that riders who didn't know the terrain wouldn't gallop onto them by mistake. The event lasted from Thursday evening to Monday morning and Walter was looking looked forward to it. It was party time.

'You better go to Twee Rivieren,' Topsy said as he arrived at Boekenhout in time for lunch. 'It seems one of their cows has got rabies. They say she's foaming from the mouth.'

Walter decided to pay them a visit straight away. Lunch could wait. A case of rabies would indeed be serious and there was no time to waste. When he arrived at the farm and saw the animal, which had

220

been herded away from the other cattle, he stopped for a moment to take in the sight. The cow was salivating heavily and her eyes had a wild, panicky look in them.

'She hasn't touched food or water in at least a day,' Hennie Terreblanche, the young farmer, volunteered. 'Please tell me it's not rabies.'

'Let me just have a closer look.' Walter approached the distressed animal slowly, carefully observing it with his head inclined to one side. Then he nodded. 'Let's take her into the crush, and then get two of your guys to hold her,' he instructed. 'One must grab the horns and the other hold on to the nose.'

He began carefully examining her, paying particular attention to her head. He ended the process by sticking his hand into the cow's mouth. A smile crossed his face.

'Just what I thought. You must give your cows more mineral licks.'

'I didn't know mineral licks had anything to do with rabies,' Hennie mumbled as he watched the vet, whose hand was still doing something inside the cow's mouth.

'Come and feel this.' Walter guided the young man's hand. 'Can you feel the tongue? And the teeth? Good. Now go a little further.'

'My *donner*! What is that?' Hennie's eyes widened.

'Wait, I show you.' With a quick manoeuvre Walter pulled a little skull out of the cow's mouth. 'You see, this is a duiker skull, what the locals here call a *pudhi*. It was stuck right in the back of the cow's throat. She obviously chewed and then tried to swallow it mouth-end first. But that didn't work, because the skull is too big. The horns are pointing backwards, so when she tried to spit it out, they got hooked in her nasal cavities and then the skull couldn't move forwards or backwards.

'To get it out,' Walter continued, 'you first have to push it in a little further, to free the horns, before you can pull it out very, very gently.'

Hennie still didn't quite understand, yet his two farm workers exchanged knowing looks. They had seen the pudhi before; according to local, traditional belief the skull was attributed with magical powers.

'But Doc, why does this cow have a duiker skull in her mouth in the first place? Cows don't eat duikers, as far as I know?'

'Well, I told you, you must give them more lick. This cow's got *pica*. You know what pica is, don't you?'

Hennie nodded hesitantly, he wasn't really sure. But unbeknown to him, he had hit on one of Walter's favourite subjects.

'Pica', he explained, 'is an eating disorder caused by nutrient deficiency and often leads to osteophagia. This means the animals chew bones in an attempt to ingest the missing minerals. That's why your cow has tried to eat the duiker skull, and that's why you need to get more mineral licks. Normally you wouldn't notice because they just swallow the smaller bones. But if they eat skulls, they'll invariably get stuck in their throats.'

Walter quite enjoyed lecturing these days, and in Hennie he had found a very attentive listener. 'Most animals chew bones, some more so than others. Pica affects livestock as well as game, and in the last couple of years I have seen a few giraffes die for exactly this reason.'

Walter turned his attention back to the cow. 'You can let her go now. I've given her some shots so she doesn't get an infection in her mouth, where the skull might have damaged the mucous membrane. And I've also given her a vitamin and mineral supplement. But you really should sort out your cattle licks.'

Hennie was relieved. Had it been rabies it would have been much worse. 'Thanks Doc,' he said, 'I'll do that straight away. But tell me, how did you know?'

'Let me tell you a story, Hennie,' Walter said, leaning against the tailgate of his bakkie. 'Some time ago, Paraffin showed me a kudu carcass on the farm and asked if I knew who had killed the kudu. He obviously did know and expected me not to. 'I am sure it was the pudhi,' I guessed. Paraffin's face fell, and I knew I was right. And lo and behold, when he showed me the kudu - well, what was left of it, because most of it had been eaten by the jackals - I opened its mouth and there was the duiker skull stuck in its throat.'

Walter had to smile at Hennie. This was clearly all new to the young man and he still had a lot to learn. He seemed to be interested to do so, Walter acknowledged, because he invited him into the kitchen for a cup of coffee. They continued their conversation, which for Hennie took some unexpected turns.

'Now, Hennie, you have seen how a duiker can kill a kudu, and nearly your cow, but can you imagine a zebra killing a giraffe?' Walter asked and chuckled quietly, when he saw the disbelief on Hennie's face. 'I've seen it with my own eyes!'

'But how did the zebra do that?'

'The zebra died first.'

Hennie tried not to show his confusion.

'The giraffe picked up the zebra's skull and chewed it, just like your cow. But somehow she got her lower jaw through the zygomatic arch, the cheek bone, and ended up with her teeth hooked into the back of the zebra's eye socket. So this poor giraffe had a whole zebra skull hanging from her lower jaw, which of course meant she couldn't eat anything.

'A ranger saw it and called me. We went out to dart the giraffe, but by the time we found her, the poor thing had already lost a lot of weight. Who knows how long that skull had been stuck to her head, maybe days, if not weeks! As she went down with the medication, she flicked her head one last time and the skull came loose. Problem solved, we thought, but unfortunately, as she lay down, she died. She was just too weak. But you see, it was indeed the zebra who killed the giraffe!'

Walter was on a roll now. He liked Hennie; his heart was in the right place and he really cared for his animals. After a short moment of silence, while Hennie was still digesting what he had just heard, Walter continued, 'You know the *kudubessie*, don't you?'

Hennie nodded hesitantly.

'It's this beautiful bush we get here, with an even more beautiful Latin name, *pseudolachnostylis maprouneifolia*. Sometimes, and only sometimes, it makes a huge profusion of yellow fruit. They only have a little bit of flesh around a hard centre, like a nut. They are very tart, but for some reason, kudu and giraffe just love them.

'One day, a couple of years back, I was called to do a post mortem on a giraffe. He was quite thin and had been sick for two days before he disappeared into the bush. They only found him again when he was dead. I had a bit of a hunch so I went straight to the digestive tract, and my suspicions were confirmed. Inside were only nutshells; from one end to the other, nutshells. So that giraffe actually had died of nuts.'

'Now I really need to go,' Walter got up, 'but have I told you the story of the *leguan* that killed the cow?'

Hennie only shook his head. This was all getting a bit too much.

223

'Well, that'll have to wait till next time,' Walter grinned as he started his bakkie.

On the road home he smiled. This had been a call-out to his heart's content; a case of rabies, which had turned out to be 'the pudhi'. The cow would be fine, there was no doubt. And Hennie, well, Hennie still had a lot to learn, but they had made a good start today.

As he approached Boekenhout, his thoughts wandered back to the Nylvalley event. There was still so much to do before the first riders arrived with their horses. Granted, it added a lot of work to their already busy days, but it was definitely worth it; they had so much fun! Topsy loved it too, he knew. A cross-country judge herself, she put her heart and soul into this event and she was the one who actually made it work.

Walter and Topsy ran the Nylvalley event as planned, and it was a great success, just as it had been every year. But on the evening after the show, they were surprised by some of their friends. All hot shots of the South African horse riding world, they wanted to show their appreciation for all the effort the Eschenburgs put into the show, and they decided to take them out for dinner. When they realised that every single shop and restaurant was closed on a Sunday in this neck of the woods, they came up with a different plan. They made arrangements with the local Greek café owner, who offered to cook for them; they turned his shop into a dining room by fashioning chairs and tables from boxes, and rearranging his shelving units and freezers. Walter and Topsy were delighted. They danced until well after midnight and the party was spoken about in the small town of Naboomspruit for many years to come.

FOLKLORE

It's a big story, that of the leguan who kills the cow. According to local belief, leguans are very powerful creatures. Also called monitor lizards or iguanas, they like to drink milk directly from the teat, with sometimes fatal consequences for the cow. Because, so folklore has it, if the leguan is disturbed, he'll bite off the teat and the cow will bleed to death.

Topsy always shakes her head at people who believe in these stories. Of course they believe them, and they have at times proved them to me.

I was called out to a chicken farmer in Naboom to do a post mortem on a cow. She was just dead, he'd said, and he didn't know why, because she hadn't been sick at all. When I found the cow, I saw that she had one teat cut off and the whole world around her was full of blood. She had obviously exsanguinated, bled to death. I did a post mortem from one end to the other, and couldn't find anything else that could have caused her death, other than that she had exsanguinated and that one teat was cut off.

An old farm worker had helped me, while a few of his colleagues had been watching. All of a sudden they started chatting amongst each other very excitedly in Northern Sotho.

'And now? What's happening?' I asked.

One of them replied in Afrikaans, '*Nee Doktor, hy is daarso*. He is there.'

'Who is where?'

'The one that killed our cow. He is there,' the man said and pointed up at a tree.

'How the hell do you know?' I asked.

'No, there he is! Look, in that tree.'

And there I saw it. A huge leguan, sitting on a branch directly above the dead cow. Now, what more proof do you want?

Sure, he didn't have the teat stuck in his mouth. That he'd swallowed it I couldn't prove, because when I tried to catch him he ran away. My point being, that there often is a lot more to learn than is initially apparent.

Take the cobras for example, who supposedly steal milk from cows. The cow's udder looks like it wants to explode due to a tremendous inflammation that appears out of nowhere within just an hour or two. This is attributed to the yellow cobra.

It is true that cobras love milk. I don't know why they like milk so much, but they do. When a cobra lives in a certain place and you put out a dish with milk for it, it will soon come and drink it; and a cobra bite will certainly cause a serious mastitis.

You know, normally we so-called clever people, we look at a cow with a huge blown up udder and we say it's a streptococcus-mastitis or a staphylococcus-mastitis. The traditional people tell us that it is the snake that has bitten her in the udder. Can you really say that they are wrong? Except that you usually don't find the bite-marks. But then a cobra's bite doesn't really leave much of a mark and can be easily missed.

Many, many a strange tale is true, and I believe that if a story has been passed down from generation to generation, then there is usually some truth, in it.

Truth, or perhaps rather wisdom. Just because we are too stupid to grasp it, doesn't mean that there is not a lesson to be learned.

LESSONS LEARNED

The older Walter got, the more he enjoyed having students with him, and he agreed with the famous James Herriot in that students were the perfect gate openers. If he got a rand for every gate he had to open and close while doing his rounds, he often thought, he'd be a millionaire.

On the farmlands in South Africa, there were gates literally everywhere and farmers who had cattle grids next to their gates were far and few between – or so it felt. He didn't really mind having to get out of his bakkie to open the odd gate, because it was an opportunity to see interesting things; animals and birds he would have missed otherwise; a family of warthogs foraging in the thicket, their tails raised like little antennae; a couple of blesbuck grazing; a swarm of carmine bee-eaters resting on a telephone line, or a green pigeon hiding amongst the foliage. But still, at times it was rather nice to just sit back and watch somebody else do the work.

Chris, Topsy's nephew, of medium height, blond and bespectacled, was one of the quickest, out and back into the vehicle in a flash. He was also a very talented young student, and he hadn't been long with Walter when a farmer brought a hunting dog into the surgery. He had an ugly, suppurating wound on his head. They anaesthetised the animal and then Walter handed him over to Chris, 'He's all yours!' He knew the young man was ready to do a bit of surgery.

Chris started exploring. As the wound wasn't fresh, it took him a while. Eventually, he looked up. 'Uncle Walter,' he said, 'there is something in there.'

'If it's loose, take it out,' Walter replied.

'It looks like a tooth?' Chris was surprised. 'But from what animal?'

'How many animals do you know that have straight canines and not curved ones?'

Chris had to think for a moment, 'Humans for one…' he hesitated, 'but I don't think a human would get into a fight with a dog and bite him on the head, so it must be baboon's tooth!' He was mightily excited. It was his first 'trophy', and Walter told him to keep the tooth for his collection.

A few days later, Chris was holding on tight and sneaking the odd glance at Walter as he thrashed his bakkie mercilessly along the rugged dirt road. If this were a normal day, they would be going through the last case they had seen, discussing the treatment they had administered and comparing the real life experience to what was currently taught at university, where other and newer methods might be practised. They would debate if any of those would be feasible when a vet was 'off the beaten track'.

However, this was anything but a normal day and the two men were traveling in silence, each engrossed in his own thoughts, in a rather sombre mood. They had been working with a herd of Brahman cattle on a farm near Marble Hall. On this hot, early summer's day, they'd had to get them into a crush to administer their annual vaccinations. But the Brahmans had proved uncooperative. After some time, the team of farm workers had become impatient and begun shouting. They'd grabbed pieces of black water pipe that were lying around next to a tank. Slowly the herd had started moving, then faster and faster. There had been shouting, cattle lowing in anger and dust rising. It had become difficult to see what was going on.

Suddenly Walter's deep voice had resounded over the yard. '*Hou op! Julle maak beeste dood! Hou op! Is julle mal?* – Stop! You are killing the cattle! Stop! Are you mad?'

Nobody would ever know what the real cause of the stampede was, but the results were dramatic. At least ten animals had piled up on top of each other at the entrance to the kraal, and the cow at the bottom was badly crushed.

'Have you ever done CPR on a cow?' Walter, red in the face and sweating, had asked Chris. He had immediately attempted cardiopulmonary resuscitation by jumping on the dead animal's chest.

The crew and Chris had been standing around somewhat sheepishly watching him. After about fifteen minutes, Walter had stopped. The cow hadn't moved. 'There is nothing more we can do,' he'd said, 'and I suggest we leave the vaccinations for another day, when things have calmed down here a bit.'

'You know, what happened happened. No point in crying over spilled milk,' Walter said eventually, breaking the silence, as he turned off onto a farm road. 'I know, it's a *kak* feeling, but there was nothing we could do for that last beast.'

'I know, Uncle Walter, it's just, I don't know,' Chris hesitated, 'it was quite dramatic.'

'It's always horrible when an animal dies while you are busy there. But let's look forward.' To change the subject, he asked if Chris remembered what their next call was about.

'I think it was a uterine prolapse on a cow.'

'Right, now I remember. I've had a few of those recently. And you won't believe what some really clever farmer did the other day. He actually caused the prolapse himself.'

Chris' interest was piqued again, so Walter continued. 'The cow had calved without problems, but then the farmer noticed that the afterbirth wasn't coming out the way it should. He knew that this could cause problems, but instead of calling me or another vet, he thought he could fix it himself. He tied a brick to the bit of afterbirth in the hope that the whole thing would eventually come loose. When he checked again the next morning, the afterbirth had come out all right, but with it the entire uterus. That's when he phoned me, to come and fix it.' Walter shook his head.

By now they had arrived on the farm and the patient, a tired looking Bonsmara cow, was already waiting in the kraal.

'I don't think she is going to give us any trouble,' Walter said.

The cow was standing motionless, almost apathetic, with the prolapsed uterus hanging right down to her hocks.

'But let me do this one. I don't like seeing students struggle.' He stripped down to his waist and put himself in position behind the cow.

Chris shook his head in disbelief when he saw how Walter pushed the uterus back in, using his full and not insubstantial weight perfectly in a rocking motion, until his entire arm disappeared in the cow, right up to his shoulder.

At exactly the right moment, he withdrew and then pushed the rest of the prolapsed organ in, expertly timing his pushing against that of the cow, whose entire body seemed to rock.

'This is crazy,' Chris said to himself. 'He looks like a middle aged golfer hitting a very long drive, the way he gets his whole weight through with perfect timing, getting his belly into the 'shot'.'

The whole procedure had taken less than five minutes. Walter just smiled, as he washed quickly and put his shirt back on. 'Ok, that's that. Let's go.'

A few kilometres down the road, with Chris still flabbergasted by how quickly they had dealt with this last case, Walter asked, 'Did you know that sometimes it is quite useful to have an empty two-litre plastic bottle with you when you are called to a prolapse?'

Chris was astounded.

'Yes, a two-litre bottle that you sew into the vagina,' Walter said enigmatically, adding that in this case, it hadn't been called for, because the prolapse had been reasonably fresh. 'But a cervix that has been out in the sun, sometimes for days, is sunburnt, hard and swollen. After you've pushed it back, you have to keep it in place, because the cow will always try to push it out again. You put the bottle in — obviously not neck first, but the other way round — and then you have to keep the vulva shut so she can't push it out. Your stitches have to be solid.'

In response to Chris' questioning look, Walter admitted that the cow might well be in discomfort for a couple of days, but that to ease the irritation, a little epidural anaesthetic should be given. The insertion of the bottle mainly served the purpose of stretching the tissue inside the vagina, and once the swelling had subsided a relapse would be unlikely, he ended his rather unorthodox explanation.

'And remember, it doesn't help at all to close the vagina with ordinary suture material, because it will cut straight through the tissue. But what you can use is some ordinary four millimetre wire. If you spend a bit more time on the road with me, you'll see that I have to do this quite often,' Walter concluded as if this was the most common piece of veterinary advice to give to a young colleague.

'At Onderstepoort,' Chris said, happy that he could contribute something, 'they use those stainless steel sticks with a screw-on ball on either side.'

'Yes, they are very useful, indeed. The problem is that you don't always have those. But on a farm in South Africa you always find a piece of binding wire. I know it sounds cruel, but it works.

'Once you've been out here for a while, you'll appreciate how much one really has to improvise. In fact, to be able to improvise is one of the most important skills to have if working as a vet in the more remote areas,' Walter looked at Chris to make sure he had his attention, before he continued.

'When you are sometimes hundreds of miles away from sophisticated medical advice, you have to keep your wits around you. Just imagine, you are on a farm in the middle of nowhere, and you have to stitch up a large wound, and after the first stitch your suture needle breaks, or the needle holder stops working; it is virtually impossible to do any kind of serious suturing with your bare hands. So now what? If you are very well-prepared, you might have a spare somewhere. But more often than not, you don't, especially if you are a damned fool like me. It happens, believe me. Then you sit there with your finger in your ear and you wonder what to do. So? Very simple.

'You use a normal syringe needle, ideally one for the large animals, with a bigger diameter. It makes a very neat and easy job. It is far easier to penetrate a thick organ, a muscle or even skin with a syringe needle than it is with a broken suture needle. You don't need that *clicked-click* needle holder or anything. This little trick will help you out of many a tight corner.'

Their next call took them to a farm near Vaalwater. An amorous donkey had tried to 'service' a mare through a barbed wire fence and hurt himself in the process, they'd been told.

Walter and Chris were greeted by a farmer in a bushveld-style cowboy hat, complete with a leopard skin hatband. Scrawny and not particularly tall, he wore very short khaki shorts, a paramilitary style two-tone shirt, veldskoens and gaiters.

'Haven't seen any of those for a long time,' Walter thought, looking at the pieces of leather wrapped around the man's shins, presumably to protect him against snake bite.

'*Hy lyk nie so goed Dok, maar hy kan pis* – he doesn't look so good, Doc, but he can pee,' the farmer informed the two vets.

The donkey looked rather forlorn, and his penis was grossly swollen. It had weeping ulcerations and was hanging down well below his body.

Walter looked at the farmer and then at the donkey. '*Nee, dit is goed dat hy kan pis* – It's good that he can pee,' he replied.

231

Under the trusting eye of the farmer, they put the donkey in the crush and tied a sack around his body; holding up the penis would reduce the painful swelling. They administered the usual anti-inflammatory as well as a broad-spectrum antibiotic and dispensed a few more doses for the following days. Before they left, Walter gave a good prognosis.

Back in the bakkie he explained, 'I think that this poor donkey was actually suffering from a bad case of cellulitis, a common skin infection with streptococcus or staphylococcus bacteria. The whole thing was most probably caused by a tick bite and not a fence.'

Chris was surprised. He was sure that Walter had not explained this to the farmer.

'That guy was so convinced about the cause, that I thought it better to leave it at that. In such situations, I have learned over the years, the imagination plays a huge role, and I didn't want to cause unnecessary confusion.' As in an afterthought, he added, 'Luckily for the donkey as well as all us men, the male organ heals very well!'

DELIGHTS

One of the lessons I try to teach my students is that there will always be mistakes. I know everybody likes to think they are perfect, but if you want to learn and improve, you must accept that you make mistakes. It happens. It is human to make mistakes. It might be devastating or infuriating at times, but it doesn't help to fret. Get on with it and learn your lesson!

Once, many years ago, I set out to spay a cat. It all started well, but then I couldn't find the ovaries. No matter how hard I looked, there was no sign of ovaries or even the uterus. Eventually it dawned on me – and I inspected the cat's backside. Well, then I quickly sewed the stomach closed and de-balled the bugger. I actually sent the owner of said cat a bill, *'One spayed tomcat – No charge. '*

Another time, I got home after having pulled a calf out of a jersey cow, only to be called back by the farmer, who asked me to finish the job. Of course, I immediately returned and pulled a second calf out; twins are not that common in cows, but they occur. Triplets, however, are really rare, but for some reason I double-checked, and believe it or not, there was a third calf. Triplets indeed.

I always thought it was a privilege to be able to teach young, aspiring vets some of the lessons I've learned over the years. When I started out as a youngster myself, I had some great mentors and I will always remember old Dr Wallander and how he'd come to the rescue when I stood behind that cow like the proverbial 'Ox'. That certainly was one of the most valuable lessons I have ever learnt, but I think I'm repeating myself here.

Over the years I've had all sorts of students. There were talented ones, like Chris who went to run his own very successful practice in East London, and then others, like Peter, who danced with the hyena, and who needed a bit of direction. I also had some students with a serious sense of humour and that I always enjoyed.

Alex was a German exchange student at Onderstepoort, but she also wanted to gather some experience in a private practice. One day, I took her along to do some pregnancy testing on a herd of Bonsmara cattle near Naboomspruit. She had some experience doing rectal examinations, so there was no problem with that, but she had never encountered South African ticks before; it seems they don't have them in Germany. The cow she was busy with, was particularly badly infested, the area under her tail completely covered in ticks of all shapes and sizes.

'I need to have a word with the farmer,' I remember thinking.

By now a small group of little boys had gathered. Sons of the farm labourers, they were always around if anything new or exciting happened. Out of the corner of my eye I saw them checking out Alex with great curiosity, when suddenly their eyes widened. Excited chattering in Se-Pedi followed. They sounded like a bunch of weaver birds with a *boomslang* trying to raid their nest.

I turned around to find out what the reason for all this excitement was, and what I saw made me gasp. There was this sophisticated, highly educated student picking walnut-sized ticks from a Bonsmara cow's bum and popping them into her mouth.

Naturally, it only took me a split second to understand that she had put on a show for her little spectators and was just pretending. What she actually did with the parasites I never found out.

RETURN TO JUCHOW

RETURN TO JUCHOW

When I picked up Rainer, the German hitchhiker in the 1960s, I had no way of knowing that this would result in some really unintended consequences. It was the beginning of a wonderful friendship; Rainer and his wife Karin visited us many times, and then, one year, they invited us to Berlin.

When Topsy and I arrived, they announced that they had a surprise for us – a visit to Juchow. I'd had no idea. And I couldn't believe my luck when we set off the next day. Juchow now, of course, is in Poland. What a surprise it was, what a wonderful journey! It brought back so many memories.

More than fifty years had passed since we'd left Germany, and Juchow; an entire lifetime. Lots of things had happened in between; good, bad and indifferent. There were times when I believed that I'd never get back, due to the political situation, the cold war, and Juchow being behind the iron curtain. But that was just the way it was.

And there we were, in November 1996, some years after the winds of change had blown over Eastern Europe, driving towards Juchow, or Juchowo, as it is called now. Our journey took us through the Polish winter landscape, with its endless forests, fields and lakes. The trees had all but lost their leaves and it was icy cold, but there was no snow yet.

The first thing I really recognised was the old railway station at Eulenburg, today's Silnowo, and I remembered the time when Tante Erica had picked us up there after the long train journey from Lübeck, at the beginning of the war. The road from Eulenburg to Juchow had changed. It had a tarmac surface now instead of cobbled stones. In the village itself, memories seemed a little blurred until we got to the castle.

That, of course, looked very familiar, and so did the old distillery and the farmyard. We had spent a lot of time there, in the big stables and barns; the same farmyard where old Herr Bohm had been killed by the bull. The buildings were all still there, if dilapidated. The lake was as beautiful as ever, it only appeared much smaller, as did the canal, the Friedhofsberg and the church. It was in good shape; once built as a Lutheran church, it was now used by the Catholic congregation. What really took me by surprise though, was that the old church smelled exactly the same as it had fifty years ago, despite all the time that had passed. The same happened as we went into the old distillery; it stank just as much as it did then. These smells, and the cold which I hadn't felt for fifty years, and the icy winds that blew from the Russian steppes, they all brought back memories and emotions, much more so than what I could see with my eyes.

Standing on the little bridge, where the canal comes out of the lake before winding its way through the park, hearing the sound of the water and the noise my feet made stepping onto the bridge, I felt like it all had happened only yesterday. As children, we used to play in the little stream in summer, trying to catch fish with our bare hands.

Somehow the winters have left more intense memories though, maybe because they are so different to what we are used to in South Africa. I'll never forget the first time I saw snow, and ice on the lake, and us skating and skiing, and tobogganing down the Friedhofsberg.

I took Topsy for a walk along the Buchengang, where Hänschen and I had carried out our first shooting experiments. It was so cold that we soon turned back, but we went far enough to see that the marks we had scratched into the bark of the trees all those years ago were still there, although mostly indecipherable. The trees had obviously grown and their roots now reached right across the road, but to me it still felt as awe-inspiring to wander through this alley-way of beech trees as it had when I was a child.

A lot had happened since then. After the end of the war the lands were nationalised and Juchow estate had become part of a co-operative. The castle itself had certainly seen better days. During the occupation by the Russians it had been used as an administration building and later, under the Polish government, as a kindergarten. Eventually the roof had needed fixing, and the authorities had preferred to move to a new building in the village. Juchow castle was deserted.

In the early 1990s, after the fall of the Berlin wall and the end of communism in Poland, the large co-operatives were privatised again, broken up into small farms, and a lot of the buildings were abandoned.

Buildings fall into disrepair quickly in those latitudes when uninhabited, the recurring frost and thaw cycles causing the brickwork to crack.

I was surprised to see that the castle's main façade was still in reasonable shape, as was the new wing, where Tante Erica had stayed with her family, but at the back the entire wall had collapsed and the first floor had caved in.

I wondered what my parents would have said if they could have seen this. Unfortunately, they had both passed away already; first my father in 1982 and then my mother in 1991. I so wished I could have shared my memories with them.

We wandered through the buildings, or what was left of them, into the big hall, where we'd celebrated the harvest festivals and which still had a feeling of grandeur about it. We scrambled over the rubble of the collapsed back wall into the park, and I couldn't believe my eyes when I saw some bright amber eyes staring at me from one of the lower branches of a large *Linde*.

It only had very few leaves left and they were exactly the same colour as the eyes of the owl that was having a good look at me. The owls in the park had always scared and at the same time fascinated me, especially when calling in the middle of the night. There had been a particularly large one, and I wondered for a second, but no, it couldn't have been the same one.

Once we returned from Poland, Topsy and I stayed for a couple more days in Berlin, before we went to Lübeck for a family reunion.

On the way, we decided to call on our friend Gerd Zieganeck, the man with the yellow bicycle. Every year after he'd spent Christmas with us at Boekenhout, he'd send a letter or postcard from faraway places, sometimes including articles about his bicycle journeys. It always made me laugh, that as soon as anybody mentioned his name in our house Topsy couldn't help herself but say, 'Gerd Zieganeck with the yellow bicycle, what a wonderful man!'

In Lübeck, I was so fortunate to meet my favourite Uncle Boli, who once was my great hero. Boli didn't hunt anymore, but he still had the most impressive 28-ender that I have ever seen in his study.

After two weeks in wintery Germany, both Topsy and I were glad to head back home again. Although I enjoyed this journey immensely, there was no question where home was. And at home, some interesting changes were about to take place.

Juchow Castle, 2009

A NEW CHAPTER

A NEW CHAPTER

The young elephant is scared. Standing at the water's edge, he has raised his trunk; his ears are flapping and his eyes wide. If he could, he would frown. The family of warthogs on the other hand seems rather content. With their tails lifted high in the air, the members of the little group are out foraging. One of the adults has decided to wallow in the mud. The shaggy waterbuck blends easily into the surrounding bushes, whilst the black rhino looks squarely at the observer. There is no doubt that he knows he is the stronger one, and certainly would charge if necessary.

It was not an easy choice. Walter had them all lined up in his office. The elephant and the rhino on the desk, the waterbuck leaning against the bookshelf and the warthogs had found a place on the window sill. He wanted to select pictures for an art exhibition, the first of its kind in Vaalwater. Annelien, his art teacher had told him about it the previous day. At first he'd thought he hadn't heard quite right, which happened rather a lot these days.

'Yes, Walter, I am serious. I really would like you to show your pictures at the exhibition.'

'*Ag*, Annelien, I really don't think they are good enough,' he'd said.

'Now don't be funny. You are by far the most talented student I've had in a long time. It would be a big pity if we didn't exhibit at least some of your pictures.'

'Do you really think so?' he'd asked incredulously.

'Of course. Your pictures are very special.'

Walter had scratched his head. 'And what exactly do you think is so special about them? If I look at them I only think that there is a lot of room for improvement.' On the other hand he couldn't help but feel flattered by what Annelien had just said.

'Look, your technique will improve over time, there is no doubt. That's just practice. And just about everybody can learn that. But what I am talking about is something different. You've got talent, and more than that, you see things differently to other people. It is hard to explain, but what I can see, no matter if I look at your elephant, the rhino, the giraffe, or any other of your paintings, is a great understanding. You understand the animals, you understand nature, there is passion and there is love. As if you know what it is like to be that little elephant, scared of the water or what it feels like for the warthog to roll in the mud.'

Walter smiled. Maybe Annelien was right. He had just never thought about it that way. Did other people really look at the world with different eyes? Anyway, he had agreed, and now he had to choose.

His eyes fell onto his most recent painting, still drying on the easel. He wondered what his teacher would say if she saw that. 'I must remember to show it to her,' he thought. It was the latest in a series of cricket playing *meerkats*. 'She is going to think I am completely mad, but I actually rather like them.' Topsy did too, and so did Debbie, Nick and the kids. They were quite simple, yet effective. The Meerkat Cricket Team. They were playing a one day international, dressed in colourful uniforms, or whatever their clothing was called. Standing upright as only meerkats can, there was a wicket keeper, a bowler and a batsman, grinning all the way to the boundary.

Another activity he finally had found time to pursue was writing. He'd inherited an old computer and painstakingly, with two fingers at a time, he had started painting pictures with words. He had begun by penning some impressions of his environment, of the seasons, of fauna and flora, and whatever else came to mind. Often, he felt, he was meandering, and one memory led to another. Maybe, one day, he could put it all together with some of the photographs he'd been taking ever since he had been given a digital camera. If he thought back, well, there were some stories to tell, they could easily fill a book. He'd also started putting some of his childhood memories on paper, the journey to Juchow, some of the adventures and experiences he remembered, but progress was slow; this project would take a long time to complete. Painting with a brush and colours was so much easier.

'It's amazing how life changes,' Walter thought while pondering over his choice of paintings. 'Who would have thought, when we were living at Weltevreden or Boekenhout, that one day I would be going to art classes, would have time to paint and write? And who would have thought that we'd end up living in Vaalwater anyway?'

But then, maybe it wasn't so strange after all. He had always enjoyed painting and drawing and writing. There had just never been time for it and he never thought he'd be any good at it either. His thoughts went to Tony, their nanny at Juchow. During the cold winter months, they'd spent many hours sitting in the children's playroom in the castle and she had shown him how to use crayons and water colours.

Life had indeed changed quite substantially for the Eschenburgs in recent years. Not long after their return from Juchow they had moved to Vaalwater, the only town situated within the Waterberg and not on its fringes. And now, more than a decade later, Walter was semi-retired. 'And strangely enough,' Walter thought, 'it all happened because a German industrialist wanted a farm in Africa.'

Hans Kunzmann had fallen in love with South Africa, and the Waterberg in particular. Exceedingly wealthy, he had acquired various farms in the Vaalwater area. But unlike many of the other foreigners who had flocked to this part of the world in recent years, he didn't follow the trend of returning the land to its natural state. In his opinion, land had to be productive, put food on people's tables. He began farming Brahman cattle, and in less than ten years had developed one of the largest and most productive herds in the region. Just over twelve hundred head of cattle roamed on Bella Vista, as his farm of nearly seven thousand hectares of bushveld was called. He could not have achieved this without Walter, who was not only his vet, but had also become a close friend, advisor and trusted translator.

Quickly, Hans had recognised Walter's abilities; that he had all the skills and experience he himself was lacking. There was no doubt Walter was the best vet in the area. He also had had a lifetime's experience of working with cattle, he knew how to manage a herd, select breeding animals, which vaccines to administer when, and how to fix things when they went wrong. Before long, Hans had offered Walter a permanent job. He wanted him to be the vet responsible for Bella Vista.

At first Walter had been reluctant to give up his independence, but the conditions were good. He could continue with his practice, and part of the deal was a nice house on a smallholding a few kilometres out of town, halfway between Vaalwater and the farm. Here he could also have his surgery, and there was enough space to keep their horses and a small herd of Brown Swiss cows. The little cottage in the garden was just perfect for George, who had been working for them ever since Paraffin and Flying Machine had retired. Part of Walter's clientele was based in the area anyway; ever since they'd moved to Naboom all those years ago, Walter had spent at least a day or two a week in and around Vaalwater. And most importantly, Topsy liked both, the idea of permanent employment and the house. For the first time in many years, they would have a secure income. No more worries about money - that was what had really clinched the deal.

It had been a great relief for Walter that from then on he could do his veterinary work on the farm without having to write a bill for every move he made. He'd never liked to deal with money, a fact that he knew was driving Topsy round the bend, and he understood it, but he couldn't really help it either. He wasn't quite sure where this aversion came from, but he thought it was a terrible habit of some other vets to enquire first if the patient's owner could pay the bill. Surely the animal had to come first?

Hans Kunzmann was the polar opposite. Money had been everything to him all his life. And he had lots of it. More than he knew what to do with, Walter had observed without envy. The two men, as different as they were, had developed a very close relationship over the years, based on mutual respect and trust. It had been a good move.

'And now, some ten years later, I am sitting here and have the peace of mind to paint.' Walter looked again at his pictures. The elephant, he definitely wanted to take to the exhibition, and the rhino. And the warthogs as well, they were quite special. 'It's actually fun to be retired, despite the old age,' he laughed quietly to himself. Of course he hadn't retired completely, he could never do that. But his workload was greatly reduced. He'd go to Bella Vista if they needed him, and some of his clients had said that they would never, ever call another vet, that they only wanted him. He still did his rounds most days, but at a more leisurely pace, with more time to chat to his clients, most of whom had become friends over the years.

He had more or less given up his activities as a wildlife vet, reasoning that it was time for the younger generation to take over. He missed the thrill of it, but the mere fact that he was living in the Waterberg guaranteed that he had his fair share of encounters with wildlife. Walter's gaze fell onto a pencil drawing he hadn't yet considered for the exhibition. It showed a fully grown elephant that looked like it was about to get really upset with somebody or something.

Walter remembered clearly what had inspired this picture. He had to laugh when he thought of Timo, who worked as a chef for the Kunzmanns in Germany. They had taken a liking to the young man and invited him to join them for one of their visits to the Waterberg. Timo got on well with Walter, loved driving around in the bush with him and never ceased asking him the most unusual questions.

'He's a city kid,' Hans had said when Walter remarked on the curiosity and naivety of some of the young man's questions. But he always enjoyed sharing his knowledge and Timo was lapping it up like a thirsty animal. One afternoon they went to the Marakele National Park near Thabazimbi, ostensibly to drop something off, but actually to have a look around.

Marakele, meaning 'place of sanctuary' in se-Tswana, was home to white and black rhinos, a host of antelope species, and on some of the rather spectacular mountain cliff faces a large colony of Cape Vultures had settled. The herds of elephant, described by travellers in the 1850s, had disappeared by the beginning of the twentieth century, but the tide had turned with their reintroduction in 1999. Since then, various family groups had been relocated to Marakele from other conservation areas.

For Timo, all wildlife was new and exciting, but seeing elephants was on top of his wish list. He had been begging Walter to show him at least one before he had to return to Germany, hence the excursion to Marakele. They had been driving around the national park for some time, when finally Timo's wish came true. Half way along a narrow tar road winding up a hill, they encountered an elephant bull coming towards them. He was flapping his ears and clearly in musth. The road was so narrow that only a single car could pass. On the right, there was a dense wall of thick bush and on the left a steep drop, down one of the precipices so often found in the Waterberg terrain.

247

Walter stopped. The elephant was approaching at a rather disconcerting speed and didn't seem inclined to turn away. 'Better we retreat slowly,' Walter thought and put the bakkie into reverse. He turned to explain the seriousness of the situation to Timo, but what he saw left him speechless.

Timo had wound down his window and, before Walter could stop him, hung his upper body out, waved one arm around while holding his nose with his other hand. He trumpeted loudly.

The elephant, in no mood to be mocked, charged. He was so close that all Walter could see was flapping ears and a raised trunk. He put his foot flat down on the accelerator and at high speed they raced down the steep hill. In reverse! At times they came dangerously close to the edge of the cliff. After what seemed an eternity, they reached the bottom of the hill, where the road widened, and with screeching tires Walter turned the vehicle around and sped off.

Once at a safe distance he stopped and looked at Timo. There was nothing left of his former bravado. He had sunk low into his seat, was rather pale around the gills and seemed to have shrunk to a quarter of his former size.

'Good,' Walter thought, 'seems he got a real fright. He needed that to teach him not to fool around with elephants!'

'My word,' Timo eventually said meekly, his teeth still chattering, 'that elephant looked like it meant business. I would have never thought….'

Walter was brought back to the present when Topsy walked into his study.

'What about the picture of the hydrangeas?' she asked and pointed at the still life he had painted only recently, a bunch of pink flowers in a blue gravy boat he'd purloined from Topsy's kitchen. 'I think it is rather lovely.'

The opening of the exhibition was a great success and all the budding artists sold some of their work. The little elephant found a new home and so did the warthogs. Walter and Topsy had just arrived home, when their phone rang. It was Patricia, one of Walter's fellow art students and a good friend for many years.

'Walter, I am terribly sorry, but I have packed one of your pictures by mistake,' she said.

Walter grinned. 'Oh, have you?'

Yes, that lovely one with the pink hydrangeas.' Patricia continued that she had found it amongst her own paintings when she unpacked them.

'Oh, did you?' Walter's grin was even wider now.

'I wonder what he's so happy about,' Topsy thought, as she was watching him.

Patricia suggested that she liked the picture so much that she wanted to buy it from Walter. She'd bring him the money the next day.

'No, you won't,' he replied.

'What do you mean?' Patricia asked, not comprehending.

'I mean that the picture is for you. I put it in with your stuff when you weren't looking. It is a present. From us to you. End of discussion now, just enjoy.' Walter rang off with a big smile. He looked at Topsy and asked, 'Why is it that giving away things makes one feel so good?'

Meerkat Cricket World Cup

FRIENDS

'Don't look at me like that,' Walter said to Frederic, the brown snake eagle, who perched on the top shelf of a corner cupboard. 'You've had your food for the day. Ja, you've been spoilt.'

He was in his surgery wiping down the old, iron surgery table. He had just stitched up the Gouses' dog, a boerbul called Tokolosh, who had been gallivanting and got caught in a barbed wire fence while in hot pursuit of a bitch in heat. It had been a nasty cut, bleeding profusely. Walter had suggested the dog be castrated, as it wasn't the first time that Tokolosh had come home from one of his excursions badly injured, but his owners would have nothing of it.

'But Doc, we are breeding with him,' they explained. 'It brings in good money.'

'Then you'd better make sure he doesn't *rondloop* so much.'

A little embarrassed, they had shrugged their shoulders and promised to do their best.

'You see, that's what happens if you chase after girls,' Walter continued the conversation with his feathered friend, while washing his instruments and getting them ready to be sterilised. His eyes fell onto the bird droppings on the floor. 'Now look at all the mess you've made here. I'll have to ask George to clean that up tomorrow. Otherwise we'll scare away our next patients.'

As well as looking after the cows, the horses and the garden, if necessary George Baloyi also doubled up as vet's assistant, the best Walter had ever had.

Looking down silently from his vantage point, Frederic did not reply to any of Walter's mutterings.

'You'll just have to be patient. Another week or so, and your wing will have healed.'

The bird seemed to understand, turning his head from one side to the other. It had been two weeks now that the Petersons asked Walter if he could have a look at an injured bird. Some holiday makers had hit it, just clipped it with the upper corner of their windscreen as it flew across the road. They'd presumed it had flown off, but when they stopped at the small supermarket in Vaalwater, they saw that the young eagle had got stuck under the roof tent of their vehicle.

'Looks like he's got a broken wing,' Walter had said after he had been called to the rescue of the battered bird. 'I think we can fix this, let me take him home to the surgery. And no, don't worry about payment. It's not your bird, is it? I'll just see what I can do.'

Frederic had recovered remarkably quickly and was getting impatient. He flapped around the surgery more and more energetically, and handling him became increasingly difficult. Walter and Topsy had taken to feeding him with braai tongs, for fear of their fingers. Yet when patients came into the surgery, Frederic somehow knew that he had to behave. He removed himself from the surgery table up onto the top of the cupboard from where he observed all activity with keen eyes.

'Ok, ok, if you promise to behave, I'll check if Topsy has some mincemeat for you. Otherwise I'll have to shoot a rat again, but you don't mind that either, do you?' Walter said. He didn't doubt for a second that the bird understood him.

Their somewhat one-sided conversation was interrupted when he heard Topsy call across the yard. 'I wonder what it is now?' he thought.

'Walter,' she yelled, 'are you deaf?'

'No, no, I am here. What did you say?'

'I said you must go and see Anna. Quickly. She says it's serious. I'm not sure what happened, but it sounds like one of her dogs had a run-in with a warthog.'

Walter grabbed the tray with his surgical instruments and dashed out of the surgery. He knew from experience that if Anna called him because there was a problem with one of her dogs, it was usually something dramatic.

He jumped into his white Toyota and sped down the dirt road, dust clouds billowing. It was the middle of winter and getting dark early now. Halfway down the road to Lapalala, where Anna lived with her seven dogs, he turned the light switch.

'Shit, these bloody lights aren't working again. I really have to fix them. Hope I get there before it gets completely dark.'

Driving in the dusky light Walter kept his eyes on the dirt road that led through the nature conservancy to Anna's house. Not long ago, at the end of last summer, he'd had a rather unpleasant encounter with a black mamba here. The snake, a good three and a half metres long, had obviously felt threatened by the passing car and reared up. It had looked him straight in the eye through the open window. He had seen the black inside of the reptile's mouth, put his foot down and accelerated away from it at speed. He'd got such a *skrik* that his heartbeat still sounded like the drumming feet of a herd of galloping buffalo by the time he'd reached Anna's house a good ten minutes later. At this time of year, there shouldn't really be any snakes on the road, but one never knew.

And Anna, she certainly had her share of encounters with snakes. She was a remarkable character, Walter mused. Somehow, the Waterberg seemed to attract all kinds of weird and wonderful people. He and Topsy had met Anna when she first moved to the area, bringing with her a motley collection of dogs and horses. Soon they had become close friends and delighted in sharing each other's life stories, their tales of adventures and lives well lived.

Having grown up in England during the Second World War, Anna's experiences had left her with some indelible memories, just like Walter's in Germany. She soon realised that she was not made to live a conventional life on the British Isles. So it was perhaps not surprising that after studying law and politics and embarking on various journeys and expeditions, she took the road less travelled and settled in Ghana, where she ran an engineering workshop with her first husband.

Ever since she was a child, Anna said, she had been an animal person, and while in Ghana she had not only trained and raced horses and acquired an assortment of furry and feathered house guests, she had also become an honorary game warden. Thus began a lifelong career and passion for nature conservation, which culminated in the establishment of a successful rhino sanctuary in Kenya, where Anna had moved together with her second husband in the late seventies. She was the driving force behind the establishment of the *Lewa Wildlife*

Conservancy, which helped secure the survival of the highly endangered Kenyan black rhino population.

She observed them regularly, learned about their behaviour and developed a special relationship with these animals. Soon, according to Desmond Morris in the foreword to Anna's book, *Rhinos – at the brink of extinction*, she was seen as being to rhinos what Dian Fossey was to gorillas, Joy Adams to lions and Jane Goodall is to chimpanzees.

The 'Rhino Lady' had settled in the Waterberg, and, strangely enough, Walter thought, right in the same area where he had darted his first rhino. She had come here to retire, she'd said. But Anna didn't stop. If she wasn't overseas giving lectures and raising funds for rhino conservation, she was out riding horses, walking her dogs or learning something new. Nothing seemed to stop her. Only recently had she come back from an expedition on horseback to Botswana, a journey that had left many of her travel companions, most of them a generation or two younger, exhausted. 'Oh, that was nothing,' she'd said, 'compared to the expeditions we used to do into the Sahara when I was younger, or riding through the Hindu Kush.'

Anna was certainly a character to be reckoned with, and beware those who crossed her path. Walter smiled. It was a well-known fact that she didn't take prisoners, as some of the snakes which had threatened the life of her beloved dogs had learned. Walter found Anna with her trusted neighbour and friend Collin, and one of her big dogs, huddled on the veranda of her house, a timber construction on stilts set in the bush.

'Thank God you are here. Fidelio had a run-in with a warthog and he's bleeding terribly,' Anna greeted him.

Walter saw immediately that she wasn't exaggerating. The warthog had injured the pointer at the shoulder, and blood was everywhere.

'You can take your finger out now and let me have a look,' Walter instructed.

The bleeding was so strong that Collin had thought to staunch it by holding his finger on the wound. 'But the hole is so big I had to stick it right in,' he said, somewhat perturbed.

'You probably saved his life.' It didn't take Walter long to stop the blood flow as he closed the gaping hole from the inside out with some tight stitches.

'These warthogs are a bloody menace,' Anna told him in the meantime. 'They used to be shy, but now they come right up to the house. And Fidelio is too brave for his own good. Not too many brains though, I'm afraid; he just went for them and of course, the big boar didn't take that lying down.'

'How is your other dog?' Walter asked Anna, after they had cleaned up and sat down on the stoep for a quick drink. 'I mean the one that your friend, the python, nearly had for breakfast.'

'Oh, Othello? He is fine and a bit wary of pythons these days. I think he learned his lesson! But,' Anna continued, 'after that incident, I got myself a Brazilian snake gun.'

'A Brazilian snake gun? What on earth is that?'

'I don't really know why and how it is different from other guns, I normally don't do guns. It's got a range of about six foot, but within that range it can do quite a lot of damage.'

'Does it work, I mean, have you used it?'

'I think you can blow it off at a puff adder, but I'd be afraid to use it for a black mamba. They are too quick and might just take retribution. In any case, six foot is far too close for my liking to being in the proximity of a snake like that.

'I have considered using it on a cobra though,' Anna continued. Some weeks previously her dogs had started barking wildly and she'd spotted a large snake on her veranda. 'It was definitely too close for comfort. So I called the dogs in, slammed the glass doors shut and ran upstairs to equip myself. But when I stepped out with all the paraphernalia, there was no sign of the snake. I searched for a while, but only half-heartedly. I wasn't really keen on testing my snake kit of gumboots, goggles and Brazilian snake gun on a cobra of that size. It was probably lying somewhere laughing at the sight of me.'

Walter grinned and got up. 'I think it's time for me to go, otherwise I'll get into trouble.' He sauntered off towards his bakkie and started the engine. 'Shit, I forgot the lights are not working.'

'Why don't you take my car so long,' Anna suggested. 'I have to go into town tomorrow anyway, and we'll swop then.'

Now hungry for supper Walter headed for home. Just before getting to the main tar road he drove over a bump, maybe a little faster than Anna's vehicle was used to, and the lights went out. No matter how much he tried, he couldn't get them to work again.

'Not much point in turning round,' he thought and looked around; he was relieved when he found a torch under the seat. He drove home slowly in the moonlight, and whenever a car came his way, he waved the flash light around wildly.

The following day, when he arrived at Bella Vista to observe the dipping process of some of the cattle, his friend Charles, the farm manager, remarked,

'Jeez, Walter, there are more and more real idiots on the road these days. You won't believe it, but last night, I was on my way home, and there was this car driving without lights and the driver was waving and shaking a torch around like a madman! Whatever next?'

Warthogs

Anna's Rhino

COURAGE

Anna is what I would call a truly extraordinary character, no doubt. We have spent many a delightful afternoon listening to her stories – and there are many. She, for one, is the only woman I know to have single-handedly retrieved her dog from the fangs of a large python.

The five metre long snake had got hold of Othello and was already squeezing him tightly. It had three curls around the dog, whose tongue was turning blue when Anna saw them. She'd heard some excited barking and then an ominous silence which had made her suspicious. When she saw the predicament her dog was in, she didn't hesitate, grabbed a kitchen knife and then straddled the snake to get a proper hold. She stabbed it a few times until, eventually, it let go of the dog. Infuriated, the snake turned on Anna.

'Let me tell you, they have bad breath, these pythons, very bad breath indeed,' she told us afterwards.

I'm not sure what happened next, but the snake changed its mind, and chose to escape into the bush rather than face the fury of this tiny woman, who was armed with a kitchen knife and a huge amount of courage.

Anna certainly has a lot of courage. She is an intrepid traveller, as well as an accomplished horse rider, a successful business woman, a dedicated conservationist and great company, but Anna is no cook. Not only is she no cook, she just doesn't do cooking. She hates it with a passion.

'I actually had it written in my marriage contract,' she told us once, and Topsy, who, as you know, has always been the most brilliant of cooks, thought she hadn't heard right.

'You had what?' she asked.

'Yes, in our marriage contract it said: I will not cook and I will climb mountains. Full stop.'

'You are mad, Anna.'

'No, I just learned from the lessons of my first marriage. No matter what men say when they want you to marry them, it's always different once you've tied the knot. And so I said, just to avoid any confusion, 'I will not cook. I will climb mountains.'

JUST ANOTHER DAY

Walter always got up early, especially in summer. Days were too short and life too precious to sleep it away. And there was always so much to do. One cool early October morning, the summer's heat hadn't yet descended on the Waterberg, he made his way out into the yard.

According to the morning ritual, he would let out the chicken, ducks and geese, and feed the horses. He'd check up on the cows, one of which he had named Topsy, and greet George Baloyi, whose company and assistance he appreciated greatly. A deeply religious man, George had been ordained a bishop in his church recently. 'I am not a big man,' he'd said after being congratulated on this honour, 'I don't have a big stomach, but I am a bishop now.'

The normal morning cacophony filled the air. The bishop was humming the melody of some church chorales while milking the Brown Swiss cows, the birds were chirping and the geese were making a racket. But when Walter approached the chicken *hok*, he stopped in his tracks. It seemed particularly quiet in this corner of the garden. Normally, at this time of day he could hear the excited chirping of the chicks, the clucking of the mother hens and the odd crow of the cock. With a slight premonition, he turned the corner and opened the hen house door.

'Oh no, not again!' he sighed at the sight of a rather large python whose extended midriff clearly indicated why all the chickens were so quiet and where they had gone.

'You know,' he said to the snake, 'you are a bloody bastard. Topsy was so proud of her hens and chicks. If she finds out, she is going to kill you!'

The python didn't even as much as lift an eyelid. It had found a gap in the fence during the night; some animal must have been digging, and there was just enough space for it to squeeze through. Only the rooster had escaped the python's appetite. An experienced old hand, he preferred to sleep on a high pole in the far corner of the enclosure. He began crowing now, probably upset and relieved at the same time, commenting on the fate of his mates and offspring.

'*Ag*, you, shut up! You should have done a better job defending these chicks!' Walter left the chicken coop and the unimpressed cockerel, making sure the door was properly closed so the thief couldn't escape. There was no way that with its full stomach it could even think of squeezing through the gap under the fence. Quietly, so as not to raise Topsy's suspicions, he walked over to the shed to fetch an empty sack and some string.

'George, George, come and help me, please.'

'*Ja* Doc, I come *just now.*'

'Not just now, George, I need you here *now now!*'

When George saw what had happened, he said, 'Jirre, if the *gogo* finds out, she is going to kill that *nhoka.*'

'Exactly. That's why we need to hurry up and get it out of here before she sees it.'

'But Doc, don't you think this thief deserves punishment? I could shoot it with my catty,' George suggested with a sparkle in his eye.

'Nonsense. Pythons are endangered animals, and they are only doing what nature tells them to do. They are not really dangerous to any of us. We'll catch it and I'll release it later at Bella Vista in the bush, far away from here.'

'*Ja* Doc, but…'

'*Niks* but, just take this sack and hold it open for me.'

Armed with a broom, he pushed the snake's head down to avoid its nasty but not poisonous fangs, grabbed it by the tail and manoeuvred it into the sack. George quickly closed it and the snake accepted defeat. They tied the top of the sack closed and heaved it on the back of Walter's Toyota.

'And George – don't tell Topsy.'

'Ok, Doc, I'll try. But you know her.'

Back in the kitchen, Walter was enjoying his second cup of coffee and preparing the daily fruit salad when he heard the scream from the yard that he had been expecting ever since catching the python. Clearly Topsy had discovered what had happened.

'Where is that bloody thief? I want to kill that snake. Where the hell is it?'

She stormed into the kitchen, her hackles raised, 'I'm going to fetch my gun. I'll find that bastard.' She looked at Walter. 'I know you! You have probably caught it again. George won't tell, but I bet it is on the back of the bakkie. I'm going to get that thief now.'

'Topsy, just wait a minute,' Walter tried to calm her down.

'No, not wait a minute; I'm going to shoot him right now!'

'Wait, I'll release it on the other side of the river. It will not come back from there, I promise.'

'No ways. Pythons always come back to their territory. That's the second time this summer they have stolen some of my birds.'

The victims of the previous perpetrator, which they had apprehended in the duck pond, had not been her chicken, but five ducklings.

'It can't be the same one as last time, because you shot that one!'

'I don't care. They are all the same anyway.'

'Tops, if Nick and Debbie hear that you shot another python, they are going to be really upset. They are actually a protected species,' Walter tried again.

'Protected species, my foot! They are not any more endangered than my left foot. But I tell you what; if they come into my garden and steal my chicken they certainly will be endangered! You let that one go and next thing it comes back and eats my bush babies. No ways. I'm going to shoot that thing. You can just do whatever you want.'

Walter turned his attention back to the fruit salad. He knew, once the bush babies were mentioned, there was no way Topsy would change her mind. She loved these little creatures dearly and he had to admit that more than once they had discovered pythons at the foot of their feeding place.

While he kept himself busy in the kitchen, making a plan for the day's activities, he kept an ear open to what was happening in the yard. There was no shooting, but instead another scream, and shortly thereafter, Topsy returned.

'Where is that bloody snake?'

'On the back of the bakkie,' he replied, hope growing.

'No, it is not! There is just an empty sack!' Topsy turned on her heel, mumbling something about being too useless to tie a sack, which Walter pretended he didn't hear.

Topsy now commanded George to look for the reptile, and Walter knew that George shared her opinion regarding snakes on the property. Rarely did they call him these days him if they found one in the garden. 'Shoot first and then check if it is dangerous or not', seemed to be their take on the subject.

The phone rang and only moments later Walter stuck his head out the back door again,

'Sorry, Topsy, Muller's just phoned,' he shouted, 'their dog has been bitten by a puff adder; they are bringing it here now.'

He got ready for the second snake victim of the day. So far, this season the snakes certainly had been rather active. 'It must have to do with encroachment of humans on their habitat what causes them to appear more and more in people's gardens,' he thought. 'Or maybe we just notice them more?'

The Labrador brought in by the Mullers was in a bad state. The tissue around the bite had swollen and before long, necrosis would set in. He could see that the dog, although calm, suffered from severe pain. There was not much he could do, other than stabilise him, put him on a drip, and give some cortisone, antibiotics and painkillers in high doses.

'What about antivenom, do you have any of that here?' Mr Muller wanted to know.

Walter replied that he didn't. 'First of all, there is no guarantee that it works. And second, you need a whole lot of it and it is rather expensive, so most people don't want to spend that kind of money. It is not viable for us to keep in the fridge because with such small demand it normally goes off before we have a chance to use it.

'If this was a cobra bite,' he continued, 'I would consider sending your dog to the university hospital at Onderstepoort to have him put on the respirator. As I am sure you know cobras have predominantly neurotoxic venom which eventually results in the animal no longer being able to breathe. But with the puff adder and its cytotoxic venom, this is the best I can do. If he makes it, we might have to operate and cut the necrotic tissue out. We'll leave him in the surgery here so I can check on him regularly and I'll phone you as soon as there is any news.'

'Please be honest with us, how much hope is there that he is going to make it?'

There wasn't really a clear answer Walter could give to the distraught owners. It all just depended, but in an attempt to cheer them up, he told them a story he had recently heard.

'You know Dr Albert, the general practitioner in town, don't you? His little Jack Russell called Felix got bitten by a snake. Nobody saw it, but from the symptoms we could only think that it must have been a cobra. He was in a really bad state but we put him on a drip and hoped for the best. And Felix, the lucky one, he made it.

'When I saw Dr Albert yesterday he told me that Felix had finally got his revenge. You must know that Felix is completely blind, but it doesn't seem to bother him much. Last weekend Dr Albert heard the birds sounding their snake alarm and Felix barking excitedly. By the time he had a look, Felix was involved in a serious fight with a large cobra. Snake and dog were so close and so concentrated on each other that Albert decided not to interfere, afraid that a moment of distraction might cause his dog to receive the fatal bite. So he left them to it.

'How Felix did it in the end, I don't know, but Albert says that not much later he saw Felix lying on the lawn and very contently devouring the large and now very dead cobra bit by bit. He said he was busy until late at night, but there was no ways he was not going to have the reward for his brave fight. He ate the whole thing!'

'Unbelievable!'

'Well, you go home now; there is nothing you can do here. I'll phone you.'

Walter walked from his surgery back to the house. Everything had calmed down now, and he was delighted that this time the snake had got away.

One that didn't get away was the python George had shot with his catty the previous year. Topsy had been so impressed by this feat that she'd taken a picture of the seemingly unharmed snake and given it to George. Only a few days previously Walter had seen it peek out his wallet.

'Oh, you still have that python picture? he'd asked.

'Ja, Doc, and I use it a lot. When you are out during the day, sometimes people from town, strangers, come to the gate here and ask for work. You never know if they are good people or *tsotsis*. So I tell them 'yes, the job is here' and then I show them the picture of this python.

'I tell them *ja, die werk is slang oppas* – you can have the job of looking after the snake. In the morning, you must take it outside, to the bush, and then the python must eat. In the afternoon, you must bring it back to the house.'

The answer is always, 'no sorry, I can't do that'. And they never come back!'

Over the many years he'd been working for the Eschenburgs, Walter had learned never to be surprised by George's ingenuity. He was not only capable of shooting pythons, rinkhals and cobras with his catty with a nearly hundred per cent hit rate, but also very adept at fixing all kinds of machines, and at building and welding. More than anything, though, he had a good eye for animals. He knew his cattle, horses and dogs well.

George assisted Walter when treating his patients and had learned to deal with smaller jobs himself. He helped with the calvings, knew what to do when a horse had colic and had acquired a certificate for artificial insemination in cattle. In a way, Walter often thought, he had the skills of Paraffin and Flying Machine combined. Slightly grinning, Walter remembered how George, in his very own way, had told his story to one of their visitors only recently.

'Doc Eschenburg and the gogo, they've known me for a very, very long time. Since I was a *pikkinin*. My parents lived and worked on Rosslene, the Spencer's farm near Naboomspruit, or Mookgophong, as we call it. After I finished school, I also worked for the Spencers and I was there when the lion came to the farm in 1972. I remember that, because that's the year I got married. That lion was dangerous; it killed a lot of cattle, and we were all very, very scared.'

When the Spencers moved to Botswana, George had decided to stay in South Africa, and Walter and Topsy had been only too delighted to offer him a job. George just adored Walter, but what he admired most in his boss and mentor, whom he liked to call "*The Number-One-Person for dogs, cows and horses*", was his ability to improvise.

'You know how the Afrikaners like to say '*a boer maak a plan*?' George would say, 'I am telling you, Doc Eschenburg, he is a proper *boer*. He always makes a plan. 'Impossible' is not possible for him.'

But George was also aware that there were certain things he could teach Walter.

No,' he'd laugh, 'the Doc, he is the best when it comes to animals. But machines? No. He is not a doctor for machines!'

As sign of their appreciation, Walter and Topsy had given their old blue Toyota bakkie to George, and he looked after it with the utmost care. And George was not only a bishop in the United Apostolic Church, he also knew one or other thing about traditional beliefs. He had a duiker skull neatly placed on the bakkie's dashboard. 'This is the pudhi. It is protection for my bakkie,' he'd told Walter.

'So, the pudhi protects your car? How?'

'Don't you remember, Doc, the pudhi that killed the kudu? The tsotsis are scared of the pudhi; that is the truth,' George explained. 'The people, everybody, tsotsis and even the police, they see the pudhi and they are scared. They say 'this man, he is a bishop, but he is also a sangoma!' Of course I am not a sangoma, but it works.'

Walter headed back into the garden to see how the fence of the chicken hok could be repaired to avoid future disasters. When he saw that it had been done already, he wasn't really surprised. He smiled.

'Really, I don't know what we would do without George!' he thought and walked over to his bakkie.

THOUGHTS

It's quite strange. Not long ago, I would have been quite happy to shoot that python myself. Now I hardly want to shoot anything anymore. I must be getting old. Or maybe it's just that times have changed. When I was a youngster, I didn't see anything wrong with clubbing spring hares or taking pot shots at porcupines. But nowadays it just doesn't seem right anymore. Why do we adore some animals and deem it right to kill others?

On the other hand, of course, I can understand Topsy and George, and our friend Anna, the Rhino-Lady too, for all wanting to kill snakes that enter 'their territories'. Particularly, if they pose a threat to their pets, or other animals they care for, or worse, to their own lives.

Conservation has become rather fashionable over the last decade or so, which is great, there is no doubt about that. Yet to live with the realities of life in the bush and the sometimes very real dangers that come with it, is a different story. It is so much easier to shout about protected species when you live in the city and don't have to deal with these creatures on your doorstep on a regular basis.

Take Anna, for example. If there was ever a conservationist, she is one, having dedicated her entire life to the cause. Yet beware the snake that sets foot on her front stoep.

Sometimes living in the bush brings some tough choices. Rarely are things as clear cut as they appear from the comfort of one's favourite urban armchair.

Still, I was glad that I'd had a hand in this latest chicken thief's escape.

CHANGES

After a somewhat turbulent start to the day, Walter got into his bakkie and headed out to do his rounds. He quietly smiled to himself, relieved that the chicken thief had managed to escape and hopeful that Muller's dog would recover from the puff adder bite. He delivered milk from his cows at the local school and the soup kitchen in Leseding, the township, where just about everyone knew and greeted the Doc with a huge smile. He popped in at the local doctor's surgery to pick up some dentist's equipment, and set forth towards Alma, to visit an elderly couple who had been his clients for decades.

Mrs Lamprecht had called the previous evening and asked him to come and have a look at her cat. The ancient Siamese was not eating well, had been losing weight and smelled rather strongly from her mouth.

'I'll be damned if that is not a vrot tooth,' he'd thought and he was right. Nothing that couldn't be fixed to Mrs Lamprecht's relief; the cat had become her most treasured companion. The old lady was a little worried when he put the cat under anaesthetic and set to work with his pliers. In fact, she was close to tears.

'But you are not going to hurt him, Doc, are you?' she asked.

'Don't worry,' Walter assured her, 'you'll see, your cat will be like new when she wakes up and realises that this horrible tooth is gone.'

Just to make sure, he stayed after the little operation and waited until the cat came around. In the meantime, Mrs Lamprecht offered him some of her most delicious *melktert*, a traditional Afrikaans dessert, close to a European custard tart but not quite the same. It was one of Walter's favourite dishes and he just couldn't resist a taste. He watched how the old Mrs Lamprecht's face lit up when he reached for the second piece.

This, he had to admit, was one of the best he'd ever eaten; the crust sweet and crispy and the sumptuous, milky filling covered with a generous layer of cinnamon.

Then, instead of heading straight home, he took a back road over Rankin's Pass. There was no real reason for it, other than that he loved the area and wanted to have a look at the condition of the veld in that corner of the Waterberg. It was dry, like everywhere, and he could see where veld fires had raged. They really needed rain badly and still, there was no cloud in the blue sky.

It was this blue sky that had attracted The Aviator, whose farm he approached now, to South Africa. One of the many foreigners who had flocked to the Waterberg in the last decade, the owner of this prospering game farm was from Holland and a pilot by trade. It must have been his sixth sense that led Walter to stop at the farm and chat to Ronnie, the manager. There was no particular reason for this call other than to say hello; he hadn't seen Ronnie and Linda for a while. When he took his leave, after yet another cup of coffee, his bakkie wouldn't start.

'Don't tell me…' he mumbled, 'come on, old girl.'

'Is everything all right, Doc?' Ronnie asked.

Walter tried once more, but the result was the same. 'Ja, well, actually no.' He couldn't believe it, but he had run out of diesel.

Luckily there was plenty in The Aviator's diesel tanks and Ronnie was only too glad to help.

'Lucky I popped in there,' Walter thought once he was back on the road, his tank filled to the brim. And Ronnie wouldn't even let him pay for it! It would have been a very long walk indeed. 'I must be really getting old if I forget to put diesel.' Then he shrugged, 'Oh well, all well that ends well.' After all, it wasn't the first time that fortune had smiled on him.

He went home for a quick bite of lunch with Topsy and checked on Muller's dog. So far so good. The animal was sleeping and seemed to be on the road to recovery. Deciding to skip today's siesta, Walter hit the road again. There was one more patient he had to see.

Driving through Vaalwater, which recently had been renamed Mabatlane, his veterinary equipment rattling happily on the back of the bakkie, Walter suddenly frowned. Something seemed different today. 'Am I seeing things?' he wondered. It was a busy day but something, he felt, wasn't quite right. Of course he was aware that the town had changed in the last decade, and not only in name. It was the transition from apartheid to democracy that he could see in the streets; the ever growing influx of foreigners, rich and poor; and the tell-tale signs of a flourishing tourism industry that had transformed Vaalwater, or rather Mabatlane. He hadn't really got used to the new name yet.

Since it had been founded as a trading post in the early nineteen hundreds, this little town had grown slowly but steadily to become a marketplace for the farmers and settlers that had chosen the uninviting yet beautiful mountains of the Waterberg for their new homes. People had been living here since time immemorial, but never in great numbers. Too sour was the grass, too steep the ravines, too prevalent the diseases. Yet they all had left their mark. Remnants of the tools of Stone Age people and the rock paintings of the Khoi and San bore witness to their presence in the area, as did the remains of the Nguni settlements, which archaeologists had discovered relatively recently.

Today there were Tswana people and Sotho; Shangaan, Ndebele, and Zulu; Afrikaners and English, plus small numbers of people from just about anywhere in the world. Not only had German and Dutch, French, Italian and Spanish settled here, Pakistani and Chinese had too, and of course Somali, Mozambicans and Zimbabweans. Things were changing indeed, or was change the only constant? Change was certainly something the more conservative people in the area struggled with. Not long ago, the language spoken in town, the lingua franca for business, was Afrikaans, and only Afrikaans. Today Vaalwater seemed like a little Tower of Babel in contrast.

Walter shook his head again. At the stop sign on the main street, he brought the bakkie to a halt, a move he normally tried to avoid. Like many drivers in these rural parts he thought stop signs were somewhat superfluous. Why stop if there was nobody coming anyway? But today he was in no hurry and he wanted to get a better look at what was going on. Was he seeing things, or were there people sitting in the trees?

The street itself was deserted, which was rather unusual for a Friday afternoon when many people were busy doing their weekly shopping or enjoying a cool drink and a chat at one of the many informal fruit and vegetable stalls, something that would have been absolutely impossible only two decades ago. Slowly Walter continued along the main street and he saw that he'd been right. People were now climbing down from the branches, chatting excitedly. He shook his head, still not trusting his eyes, when he noticed a commotion in front of the co-op and a Land Cruiser coming towards him. It was Charles, his colleague from Bella Vista. Walter signalled for him to stop.

Over the rattle of his diesel engine he shouted, 'Hey, Charles, what the hell is going on here?'

'You won't believe it, Walter, but one of Viljoen's rhinos escaped. You are a bit late; you've missed all the action. A short while ago that beast was running up and down the main street here.'

'That's why everybody is sitting in the trees.' Walter finally understood.

'Exactly. You should have seen it. The rhino was obviously upset and it went after quite a few people, but luckily nobody got hurt. Just as well we have so many trees here!'

Walter nodded. He had darted his fair share of rhino and been charged a few times. A rhino in distress was nothing to scoff at. Funny how everybody always said you should climb a tree. Whenever he was chased, there never seemed to be a tree anywhere near!

'Viljoen darted it. He got it over there, next to the co-op. Now they are busy loading it,' Charles continued with his explanation.

A car came up from behind, hooting. 'I'd better get back to the farm. See you tomorrow!'

At the co-op, the crowd was slowly dispersing. The rhino, its eyes hidden under a blindfold of green cloth, was safely stowed away on the back of a truck. Walter saw Viljoen, the proprietor of the local game capture outfit, standing next to the truck, his stomach protruding over his shorts and a look of satisfaction on his face.

'Ten years ago, it would have been me,' he thought. He and Reuben Joubert had darted a lot of game together. One of their first expeditions had been to the Zambezi. They had been asked by the Zimbabwean nature conservation authority to help with the relocation of a herd of elephant. The area was flooding and the elephants were trapped on a relatively small island in the middle of the Zambezi River. Or so everybody had thought.

It had taken them some time and effort, but eventually, with the help of the helicopter, the men had managed to herd all the elephants together close to the shore. They had darted and loaded them onto a barge and moved them across the flooding Zambezi. Walter still felt like laughing out loud when he remembered the whole procedure and what had happened afterwards. As soon as the animals had been given the antidote and had recovered, they reoriented themselves, seemed to shake their heads and took to the water. Within a couple of hours they had all swum back to their little island in the middle of the flooding river.

But that was a long time ago. Now Walter had left these kinds of wildlife adventures to a younger and fitter generation. He had to admit that when it came to running he was not quite fast enough anymore. He'd even struggle to climb up a tree these days. Too much good food.

Game capture had become a big business, with lots of money involved, and a new generation had taken over. More and more landowners had followed the trend and started farming game. In the beginning, of course, there were many who thought these people were mad. 'Bunny Huggers', they had called them, but now many a doomsayer had been converted and joined the ranks of the conservationists.

Evidently this move was not only about conservation, but also about making money. And it had all hinged on South Africa's changed political climate, the release of Nelson Mandela, the unbanning of the ANC, and the move to democracy. Tourism was on the up, and hunting had become big business; trophy animals were sold for vast amounts to hunters from overseas, and these funds could pay for the conservation efforts – or they went straight into somebody's pocket. For some, Walter realised, this was a controversial issue. However, breeding game for restocking farms and national parks in other parts of the country also helped to pay the bills.

Over the years, elephant, buffalo, rhino, lion and a variety of rare antelope had been reintroduced into the biosphere of the Waterberg, mostly with success. Populations were flourishing.

The exception was the rhino. All over Africa rhinos were under serious threat of extinction. They bred very slowly and population numbers were low, particularly for the black rhino. But the big problem was poaching. The powder made from rhino horn, celebrated as an aphrodisiac and a remedy against cancer in the Far East, was worth a lot more than its weight in gold.

The situation was getting seriously out of hand, if reports were to be believed, with a dramatic annual increase of poached and mutilated rhinos. And it seemed that the poachers were highly organised gangs of criminals with all the equipment that one could possibly need, including helicopters, dart guns and drugs.

In some incidents it was said that even vets were involved. Walter shook his head and pondered, as he drove along. It was definitely a different generation that had taken over.

He turned onto the Melkrivier road on his way to Triple B Ranch, one of the most successful and long established farms in the Waterberg. He was on the way to check up on a horse that had had a rather unpleasant encounter with a rhino. Old Diana, one of the dominant mares in her herd, had been gored and the back of her leg ripped open. It had taken him a good two and a half hours to stitch her up again. And in the end he'd even had to resort to his old tricks of using a hypodermic syringe needle because his normal suture needle had become blunt; it was rare that he had to put so many stitches into one patient.

On the right Walter passed the turnoff to Boschdraai, the heart and soul of Triple B, where their old friends Charles and Nina Baber lived. Their farm was a good example of how things had changed over the years. What had started off as a small cattle farm a hundred years ago had grown over time and, in its heyday, had been home to a good few thousand head of cattle. Walter remembered endless hours spent doing pregnancy diagnostics here, often from dawn to dusk; hundreds and hundreds of Bonsmara cows at a time.

On the way home he should definitely make a *draai* there, stop to say hello and have a cup of tea with Charles and Nina. He hadn't seen them for a while and, like himself, he felt, they were remnants of a time gone by. Charles' two sons had taken the reins now, and they had gone with the times and diversified. Cattle were still farmed, but there was now also Horizon, a horse riding and tourist enterprise, and another portion of their land had been turned into a game and hunting farm.

'Has going over to game been a good move?' Topsy had asked Charles and Nina in her characteristic, direct way when they had last seen them.

'Well, it is very hard work,' Nina had replied, 'and marketing is so important, something we never knew about when farming cattle.'

'And the value of the animals is immense,' Charles had added, 'which obviously means that you worry a lot more about them. There are eleven rhinos on the farm now. You can imagine the constant worry with all the poachers around. And you don't know who you can trust.'

He really should pop in there on the way home, Walter thought. He liked the old couple, and Nina hadn't been too well recently.

Sometimes, if he was completely honest with himself, he felt a little tired too. Not that he was sick. There was nothing wrong with him, other than the usual. The heart didn't work quite the way it should, and the fluid in his lungs was at times a little worse, especially if he forgot to take his pills. But it wasn't that either. It was more like a general tiredness, a weariness, he felt. He'd always had the ability to just close his eyes for a one-minute nap anywhere, preferably when it was getting late during a dinner party, just like his Dad had, and when he opened them again he felt refreshed. This was different.

But maybe he was just imagining things, getting paranoid in his old age. Only the other day, their old friend Patricia had said to him, 'My God Walter, but you are still so strong!' after he had pulled a calf out. And it was true, when push came to shove, he was still strong. Anyway, to think too much about these things didn't help. After all, he was only just on the wrong side of seventy.

He arrived at Horizon and was delighted, as always, to see 'young' Shane. 'Well, not that young anymore either, he must be well into his forties by now,' Walter thought.

Shane had an extraordinary connection with horses and from the minute they'd met, nearly twenty years ago now, they had clicked and become close friends. Their relationship was based on mutual respect and common interests, and often the two men could be seen sitting on the fence, discussing ways of dealing with diseases, injuries or snake bites.

Both were open to suggestions and always prepared to try something new. These discussions were interesting because they each approached problems from very different angles. Walter drew from his wealth of experience as a bush vet, his intrinsic understanding of nature and animals, his ability to see straight to the point – and also a good portion of sixth sense. Shane on the other hand, who had also spent the better part of his life working with horses and had lots of hands-on of experience, lacked the medical background, the years spent sweating and swotting at Onderstepoort. But he had discovered that the internet could provide him with a wealth of information.

'Walter, this is a revelation,' he'd say. 'Suddenly I have it right at my fingertips how they treat strangles or biliary or snake bite in other parts of the world. It is not only a revelation, it's a revolution!'

Walter listened carefully. He thought these new ways were fascinating, yet he'd never actually managed to get into this internet story. Maybe one day he would.

However, often they acted as each other's sounding boards, discussing new or refined ways of treatment. Neither of them was set in their ways and they were both prepared to give the ideas of the other space to develop.

They had recently come across an ingenious solution to treat a puff adder bite when it occurred on a horse's head, which was not unusual. The biggest problem in such a case was the extensive swelling. It could become so severe that it would eventually block the airways and cause the animal to suffocate. They realised that to cut two pieces of hosepipe and insert them into horse's nostrils would allow the animal to breathe until the enormous swelling of the head had subsided. It seemed too good to be true.

The biggest headache for anybody keeping horses in this part of the world though was African horse sickness. This viral disease, transmitted by *culicoides* midges, was a challenge and a curse, and somewhat unpredictable. They'd had good years and bad years – and they had horrendous years, when they lost a lot of horses, no matter what they did. Walter never gave up on horse sickness though, just as he never gave up on an animal; nor did Shane. They were always on the lookout for an innovative way to treat the disease, be it based on either conventional or alternative healing methods. 'When it comes to horse sickness, one has to be pragmatic and use whatever works,' Walter and Shane both maintained, 'it doesn't matter whether you understand why and how it works, as long as it does.'

Walter had always loved to impress people with his bush cures, and he knew Shane appreciated them. When he first had started working on his own in the rural areas, he had to get along with a minimum of veterinary equipment, and he had to be completely self-reliant. He had learned to make a plan, to improvise. And he'd always loved the challenge. More so, over the years he had come to the conclusion, that the simplest solutions were often the best.

After a good chat, Walter and Shane had a look at Diana and she was given the all clear. The wound, inflicted by the rhino some of weeks previously had healed surprisingly quickly.

Walter was about to leave the farm, when he remembered. 'Shane, just hang on a sec. I nearly forgot, I brought you some of my most recent creation.'

'What, some of your homemade cream cheese? The last one was just delicious!'

'Ja, that as well. But here, take this too.' He passed a packet wrapped in greasy paper to his friend. 'It's some kudu meat that I smoked. New recipe. Tell me what you think!'

And with this he was off, leaving a cloud of dust behind.

Shane stood in his yard for a moment and then turned to his wife Laura, who had come out of the office to see Walter off.

'You know,' he said, 'Walter is a big person. In fact, the biggest I've ever known. Sometimes I think they don't make them like that anymore. There is an old school of bush people which is dying out,' he continued, more talking to himself now, 'and it's not that the younger generation are not very knowledgeable or anything, but they just don't seem to be made from the same cloth.

'People like Walter live the bush. You couldn't separate them from it, even if you wanted to. For the new breed, the bush is more where they work, not who they are. There is something that makes these old bush people very special, very strong. Most of them have lived very frugally all their lives.

'Look at Walter. He's never lived in a fancy place; his bedroom is a cell. Nowadays he has a computer, but other than that, he's got his gun-safe and his shoes and that's it. And it doesn't matter, that's not what life is about. Maybe it's got to do with hardship and trying to make ends meet in a difficult environment. And the Waterberg, beautiful as it is, is a hard place. Your livestock dies easily. People die easily. Maybe living on the edge like this makes for strong people and strong relationships. You understand that life is fragile and that it is tough and that you have to work hard to get through it. I think that makes for bigger people.'

IF THERE IS NO FISHING IN HEAVEN…

'Oupa, Oupa, let's go fishing!' Luke had been nagging Walter the entire day. 'Please Oupa, I want to try the new fishing rod I got for Christmas.'

'Do you really want to go fishing? Today?' Walter teased his grandson.

'Yes, of course, Oupa, you promised yesterday!'

Walter stood at the kitchen table making cream cheese. He sold most of the milk from his cows, but what was left, he passionately turned into cheese. 'We'll put some garlic and black pepper into this one, and what do you think, Luke, shall we put some chives and parsley into the other?'

'Yes, Oupa.' Luke sighed. All he was interested in at the moment was fishing.

'Dad, the cheese is divine, especially the one with garlic and dill.'

Walter turned and saw that Debbie had walked into the kitchen.

'And Dad,' she looked at her father, 'if you don't feel like it, you don't really have to take Luke fishing.'

'Don't worry, Debs, of course I will. Just making him suffer a bit,' Walter grinned.

'Thought so.' Of course Debbie knew that her father loved fishing as much, if not more, than her son Luke. Her eyes fell on a little framed picture on the kitchen wall. *'If there is no fishing in heaven, I'm not going!'* it said, and it was one of Walter's favourites.

'Luke has been driving us mad for the last two weeks,' Debbie said. 'There we were driving through the Okavango Delta, seeing the most amazing birds and animals, and the only thing he's thinking about is fishing. If he could, he'd breath and sleep and eat fishing.'

'I know, I was the same at his age. As soon as I'm finished with this batch here, we'll go.'

Debbie and Nick had arrived the previous evening, together with Jade, Hannah and Luke, their youngest. They were on their way home from a holiday in Botswana. Walter and Topsy absolutely loved having 'the kids' around; the house was buzzing with life. Hannah and Jade now joined the little group in the kitchen and related excitedly what they had seen; tsessebes, giraffes and hippo, but most impressive of all had been a fresh lion kill.

'And Dad, the birds were unbelievable!' Debbie added, knowing where her father's priorities lay.

'So tell me,' Walter asked while putting the tubs with cream cheese into the fridge, 'did you see the Pel's fishing owl?'

Debbie laughed. Every time they came back from a trip to Botswana or the Kruger National Park, Walter asked about this elusive bird. 'Unfortunately not. But we saw some lovely pearl-spotted owls.'

'They are so cute!' Hannah chirped, 'and so tiny!'

'They look as if they have two eyes on the back of their head,' added Jade.

'We also saw the giant eagle owl and, Oupa,' Luke winked, 'lots of fish eagles. We actually watched how one of them caught a fish!'

'But no Pel's fishing owl? Do you know what they look like?'

'Yes, Oupa, of course,' the children answered in unison, humouring their grandfather.

'It's large, like a giant eagle owl,' Hannah said.

'But it's brown; sort of ginger coloured with large black eyes,' Jade added.

'And the Latin name is *Scotopelia Peli.*' As usual, Luke impressed everybody with his knowledge of Latin names; 'And it lives in large trees close to water, so it can go fishing!'

Walter was delighted; he had taught them well.

Debbie and Nick often commented on how much they'd all learned from Walter. His knowledge of flora and fauna was encyclopaedic, and they'd never met anybody who knew quite as much. But Debbie felt that there was more to it; her father seemed to understand the inner workings of nature, how everything was connected, and how one part always depended on another. And he had the keenest eye.

He just noticed everything, be it a kudu hiding behind some bushes, a leopard in the trees, or a rare bird. He even seemed to have eyes in the back of his head, and although sometimes hard of hearing in daily life, there was seldom a birdcall or an animal noise that escaped him.

Walter often seemed to think like the animals he was watching, and he spoke to them. He had regular conversations with the giant eagle owls living on their property, and not only here at Vaalwater, but also at Weltevreden and Boekenhout. He'd had a special relationship with owls of all kinds all his life, ever since their call sent goose bumps down his spine in the forests of Juchow. The Pel's fishing owl though, somehow, had eluded him son far.

'Ja, we might not have seen the Pel's fishing owl,' Nick said now, while licking some cream cheese of his fingers, 'but have you ever asked your Oupa about his encounter with the owl on the long drop?'

Walter pretended he didn't hear, so Nick continued.

'Once upon a time, he was doing the rounds, visiting patients on some of the outlying farms, and it so happened that he needed to go to the toilet really, really badly.

'He stopped at a farm stall near Moordrift, somewhere in the middle of nowhere, hoping they'd have a loo that he could use. 'Yes' they told him, 'there is one out the back. We don't use it very much, but here is the key.' So off he went, opened the door of the rackety outhouse and was surprised to see a barn owl sitting on the wooden seat. He obviously really was in an urgent need, so he sat down right next to the bird.'

'Didn't the owl move off?' Luke asked.

'No, she must have been sitting on eggs. Anyway, he sat there together with the owl hissing at him all the while. When he was done, he just locked the door and returned the keys.'

'Who wants to come fishing?'' Walter asked, changing the subject.

'Yeah!' Luke darted off to get his fishing rod, while the girls declined the offer.

'But bring us a fish for supper!'

Half an hour later, Walter and Luke were rattling down the dirt road towards the Bella Vista farm dam. On this beautiful late summer's afternoon, they passed the fields where the Brahman cattle grazed. The rains had been good this year, there was plenty of grass and the calves looked fat and healthy.

'What a joy to see the veld like this,' Walter thought. Although mostly retired from his duties, he always checked on the cattle when driving around the farm. 'Looks like we are slowly getting things right. The management of the farm is working like a well-oiled machine.' It wasn't really his responsibility anymore, yet he couldn't help but still care.

'Oh, look there,' he called out and stopped. He had spotted a small group of kudu standing in one of the cattle kraals. The graceful antelopes pricked their ears and gazed at them. They had long spotted the old bakkie but remained calm. They seemed to verify who was approaching before they returned to their browsing.

'They have become really tame here on the farm, as if they know that nobody is going to harm them. There is no hunting here, and I'm sure they know,' Walter explained. They silently watched for another couple of minutes, but Luke was keen to get going again.

When they reached the dam, Walter parked next to his favourite fishing spot. They got their gear ready, baited the hooks and cast them into the water. Sitting in silence for a little while, they watched a pied kingfisher swoop down from his perch on a nearby branch and dive into the water. They had a few nibbles on their bait, the odd tug on the line, but no fish yet.

Weavers were chirping in the nearby reeds, a pair of Egyptian geese flew by and the red chested cuckoo called out his loud '*Piet my vrou, Piet my vrou*'.

'Why is he calling 'Peter my wife', Oupa?' Luke asked.

'I really don't know,' Walter replied. 'It's obviously the translation of what his call sounds like in Afrikaans, but it has never made any sense to me.'

Before he could get into any further explanations, Luke's reel started to buzz. After a long struggle that left them both completely soaking wet, Walter and Luke managed to land a bass, and then another one, and after the third fish they decided it was time to go home.

Soaked in dam water, and with fish flapping on the back of the bakkie in the midst of all the veterinary supplies, they headed off into the sunset, a big smile on each of their faces.

Waterbuck

EVERYTHING IS CONNECTED

Some people might drive across a farm and just see cattle, but if you look closely, you'll realise that the cows and their calves always have company, and that they are sharing their space with countless other species. There are egrets feeding literally off the back of the cattle, and pewits, larks and dozens of grassland and savannah birds. The Burchell's coucal calls for rain, while eagles, buzzards, kites and other raptors watch them from above. They are out hunting the many rodents, insects and other small creatures living in the grass. Thousands of swallows and the most colourful bee-eaters dart through the air plying their trade, or we see them resting on fences or other high vantage points. Even fish eagles are not rare; the picture wouldn't be complete without their call.

As if this wasn't enough, there are kudu, as well as reed-, water- , bush- and blesbuck who keep the calves company. But perhaps the strangest creature of them all is the springhare. Looking like a miniature kangaroo, he reminds one of Australia and seems somewhat out of place here. He hops along on its hind legs and only uses his short front limbs to scratch for food and dig up grass roots.

These are also enjoyed by bush pigs, who make night time pilgrimages to the green pastures to graze and dig. They are rarely seen, unlike their more bold cousins, the warthogs. Diurnal animals, they bring a smile to one's lips if they march across the veld with their thin tails held vertically like little antennae. Over time they can become habituated to humans and their companions, which, as our friend Anna would know, is not necessarily a good idea.

The farm dam provides another entire spectre of bio-diversity, with its countless amphibians and reptiles, and at least twenty species of fish, some of them most delicious to eat. There are crocodiles, snakes, monitor lizards and terrapins, and an incredible number of insects, scorpions and spiders. The '*Kommetjie's Gat Kat*' lives by the water, and so do otters and occasionally brown hyenas.

It's one of life's delights to experience the bushveld, at any time really, but particularly after the first summer rains. Every creature under the sun seems to rejoice when clouds begin to move in from the north and burst open with heavy thunder and lightning. When the weather clears up again, the ground is steamy. New clouds build up almost immediately and there is another heavy cloudburst. It seems it is raining grass too. Where there was only parched earth yesterday, there is a green sheen on the ground today. With every falling drop the blades of grass grow.

Slowly, little springs appear on the hillsides and cliff faces. Big rivers that have been dry for months, sometimes even years, start flowing again. Water holes and dams are filling up and start overflowing. That's when the Waterberg lives up to its name. Water appears everywhere and glitters on the shiny rock faces.

When the first settlers of European descent arrived here from the Cape, it must have been a wet year, with clean streams running down the mountainsides. It would have seemed like paradise to them after the scorched landscapes of the Karoo and Highveld they had trekked through. Soon though, they were to realise why the Waterberg was so sparsely populated. Paradise has its faults too. Ticks, mosquitoes and flies love hot and humid conditions and can become a burden to man and beast by transmitting diseases.

But who wouldn't be happy if the whole world is flowering and flourishing, even if there is the odd problem. Suddenly dung beetles are toiling, digging dung balls into the wet earth; it seems to be hard work. Flame lilies, *schistozylis coccinea*, are flowering, and so are indigofera and cotyledons, *ricinus communis*, and lobelias. And the trees! There are white and green flowering dombeyas, and more scarce, the pink variety; bush willows are sprouting pale yellow flowers, and the boer boon tree, *schotia brachypetala*, dazzles with its bright red flowers. It seems like a miracle, but there is no dust anymore and every last piece of ground is covered by vegetation.

Birds are building their nests and attracting partners with their mating calls. One of the more conspicuous amongst them is the red chested cuckoo. Even on the hottest days his call can be heard from sunrise to sunset, while his wife is looking for an adequate nest to lay her egg in. In our garden we have observed more than once a pair of bulbuls feeding a young cuckoo at least twice their size.

Watching the cuckoos, we are amazed at their ingenuity and at the same time feel sorry for the bulbul, who ends up raising the cuckoo's chick instead of his own. Just like the cuckoo, squirrels, koggelmanders, snakes and owls are nest robbers, yet they all have their place in the garden – and in nature. How much poorer would our life be without them? Yes, whoever wants to live disturbs someone else's life.

We admire the eagle owl for her wisdom and grace, yet at the same time we feel for the bush babies she preys on. Insect eaters have become our friends, yet they prevent beautiful butterflies from hatching. Butterflies lay their eggs and caterpillars hatch and devour the leaves of our beloved trees. Seed eaters disturb freshly sown flower and vegetable beds. Even the pretty sugar birds destroy the flowers to get to the nectar, use cobwebs to build their nests and feed spiders to their young.

In the end, everything is connected.

THE END

THE END

Everything is connected – Walter understood the connections, perhaps better than most. The sense of urgency that had permeated our recording of his memories was palpable then, and now seems justified.

Today, his favourite blue armchair is unused. He no longer sits in it and will never read this book, his life-story.

On the 16th of September 2009, a great sadness descended upon the Eschenburgs' home, the Waterberg, and wherever else people had known, loved and respected Walter. Their only consolation was that his had been a life lived to the full, and that he'd appreciated every single aspect of it.

While writing this, far from Vaalwater, I often heard the owl. An eagle owl, its calls accompanied my attempts at patching together Walter's words and memories with friends' stories and family anecdotes.

Walter had a special relationship with owls all his life, and the night after he died, the eagle owl in the terminalia tree outside his house in Vaalwater called incessantly, until the early hours of the next morning. A week later, Nick, Debbie and the children saw the Pel's fishing owl for the first time ever; a bird that had eluded Walter all his life.

EPILOGUE

More than a year would go by before my next visit to the Eschenburgs' house. A lot had happened in the meantime. Topsy had to learn to manage life on her own. It wasn't easy, but life carried on. It had to carry on. George stayed with her and helped with the daily chores, and the menagerie, diverse and plentiful as ever, kept her company.

As I arrived, I was greeted by Tessa, Walter's old Labrador, Domino the Dalmatian, and Duffy the Maltese poodle. The herd of Brown Swiss cows had been sold, but the families of chicken, geese and ducks had grown, and a handful of horses grazed in the back yard. Every evening the bush babies appeared for their supper of strawberry yogurt and worms, before heading off into the night with prodigious leaps. They had become so tame, that not even the excited barking of George's dogs Sam and Bullet disturbed them.

They were, of course, also part of the family. Sam had been brought into the surgery one evening by a neighbour who had found him next to the road. He had been run over and left for dead. Things didn't look good for Sam, but Walter had put him on a drip and vowed, 'If he makes it, we keep him.'

His best friend and companion, George had picked up in the nearby township. 'I'll call him Bullet,' he'd said when he introduced the little white and grey dog with the big ears to Walter and Topsy, 'because he's as fast as a bullet, and he will chase all criminals away.'

Although Topsy and George still persecuted any snake that dared set foot on the property with fierce determination, José, an American corn snake and thus not venomous, had taken up residence inside the house.

'He is for security, that's his job. But I've actually quite got to like him,' Topsy was amazed herself. José could often been seen resting leisurely around Topsy's neck, while Parrot, the African Grey, chortled away, entertaining anybody who cared to listen.

When it came to picking up strays and welcoming visitors, nothing had changed, and the latest addition to the family was Buddy, a young Labrador.

'It was uncanny,' Topsy said, 'I was just considering getting another dog, when Buddy appeared out of nowhere. He was about four months old and just a bag of bones. He fitted in immediately as if he'd always belonged here.'

As had become a habit, we had lunch together with Anna, the Rhino-Lady. A great friend of Walter and Topsy's for many years, she had become a mainstay for Topsy during the difficult times. At the Bush Stop Café in Vaalwater, Anna indulged in her staple of apple pie and ice cream.

'No, I don't do salads,' she'd say to anybody who questioned her choice, and thus the subject matter was closed. There were more important things in her life than food — she who had written into her marriage contract that she didn't cook!

Topsy and I listened to the tales of her latest adventure, a camel safari in northern Kenya, only weeks before her eighty-first birthday.

'Camels are actually very comfortable; they are wonderful animals,' she said when we asked how she'd coped; after all she had broken her hip earlier in the year. Mopping the last bit of ice cream off her plate, Anna continued, 'People ask me all the time, '*Isn't it dangerous, all these things you are doing?*' and I can tell that they think I am completely mad.

'I then ask them, where they think I broke my hip. Riding horses? Traveling in Africa? Climbing mountains? No. In the bloody kitchen — of all places. Nothing actually happened; I just slipped and broke my hip. Easy as that. So why on earth should I stop doing what I love?'

The conversation meandered, touching on the tragic accident of a young game ranger who had been killed by an elephant, continued to pirates off the Somali coast and eventually reached the subject of rhino poaching that was rampant in the area.

'Did you hear,' Topsy asked, 'they've arrested a ring of alleged rhino poachers. And one of them, believe it or not, is a vet.'

'I know. These are not your run of the mill thugs. It is a really sophisticated set up; it's infuriating,' complained Anna.

'Yes, but a vet? A vet slaughtering rhinos? If that is true, it is unbelievable. It is against everything a vet stands for. If Walter knew, he would turn in his grave.'

When on the last evening of my visit, which we spent sitting until late at the dining room table chatting, Topsy and I eventually decided it was time to let the dogs out and call it a day, there was a commotion by the fence followed by loud and angry barking.

Topsy switched on her torch and just beyond the fence, less than half a metre above the ground, we could make out two pairs of bright orange eyes. They were surrounded by a black and white halo.

'Porcupines!' Topsy shouted. 'Porcupines, these bastards! Just look at them!'

Standing on the other side of the fence, they stared us squarely in the eye. With all their quills erect they offered a formidable sight. As we stepped closer, so did they, causing the fence wire to ring metallically.

'Here, hold the torch while I go and get my gun!' Topsy whispered.

'Get your what?'

'My gun. I'm going to shoot these buggers.'

'You can't just shoot them?!' I was fascinated by the sight and the fearlessness of the two animals.

'No, bullshit. I have to shoot them. Otherwise they'll kill my dogs. In no time. If the dogs get anywhere near them, they will get spiked by the quills. If it doesn't kill them immediately, they break off and cause a septicaemia that *skriks vir nix.*'

Topsy went to fetch her gun. When it came to protecting the life of her feathered or four legged friends, nothing and nobody could stop her. The porcupines had no intentions of fleeing the scene. Bravely they stood their ground when she reappeared, ready to shoot.

'Take the dogs out of the way and shine the torch!' she commanded, before she changed her mind and said, 'No, give me the torch and take Duffy.'

The shot rang out loud in the otherwise still night. Now there was action. Porcupines were running and quills flying. Sam and Bullet came scrambling out of the cottage, with George in hot pursuit.

'George! Porcupines! I shot the bastards.'

'Oh, I see.' George was clearly relieved. 'And I thought it was time for the tsotsis now.'

293

The porcupines certainly got a big fright and lost some of their quills, but otherwise they seemed unharmed, as we saw them diving down the bank towards the river.

'The fun is over, let's all go to bed,' Topsy suggested calmly. 'Thanks George and good night.'

The next morning, George confirmed that indeed the porcupines had got away.

'Perhaps just as well,' Topsy said. 'Walter and I would often take a pot-shot if there was something creeping and crawling around at night. Don't think we ever hit anything though. That wasn't really our intention. And you know what, we shouldn't really mention this to Nick and Debbie, it would just upset them unnecessarily.'

Indeed, life wasn't always easy, but it carried on. It had to carry on.

JOURNEYS WITH WALTER

A TRIBUTE BY BOWEN BOSHIER

JOURNEYS WITH WALTER

I was blessed to have Walter as my Godfather. During my formative years I often spent my school holidays with him, Topsy, their menagerie of interesting creatures and the many visitors at Weltevreden. Topsy and Walter loved socializing, and were famed across the district.

I would get a lift or catch the train up to Naboomspruit, the centre of adventure land. The Springbok Flats were in a magical time capsule – Bushveld with its long grass, snakes and retreating warthogs – offered cool, secret thickets, or miles of distance made mysterious by shimmering heat waves.

A marvellous diversity of birds and insects filled the days and seasons with sounds and colour. An array of bright characters populated Weltevreden. Besides Walter, there were a group of strong headed women: Topsy, Pina and Mrs Graham, whose screen doors would wheeze open onto the Eden of savannah leading down to the Nyl floodplain with its tea-coloured water.

Africa still felt enormous in those days. The many dirt roads were veins that went on forever through the body of one mysterious landscape after another. At the end of each track you would find interesting people who lived with their assortment of animals needing the occasional attention of a country vet.

Everybody loved Walter, from the hardened farmers to the townsfolk. Even the traffic cop, who flagged us down for speeding said, '*Oh, Middag, die Doctor moet maar ry.*'

People out here dearly love their pets and animals. And Walter was their advisor, saviour and consoler. I remember a large man weeping because his little *stoep-kakker* had died, while Walter stood by him.

Courtship

It was still early in their strengthening relationship when Walter took Topsy for a trip to the Kruger National Park. One evening while having genteel drinks overlooking a wide sand river, Walter picked up his binoculars to peruse the far riverbank. He involuntarily gasped out loud. Instantly curious, Topsy asked what he had seen.

'Oh, it's nothing…' he tried.

'Let me see!'

Reluctantly he handed over the glasses.

Topsy scanned along the far bank while Walter fidgeted.

'Where is it?'

Walter stayed mum.

'I see an elephant… what's it doing?' she asked innocently.

Topsy burst out laughing as she focused on the big bull elephant standing amongst the shadows. He was idly kicking the long trunk that stretched down between his back legs.

Birds and Bees

We trod across the field of long veld grass, which was waving in the wind.

Walter pointed: 'European Bee Eaters…'

'Aren't they White Fronted Bee Eaters…?' I ventured.

Walter was probably right; I was distracted by the rather large bull that had no doubt registered that we were striding his way.

'Walter, have you seen the big fellow over there?'

He ignored me and we angled in closer.

I've had too many bad bull experiences, I was thinking, please not another.

The monster turned his massive horns, his boss targeting us, nice and square. Walter nudged me with his powerful shoulder: 'You head across the front, I'll get in behind.'

What? my poor mind cried out, but no sound came from my mouth.

Wait! my brain shouted.

Too late, it was already unfolding… The brute lumbered towards the messy mark on the field that was to be me. Walter closed in behind and grabbed the tail.

'Pull the ring in the nose!' he yelled.

Yes, that's what he said - I told my body.

The fractions of the second dragged out while I willed my arm to reach out as the bull moved in swiftly. I watched remotely as my skinny arm darted its hand towards the slippery brass ring … and miraculously took hold. More fractions of time, as I felt my life teeter on the brink.

Pull the mountain towards you - I told my hand.

I could feel raw power through the ring. A mountain avalanching.

Somehow my hand slowed then stopped the avalanche.

I was on the threshold of a portal of fear. My fortunate hand was on the other side. But I was still standing in terror over here.

Then I crossed over.

My fear turned to awe of this amazing beast.

I was mesmerized by his massive head, the large tube of an ear, his eye – staring at me. Then, out of my peripheral vision I watched aghast as Walter reached for the big fellow's you know what…

'Hold him steady while I…'

Around us the bee-eaters were swooping and the grass glowed a luminous gold.

'Friendly fellow, isn't he?' Walter laughed.

He held up a test tube of semen.

Co Incidents

Walter used to drive at high speed because 'he had vast distances to cover'.

One day he was whizzing along the dirt road that skirts the lovely Nylsvlei Nature Reserve in his old tan Merc, hurrying to get home to his darling Topsy. As the road crosses the Nyl River it narrows to a one-car-width bridge.

Approaching from the other side was another Mercedes, also flying at high speed with its attendant plume of dust.

Walter put foot to be first on the bridge. The other car also accelerated. They both roared onto the narrow bridge at the same instant. To avoid collision they yanked on their wide steering wheels and each swerved one wheel up onto the pavement.

But because the cars were now tilted towards each other, their roofs touched as their clouds of dust merged.

Walter's windscreen suddenly turned white as the shatterproof glass fragmented. He slammed on anchors as he felt the car straighten back onto the road. Then he leapt out to clear out the windscreen. When the dust settled he glanced back and saw the other man breaking out his own windscreen. When they had finished clearing the glass, they jumped into their cars and roared off.

Bakkie Ride to Heaven

Walter chuckled when I asked where his Nomad bakkie was…

'Got hit by the train …'

The Great North train track ran just past Weltevreden. I remember steam trains leaving long plumes of smoke as they thundered past with their whistles blasting.

One night Walter had roared up to the train crossing. He hit the brakes when he saw an approaching train. Noting he was a little too close to the tracks he slammed the gear lever into reverse to back away. Unfortunately the first and reverse gears lie close together. His Nomad jumped onto the track.

'Next thing I was spinning through the air…'

The bakkie had been flung high to the tune of the train's whistle, and landed badly damaged, but Walter was fine. The train driver did his emergency stop manoeuvre and rushed back up the track. He was very agitated. Walter tried to console him but to no avail; the man continued jabbering about what he had seen.

'The poor guy had to radio for another driver as he was too upset to continue!'

In the moment of impact, the driver had seen a bakkie load of people going round and round on their way to heaven.

Dream Riding

Some dear soul gave Walter a tower of a thorough-bred horse. Seventeen and a half hands high. Walter would rise before dawn, saddle up and I would hear him galloping off across the *veld* in the pre-dawn light.

By this stage Walter had tactfully given up trying to teach me how to ride. But I was intrigued as to how he managed to get up onto its high back, and then ride such a massive beast.

'*Ja*', he said. 'At night I dream about riding, and try out various manoeuvres. Then I wake up, and while the dream is still fresh, I go and do the ride on the real horse.'

How to Catch a Giraffe

We headed out into the Waterberg, through a Nature Reserve, and pulled up at some wooden railing. In this paddock stood a young giraffe, a good fourteen foot high. It gazed down on us steadily while its skin twitched at the attendant flies. Walter greeted a farm hand and asked for the dart gun...

No dart gun.

Walter quickly hatched a scheme in which I was to sneak up with a large syringe and plunge the needle into the shoulder of the, no doubt, sick and grumpy fellow.

He would 'distract the giraffe.'

Walter and a group of enthusiastic workers shouted and waved sacks while I did my best to be invisible. I raced in from behind with the syringe, thumb ready to plunge, leapt, and stabbed: all good... except the needle just bent as I struck bone.

The giraffe went berserk. Lashing out with its sharp, lion-slaying hooves, the size of soup plates. I moved out of reach swiftly.

Plan B...

Walter mixed up another syringe of sleeping *muthi* and placed it in my reluctant hand. This time they would 'subdue the giraffe'. By now the giraffe was pretty wired.

They tried to blind-fold it with a sack on a long pole, but the beast easily avoided the offer of darkness.

Then Walter called for rope. He stationed the men so that they could cross the ropes over its neck, and then pull tight to hold it still.

301

Ja...' I thought. I looked into the eyes up high and knew that the giraffe knew.

Luckily for me, sanity prevailed.

I heard the sweet words: 'We wait for a dart gun...'

Stalking Giraffe

Walter always had plenty to do, but he often made time for me. Once, when I was around ten years old, as we were leaving a reserve, watching and naming birds, we spotted two giraffe. He drove a little closer and stopped gently. Everyone knows you cannot really stalk a giraffe. They simply stand stock still with their large eyes staring, seeing everything from their lofty heights.

However, Walter checked the wind then advised me how I could get close to them. I snuck out and, bent double, headed for the first bush. I glanced back and Walter's arm directed me on. I came to a thicket. Walters hand motioned me to be quiet. The giraffe were on the other side. I held my breath, crawling as quietly as I could underneath the bushes, doing my best to avoid thorns. As I approached the edge of the thicket, and peered through the leaves, their legs were starting to scissor away.

I heard the sound of my heart beating, and then realized it was the drumming of their hooves, through the ground.

Curiosity

One night we returned after the varied adventures of the day to an empty house. Topsy was away but had kindly left us dinner. We sat down to a meal which centred around a rather large pot full of kudu meat. We chatted away while we ate, Walter imparting some more of his useful information to me.

'If you ever have to punch someone, be sure to aim for the opposite side of their head.'

'Why's that?' I asked around a mouthful. The slabs of meat were delicious.

'If you are aiming for the side you are going to hit, your fist will start to slow down just before connecting... If you aim for the opposite side, your fist is still moving at full speed when it connects.'

I better not ever push you too far, I thought.

Walter offered me 'another piece of kudu?' which I humbly accepted and tucked into.

We chatted on between 'how about another piece?'

It wasn't long until the pot was empty…

Walter then remarked, 'That was our meat for the week!'

I was mortified, 'Why didn't you say so before I ate it all?'

'I was just curious to see how much a human can eat.'

First Hunt

Walter wanted to test some young puppies for a career as hunting dogs. He had them tumbling and playing around his feet while he pointed a shotgun to the sky and let rip. Then he looked down to see which ones could handle the loud thunder. I saw the moment as an opportunity and pestered him once again to take me hunting.

He looked at my skinny twelve year old form… my eager pleading eyes.

'Ok.'

We went into his room and he opened his gun safe. The distinctive masculine smell of gun oil wafted out. Walter showed me a variety of classic rifles and shotguns. He broke and placed empty cartridges in the chambers of a rather heavy looking piece, then handed it to me. My arms groaned as it was even heavier than it looked. It had three long barrels: a double-barrelled shotgun and a rifle beneath it. Between the barrels and the stock were two large antique-looking hammers.

I held it gingerly.

'Pull the hammers back.'

I tried and could just, at the limit of my strength, cock them.

'Now squeeze the trigger slowly… smoothly, don't jerk it.'

My head twitched a little at the dry 'click'.

We set off early the next morning, the shotguns propped between us. The bakkie eased down the rails of a sandy track, the middelmannetjie's grass offloading sluggish insects and seeds. Then out we climbed. I managed to calm my boyish excitement as Walter handed me the sacred paper cartridges, watched me load and checked the safety. We set off through the high grass, which was still wet and draped with spider webs. The cold blue steel was absurdly heavy and after a short time my arms were aching, my legs wet and my shoes soaked. I followed Walter, taking care to tread quietly and keeping the long barrels pointed safely at the ground without getting them wet. On the edge of miserable, I couldn't help noticing that Walter seemed oblivious to the discomfort; he seemed in fact to be thoroughly content.

Walter raised his arm bringing us to a stop. He then positioned me on his left flank and we started off across a field of long grass interspersed with thorn trees.

I was beginning to really feel the effects of a restless night and an early morning. The sun was starting to dry out the pools of dark shadow, and sweat was running down my back. Walter moved steadily on my right; his shotgun seemed light in his hands.

The startle of exploding pheasant shocked me. The whirring birds fanned out high across the sky. Before I knew it I had raised the stock to my shoulder, cocked a hammer and squeezed the trigger.

Wump!

One of the flying forms exploded feathers that drifted down long after it had plummeted to the earth.

'Good shot!' said Walter

We gathered together at the pile of soft feathers. The sand was cool and white.

Walter stood at my side as I picked up the warm bird, and held life and death in my hands.

Going Solo

One afternoon we were out hunting pigeons for a pie. Walter had placed us amongst thorn bushes so that the birds were channelled as they headed for their evening drink. I was enthusiastically pointing at the speeding grey forms and shooting quite wildly, when Walter's calm voice suggested I stop shooting in his direction...

That evening while we were cleaning the shotguns, I brought up the next item on my wish list. I wanted to do a hike in the Waterberg, on my own. Instead of the expected 'but you're only twelve!' Walter was immediately enthusiastic, and said he would take me out to the mountains. The mysterious Waterberg marked the edge of the

Springbok Flats universe. It sat in the distance, reminding us that the world was not quite flat.

I packed food for a week and Walter drove us along the winding road that led to the peak of Hanglip. He dropped me off near its looming height, and I stood and listened to the sound of his truck getting quieter and quieter.

What have I done? I thought. *A whole week without Walter?*

I shouldered my old canvas pack, and headed towards the mountain. Seven days and nights later, he picked me up again. He was keen to hear my stories of searching for water, coming upon leopard tracks and making fire.

The Rounds

Over the years, many cars and bakkies carried the vet across the Springbok Flats and into the Waterberg. The back was always full of metal boxes containing a jumble of stainless surgical instruments and other medieval-looking implements that would rattle away merrily. I think the noise warned off the kudu that waited patiently to leap out from the sides of the 'green tunnels' that line the dust roads.

Sometimes a cheeky Jack Russell would snuggle across Walter's shoulders, waiting to dash off and sniff through some new farm yard or field.

It was always with great excitement that I would stumble around in the pitch dark of the early hours when Walter had roused me to join him on a mission to save some distant animal in trouble. We would head out, clearing the misted windshield so that the stars would appear above the pale dirt road. Walter was a great storyteller, and the miles would speed by too quickly.

Every farm house and its family were different, but they all greeted the vet with the same genuine warmth and affection. It was easy to see that he was honoured, respected and loved. They would give us hot cups of coffee and *beskuit* as they gently probed him for advice.

Then there were the herds of livestock, some of them massive. Paddocks full of lowing cattle would be herded into a crush, their eyes wild and heads straining against the creaking poles. Walter would then take blood, or check them for pregnancy.

Unfortunately Walter was sometimes called in too late and we would squeeze through barbed-wire fences and walk across fields, or enter gloomy barns, to find a cold and lifeless animal.

The deaths would need explanations and Walter would carry out an autopsy. He felt it was important that I should learn the inner workings of the different animals, and would get me to grope amongst the organs and viscera while he explained their varied functions.

Every day would be different, every situation unique, always an adventure.

Do It

Among the many life skills I learned from Walter early on...

One evening we pulled into a café for something to eat. I waited in the car and peered at Naboomspruit street-life through the bakkie windscreen. The gummy mix of dust and splattered insects made everything rather interesting. Street lights starred and merged with neon colours. I wondered at how Walter could actually see through the paste.

When Walter returned he chastised me for not cleaning the window.

'If you see something needs to be done, do it! You don't have to wait until you're asked.'

I leapt out and got it done.

Then we headed out onto the starlit road, Walter chatting away.

Whodunnit?

One day while we were eating lunch the party line did its particular ring. Walter went to answer. He then rushed out to his bakkie shouting to me to open the gate. We hurtled along the maze of dirt roads while Walter explained that a farmer's breeding bulls were suddenly dying. We arrived at a dramatic scene ...

Workers were standing around in a field of dejected bulls. Heads hung low while long streamers of mucus dragged across the stubbles of grass. Spasms moved across their great muscles while wide eyes stared at us madly. Scattered amongst them were six large still bodies. The farmer rushed across to us, and hurried us to his beloved animals.

Walter moved quickly from bull to bull, examining their mouths and eyes.

What could have caused this nightmare? I could see Walter's mind was working in overdrive.

He looked around and spotted a great concrete ramp leading down to a pool of muddy water. Another ramp on the other side allowed the beasts to return to the surface after they had swum through the mix.

'Have they been dipped?'

'Ja, but we used the usual mix.'

'Hose them down with fresh water!' he instructed.

Walter asked to see the dip concentrate. The containers were gathered together. They seemed to be standard tick dip, and shouldn't cause this kind of reaction. But then he spotted that one of the containers was missing a label. He opened its lid and sniffed the contents.

'Where do you store the dip?' Walter asked.

The farmer led us across to the store and on the floor I spotted a tatty old label. Walter studied it with his head tilted back. 'Way too strong a concentration,' he muttered. It was pure organo-phosphate insecticide, intended as a crop spray.

'Quick,' said Walter, 'we need atropine fast.' He instructed the farmer to phone the chemist in Nylstroom.

Walter rummaged through his boxes and found a single glass vial of the magic potion. He selected a dusty syringe and thrust a blister pack of needles at me to open. Plunging the needle through the rubber stopper, he inverted the bottle and held it up to the light while he filled the syringe. He chose the sickest of the herd and jabbed into its quivering neck. Almost immediately the shuddering slowed.

The farmer raced off to Nylstroom and returned with more *muthi*. Walter moved quickly treating each bull.

The lives of the remaining bulls were saved.

Day Out

'Let's go for a walk.' Walter suggested one Sunday. 'I hear there are Bushman paintings amongst some koppies not too far away.' Both Walter and I were budding artists. Hopefully we could glean some wisdom from the great masters of old.

We climbed into the bakkie and chugged off at a leisurely pace, enjoying a mild summer's day. I had recently achieved my driver's license and Walter wanted to impart some of his experience on driving.

'If you find the clutch isn't working, you can still drive by getting the revs of the engine to be the same as the gearbox before you change. So rev up to change down, and let go of the accelerator to change up.'

I noted that he didn't demonstrate the action, but I filed the info away under 'mechanical knowledge'.

We then became engrossed in the life around us. We were soon swimming in a verbal soup of Latin names. Trees and birds, even grasses were spotted and pondered. Up along a river we strolled, and then entered the hills looking for overhangs with their galleries of art. Dassies noisily protested our presence, and we caught a glimpse of a bounding klipspringer. Then the beautiful rock art; animals portrayed with such sensitivity that they seemed still alive even though eons old.

On our way back we spotted a hare warming itself in the late afternoon sun. Its soft pelt was lit like a halo and glowed a warm red. We stalked a little closer but it was off in an instant, dodging away amongst the rocks and through the long grass.

'Lepus… Scrub hare,' I whispered,

'Saxatilis,' Walter finished, then said 'Nah'.

'Riverine?' I suggested.

'Nah … Shouldn't occur here. Definitely Order Lagomorpha, maybe Genus Pronolagus…'

Back at home we concurred that the find was probably a Jameson's red rock rabbit.

Altogether a rewarding treasure hunt.

Solving a Habit

I had always been concerned with Topsy and Walter's rather large consumption of cigarettes. I was forever getting into trouble by hiding or even destroying packs of the smelly things. I vaguely recall myself as a child inserting a firecracker into a pack and then lighting the fuse...

One day I noticed Walter wasn't lighting up one cigarette after another. I kept quiet in case he had just somehow forgotten his habit. At the end of the day I had to ask.

'What happened to your smoking?'

'I stopped.'

'You went through a Smokender's programme?'

'Nah, I just stopped.'

Ghosts in the Desert

On some of my long trips up into the Kalahari I would stop off for a few days with the Eschenburgs. Walter recalled how he also used to travel far and wide. He described a desert landscape up in Namibia where a life-size engraving of a giraffe spanned a path down to a water hole. Near this source of life someone had once had enough energy to construct a rock bunker. It was a well-built structure and Walter felt safe in the cool room as he looked out from its window straight onto the little pool.

The landowner suggested they spend the night camping there and that they may get a chance to see some of the elusive desert elephants. That evening they headed to the water hole. Walter started towards the rock structure, but the old man said they should rather camp up on a nearby hill. A little sad at having to be some distance from any action, he helped set up camp looking down on the scene. They had dinner and watched a splendid moon rise silently, its light thrusting fingers of silver amongst the dark shadows.

And then there they were: giant ghosts that made no sound. He watched them approaching, then the herd stopped and the large matriarch cautiously moved up to the pool. As she drew level with the rock shelter she suddenly knelt down and thrust her trunk deep through the window and into the building. Walter watched aghast as she carefully and thoroughly searched through the room.

If they had been in there...

The old man chuckled quietly as the herd gathered to drink.

A Day with Walter and the Birds

My most recent memory of Walter was of a day we spent together in Cape Town. It was a treat to have a whole day with him.

We started with a breakfast picnic on the cliff edge of Table Mountain. The cable car carried us high above the city. We walked some way along the table edge. Walter enthused about the wonderful plants and birds.

As we sat eating, a black eagle drifted over and hung in the updraft some ten meters away from us, watching us intently.

We then went for lunch at Cape Point. I took Walter on one of my favourite walks above False Bay. Out of a beautiful sky a rock kestrel swooped down and hovered in the air – just in front of Walter. Its rapidly winnowing wings held it in place as it faced him, opened its beak, and trilled out its shrill call: *Kreeeeee*.

It felt to me like the birds were honouring and blessing Walter.

ILLUSTRATIONS

1. Juchow, 1930s; p 35; courtesy of Frau B. Hannig. All rights reserved.
2. Elsa, Walter and Comtesse, p 95; courtesy of Mrs E. Mortimer. All rights reserved.
3. Graduation, p 115; Getting married, p 116; 'His first rhino', p 175; microscope, 205; courtesy of Mrs T. Eschenburg. All rights reserved.
4. Drawing, p 176; courtesy of Tiger Solomon. All rights reserved.
5. Juchow Castle 2009, p 240; by author. All rights reserved.
6. Meerkat Cricket World Cup, p 250; Warthogs, p 257; Anna's Rhino, p 258; Waterbuck, p 282; courtesy of Mrs T. Eschenburg. All rights reserved.

A TRIBUTE

GLOSSARY

Aardvark: ant bear (South Africa)
Amsel: black bird (German)
Baie dankie: thank you very much (Afrikaans)
Bakkie: a pick-up truck with an open body and low sides (South Africa)
Beskuit: biscuit (South Africa)
Blerry: bloody, mild swear word (South Africa)
Boomslang: tree snake (South Africa)
Bowle: punch bowl (Germany)
Buchengang: alleyway flanked by beech trees (Germany)
Dok: informal; Doctor (Afrikaans)
Donnerwetter: mild swear word; thunderstorm (Germany)
Draai: turn (South Africa)
Drilling: triple barrelled gun (Germany, South Africa)
Dubbeltje: little devil; desert plant (South Africa)
Eina: informal; expression of pain (South Africa)
Emasculator: veterinary instrument for the simultaneous crushing and cutting of the spermatic cord during castration.
Embryotome: a cutting instrument/wire saw for removal of a dead foetus in cows or mares
Engelsman: Englishman (South Africa)
Förster: forester, forest ranger (Germany)
Fräulein: Miss (Germany)
Frau: Mrs; woman (Germany)
Gänse: geese (Germany)
Gänseköpfe: goose heads (Germany)
Gänseschlachtfest: celebration during annual slaughtering of geese (Germany)
Gänse-schwarz-sauer: a particular dish made from goose blood and innards (Germany)
Gänseweide: geese paddock (Germany)
Gatvol: fed up (South Africa)
Gogo: grandmother (South Africa)

Goue Bad: Golden Bath (Afrikaans)
Herr: Mister (Germany)
Hok: coop, as in chicken coop (South Africa)
Jagdstube: hunting chamber (Germany)
Jammer: pity; I'm sorry (South Africa)
Jirre: mild swear word (South Africa)
Just now: colloquial expression meaning *'soon'* (South Africa)
Kaiser: emperor (Germany)
Kaiserliche Yachtregatta: Emperor's sailing race (Germany)
Kalahari Gemsbok National Park: large conservation area in South Africa; today part of the Kgalagadi Transfrontier Park, together with the adjoining Gemsbok National Park in Botswana.
Kartoffeln: potatoes (Germany)
Kartoffelschnaps: distilled alcoholic drink, made from potatoes (Germany)
Klapperstorch: European stork; brings babies, according to traditional belief (Germany)
Kommetjie's Gat Kat: water mongoose (South Africa)
Koppie: small hill; rocky outcrop (South Africa)
Leguan: iguana; monitor lizard (South Africa)
Liebling: favourite, darling (Germany)
Linde: Tilia, lime wood tree (Germany)
Mak: tame (Afrikaans)
Mamsell: chef; head of kitchen (Germany)
Melktert: milk tart (South Africa)
Meneer: Afrikaans title of address, meaning *Sir* or *Mr*
Middelmannetjie: central ridge of an unsurfaced road (South Africa)
Mielies: Maize (South Africa)
Muthi: medicine (South Africa)
Naboom: see Naboomspruit
Naboomspruit: today   Mookgophong, town in South Africa's Limpopo province
Nagapies: bush babies (South Africa)
Nhoka: snake (South Africa)
Nigdy: No (Polish)
Niks: nothing (South Africa)
Nou gaan Menheer julle donner: now the teacher is going to hit you (slang; South Africa)
Now now: colloquial expression meaning *'immediately'* (South Africa)
Oom: uncle, used when respectfully addressing an older man (South Africa)

Opa: grandfather (Germany)
Oupa: grandfather (South Africa)
Pfingsten: Pentecost (Germany)
Pica: eating disorder caused by nutrient deficiency
Pietersburg: today Polokwane; town in South Africa's Limpopo province
Pikkinin: little boy (South Africa)
Plaas: farm (South Africa)
Plumeau: down blanket (Germany)
Pudhi: skull of small antelope, attributed with magical powers (South Africa)
Rinkhals: a venomous Southern African snake, similar to cobra
Rondloop : gallivant (South Africa)
Rumenitis: inflammation of the rumen, the first compartment of the stomach of ruminants
Sangoma: traditional healer (South Africa)
Schlosshalle: castle hall (Germany)
Schlucht: gorge (Germany)
Schnepfenstrich: snipe hunt (Germany)
Sjoe: expression of relief (South Africa)
Skaapsteeker: a small Southern African snake
Skedonk: an old, battered car (South Africa)
Skriks vir nix: shy of nothing (South Africa)
Snaaks: strange (South Africa)
South-West Africa: today Namibia
Springbok: National Rugby team (South Africa)
Stoep: veranda (South Africa)
Stoep-kakker: colloquial; lap dog (South Africa)
Strasse: street (German)
Tak: yes (Polish)
Tante : Aunt (Germany)
Tier: leopard (Afrikaans)
Tsotsis: thugs, criminals (South Africa)
Uhlenhorst: owl's nest (Germany)
Vater: father (Germany)
Veldskoens: ankle-length boot or walking shoe made of rawhide, suede or leather (South Africa)
Vrot: rotten (South Africa)
Weidenflőten: flutes made from the branches of willow trees (Germany)
Wurst: certain type sausage, cold meat (Germany)

ABOUT THE AUTHOR

Stephanie Rohrbach is a traveller, writer, translator and free spirit. She grew up in Germany, has a degree in veterinary medicine, and has worked as researcher, waitress, bicycle travel guide, conservationist, language practitioner, tourism consultant and farm hand. Having lived in the south of Spain and on a Mozambican island, she currently calls South Africa home, where she divides her time between plotting the next journey and writing.

Printed in Great Britain
by Amazon